HOME REMODELING
DESIGN & PLANS

HOME REMODELING DESIGN & PLANS

HERB HUGHES

CREATIVE HOMEOWNER PRESS   A DIVISION OF FEDERAL MARKETING CORPORATION, PASSAIC, NJ

Manufactured in United States of America

Current Printing (last digit)
10 9 8 7 6 5 4 3 2 1

Editor: Shirley M. Horowitz
Art Director: Léone Lewensohn
Proofreader: Marilyn M. Auer
Technical Assistance and Review: Frederick Jules, Asst. Professor,
School of Architecture and Urban Planning, University of Wisconsin-
Milwaukee

Cover: Three photographs of siding remodeling courtesy of Lumaside,
Inc., Milwaukee, Wisconsin

Library of Congress Cataloging in Publication Data

Hughes, Herb.
  Home remodeling design & plans.

  Includes index.
  1. Dwellings — Remodeling. I. Title.
TH4816.H84   643'.7   79-23347
ISBN 0-932944-11-6
ISBN 0-932944-12-4 pbk.

CREATIVE HOMEOWNER PRESS™
A DIVISION OF FEDERAL MARKETING CORPORATION
62-70 MYRTLE AVENUE, PASSAIC, NJ 07055

Acknowledgements

I have always wondered why every book was dedicated to the author's
wife or husband. I couldn't understand why they didn't do something
different, something unique. Now I no longer wonder why. This book
will be no different; it is dedicated to my wife, Charlotte.

I must thank the manufacturers and professionals, too numerous to
include all their names, who offered material and technical information
for the book.

A special thanks goes to Russ Eckley, a very talented draftsman,
whose hands appear in a number of photographs and whose neat
freehand lettering appears on all my drawings.

I must also thank Rick and Nancy Anderson for allowing me to use
their home as the sample home for the book, and for posing in several
photographs for Chapter 2.

And, finally, thanks to Shirley Horowitz, the publisher, for asking,
pleading, demanding, requesting, badgering, ordering, soliciting, commanding, urging, and begging this book into reality.

H.H.   1979

Contents

Introduction

Remodeling became a major trend during the 1970s due to dramatic rises in costs of new homes and in mortgage interest rates. Unfortunately, many remodeling projects will never get beyond the wishing stage because of the difficulty and cost of acquiring plans.

Plans are essential, whether contemplating a few simple changes or major additions. Even a small job will cost less in time and money with a well-thought-out set of drawings from which to work. But unlike buying or building a new home, where you can select from prebuilt samples or choose from catalogs of home plan designs, there are no books with page after page of remodeling plans. The reason is obvious; remodeling plans must be adapted to each existing structure. And the one who knows this existing house best is you, the homeowner.

Drawing your own remodeling plans is not as difficult as it may at first appear. With a little instruction it becomes easy and enjoyable to plan your family's future wants and needs. As a self-planner, you will find a great many advantages in doing the work yourself.

The most immediate advantage is the dollar savings. Drafting tools require an investment that is far less than that of hiring an architect. You can save hundreds or even thousands of dollars, depending upon the extent of the work to be done.

By developing your own design, your home is remodeled to your particular requirements, not the ideas of someone who knows little about you and your family. A large part of the architect's fee is for the time he spends learning and understanding what you need.

One of the biggest benefits of making your own construction drawings is that of becoming intimately familiar with the work to be done. This will enable you to sit down with your contractor and discuss what is to be done and what you expect in the way of workmanship and materials. It will also help during construction as you inspect the work's progress. If you will be doing most or all of the construction yourself the benefits are even greater. Once you have spent the time required to draw the plans, your familiarity will make the construction quicker and easier. Instead of wasting hours trying to decipher the meaning of someone else's drawings, you will need only occasional glances for reference.

THE PLANNING PROCESS

This book begins with the fundamentals — design development and selection of drafting tools — and carries you step by step to the finished drawings.

Much more is involved than just drawing lines on paper; the planning process begins with the desire to remodel and continues until the start of construction. Some aspects of the planning may not be completed until furniture is in place. The process includes selection of materials, working with contractors and building material suppliers, meeting codes and other legal aspects, determining the timing of the various elements of construction, and more. This book is designed to help you through the entire planning process.

From the discussion of each tool and how it is used in the first chapter, succeeding sections will help you to design and prepare a professional set of plans and carry out the remodeling stages. This book will cover:

- how to assess your home, what you have and what you need;
- how to set up your home office on a "permanent" basis if you have the space and on a "temporary" basis if you don't;
- each tool, what it is, what it looks like, and how it is used;
- ideas and where they come from, with a discussion of the fundamentals of design and specifics to help you apply these concepts;
- how to begin drawing and how to make your drawings look professional;
- each aspect of the plans such as floor plan, exterior elevations, cabinet elevations and details, and site plan;
- a full section on codes to help you design a livable home and to help you get your plans approved by any government agencies involved;
- the process of getting construction started, whether you are using a contractor, subcontracting the work, doing the work yourself, or a combination of subcontracting and working yourself.

Once you have completed the total planning process, you will be in the position of knowing what will happen even before the first nail is nailed. This will save tremendous amounts of money, time, and aspirin. Problems will arise, as they always do even for the most experienced contractor, but you will be better equipped to solve them.

USING THIS BOOK

Even if you never draw a line, this book will be invaluable in helping you through the planning process. You will become knowledgeable about remodeling and construction before the job starts. You will be able to understand construction drawings and will find it easier to get your ideas across to whomever is drawing your plans. If you do decide to draw your own plans, this book will become your home remodeling bible.

Read the book throughout before you buy equipment or begin drawing. It is important that you have as full an understanding as possible of the planning process and what you must do before you start.

Once you are ready to draw your plans, go back to the beginning of the book. Take the tool list in Chapter One to a store that sells drafting supplies. Discuss your purchase with the salesman; he can offer valuable information. Then set up your work area and follow carefully through the book. Where possible, the chapters are arranged in a chronological manner, so that each chapter builds upon the preceding one. Certain sections will become references. You will find yourself going back to them repeatedly. You will even find some sections that will help you during construction. The book may become ragged and dog-eared, but that's all right; it is meant to be used.

For Your Own Protection

When working out your plans with your contractor, specify the performance rather than the "how to" of the construction. For example: walls must adequately support ceilings, insulation must prevent drafts, and foundations adequately support the house. This will protect you in the event that any problem occurs, so that the contractor is held responsible; otherwise he may try shifting the blame to your plans and to your original concept.

1 Before You Draw a Line

DRAFTING TOOLS

If you don't believe you can draw a set of plans, it is only because you are not familiar with the tools available to you. Drafting tools are precision instruments with which you can draw your remodeling plans even if you have absolutely no artistic ability. And it doesn't cost a fortune to set up your work area. You must have the proper equipment to work with, but you can put together a complete drawing office for between $100 and $150.

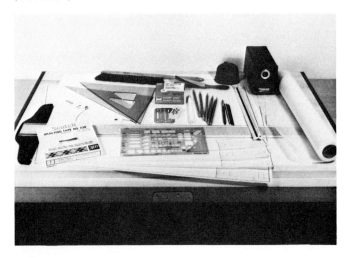

The Essentials

Following is a list of the drafting equipment you will need. There is a full explanation of what each piece is, how it is used, and approximately what it will cost. When you begin drawing, refer to this section as often as you need until you fully understand the function of each tool.

- Drawing board (recommended size 24″ x 36″)
- Vinyl mat (optional)
- T-square or parallel rule
- Triangle (45° and 30°-60° or adjustable)
- Architectural template
- Architectural scale
- Engineering scale (optional)
- Pencils (2H, H, & HB) or lead holder with same wt. leads
- Pencil sharpener (depending on type of pencils used)
- Eraser and erasing shield
- Drafting brush
- Vellum (precut 18″ x 24″ sheets recommended)
- White or yellow ''rag'' tracing paper (18″ roll)
- Drafting tape or dots

Drawing Board. This is a wood board with a perfectly level surface and precision straight metal sides. A small or medium size board will be sufficient for home use; recommended size is 24″ x 36″, which is small enough to be easily handled and large enough to be useful for drawing. The board can be set up on top of a desk or table. Use two equally thick books or other supports to prop the back corners up so that the working surface is slanted toward you.

Vinyl Mat Surface. Since the paper you will be drawing on is semi-transparent, the wood grain of the board could cause visual distractions. If you don't mind a little additional expense ($10 to $15), a vinyl mat will eliminate this problem and will give you a slightly softer surface to work on. Allow the vinyl mat to lay on the board in a warm room (80° to 85°) until it is completely flat; this might take a day or two. Then apply double-stick tape around the edge of the side that will go against the surface of the board. (Mats have a green surface on one side and a yellow surface on the other. You may use either side.) Do not place the tape anywhere besides the very edge of the mat. Even something as thin as tape can cause a permanent ''lump'' in the mat's surface. Be sure both the board and the mat are completely free of dirt and dust, then place the mat in the proper position on the board and allow it to remain for another two or three days in a very warm room before the board is used.

If you decide not to use the mat, an adequate substitute would be a thin piece of poster board or a large sheet (slightly less than the size of the board) of white 24 lb. (or heavier) paper. A sheet of this size can be purchased at any paper supplier. Tape the paper or poster board securely to the clean drawing board with drafting tape to provide better visibility and a softer drawing surface. While the vinyl mat is washable and will remain permanently affixed to the drawing board, the paper will require replacement from time to time.

T-Square or Parallel Rule. The T-square is, appropriately, in the shape of a capital ''T.'' The short cross member, a 90° angle to the long body of the T-square, is held snugly against

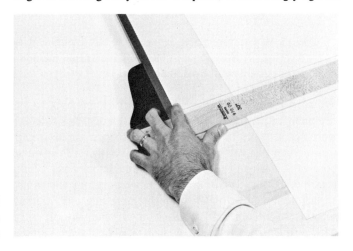

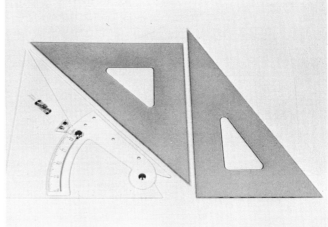

the metal edge of the drawing board and will slide along this edge easily so that all lines drawn against the body are parallel. The cross member should be held on the left side of the board by righthanders and on the right side for lefthanders. The length of the T-square should be slightly less than the drawing board for maximum ease in handling. The cost of this instrument will vary depending on size and quality.

While the T-square is fine for home use, most professionals now use what is called a parallel rule. This consists of a long rule set up on a wire track system. The wire track holds the rule exactly parallel to the length of the drawing board while letting it slide smoothly up and down. Since you do not have to hold the rule against the side of the board it is easier to use than the T-square and is more accurate. But it also costs more. If you will have future need for such equipment, you can invest the money, but for drawing your own remodeling plans at home the T-square is a sufficient investment.

Triangle. A triangle is a clear or tinted plastic instrument, in the shape of a triangle, with one 90° angle. You will need two: one 45° triangle and one 30° to 60° triangle.

A tinted triangle will be more visible and easier to use than a clear one. Six- or eight-inch triangles are good working sizes. When the leg of a triangle is placed against the T-square, lines drawn against the other leg are perpendicular to lines drawn against the T-square. Lines drawn against the hypotenuse, or long side of the triangle, are at a 45° angle from the T-square for the 45° triangle and either 30° or 60° for the 30°-60° triangle, depending on which leg is placed against the T-square. By sliding the triangle along the T-square a series of parallel lines may be drawn.

When drawing lines at an odd angle, place the two triangles together so that the top triangle is along the line to be drawn. (See accompanying photo.) By holding the bottom triangle firm and sliding the top triangle along the bottom one, a series of lines may be drawn which are parallel.

As is the case with most instruments, there is a more expensive version of the triangle; it is called an adjustable triangle. This is preferred by many (but not all) professionals because the hypotenuse may be adjusted to any angle desired and

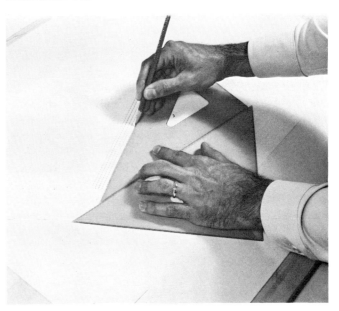

eliminates the need for two triangles. But the cost can be high. Since this book is not directed to the professional draftsman, all instruments shown in later chapters are the more economical types.

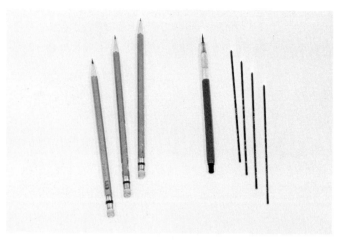

Architectural Template. The architectural template is a useful shortcut to drawing many difficult-to-draw items on the floor plan. It is a tinted plastic sheet with a series of cut-outs in the shape of various plan items such as tub, sink, etc. Simply place the item you need in the proper position on the plan and trace along the edge of the cut-out. The scale of the items on the template is 1/4 scale, which is the same scale used to draw the floor plan (see architectural scale, below). The cost is usually low for this essential tool.

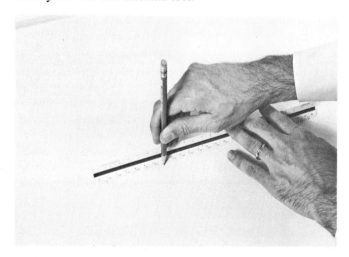

Architectural Scale. The architect's scale is a three-sided ruler, twelve inches long, with 2 scales of measurement shown on each side. The scales are for reducing actual size down to drawing size. The most commonly used scale is the one-quarter scale. This means that one quarter inch on the drawing is equivalent to one foot actual size. The one-quarter scale is marked so that one inch on the scale will read 4 feet. From the zero on the scale, feet are read in one direction and inches in the other. For instance, if a room measured 12 feet-4 inches you would put a light mark at the 12 on the scale for twelve feet. On the other side of the zero, count the small lines, which represent inches, until you reach four and place another light mark. Because some scales are very small, the inch marks might represent more than one inch. For large scales they might represent fractions of an inch. Be sure you determine which is the case before you try to use any scale.

Engineering Scale. This is particularly useful for site planning, since it enables you to fit more onto your paper.

Pencils. Common pencils are too soft and will not hold a

fine point, so you must purchase drafting pencils. You will need three different types of lead: hard, medium, and soft. The recommended designations are 2H, H, and HB; however, with a little practice you may wish to adjust these to your own drawing habits. The hard (2H) pencil makes a light line and will be used on initial drawings so lines can be easily erased. The medium (H) pencil makes a darker line and will be used for the final construction drawings. The soft (HB) pencil makes a very dark line and is good for sketching ideas.

A slightly better system for keeping fine points is the mechanical pencil. It consists of a single lead holder and leads of the same weights as mentioned above. The leads are interchangeable in the holder and can be sharpened to a finer point because of the different type sharpener used (see below). Although the mechanical pencil may cost slightly more initially, it could prove more economical in the long run. It also gives a more accurate line.

Pencil Sharpeners. The final deciding factor on which pencil system to use could be whether or not you already have a

pencil sharpener. If you do, you may prefer the wooden pencils to the added expense of a different type of sharpener. If you don't and still prefer the wooden pencils, the sharpener you buy should be a good enough quality to assure fine points. An electric sharpener is quick and easy and gives an extremely fine point, but can run much more.

The mechanical pencil uses a different sharpening system. There are several types available, but all work on the same principle. About a half inch of lead should be exposed from the mechanical holder and inserted into the sharpener, using a circular motion of the pencil. The lead brushes against a band of sandpaper on a scraping edge on the inside to give a needlesharp point.

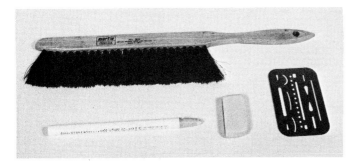

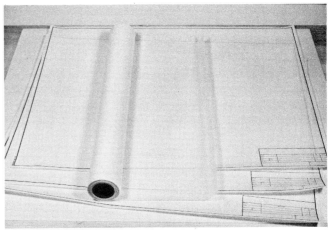

Eraser, Erasing Shield and Brush. Although there are many different types of erasers, a soft white vinyl is the most efficient for all types of lead. The common pink household eraser is not a good choice. Exclusive use of the white vinyl eraser will avoid the confusion of trying to remember what type to use with 2H lead or with HB lead. The erasing shield is a thin sheet of metal with several sizes and shapes of cut-outs. This allows you to erase only what you want to, while the rest of the drawing remains intact. Select a cut-out in the shield that exposes what you want to erase and nothing else. You may then erase the mark while protecting the remainder of the drawing. The cost of eraser and shield together will be low.

The horsehair drafting brush is used to remove eraser shavings and graphite dust from the drawing. The brush is not only

Drafting Tape. Drafting tape is used to secure the drawing to the drawing board. Place a strip about an inch long on each corner of the paper. Don't place it across the corner, as this may cause you to tear the drawing when you remove the tape. Instead, place the tape on the corner as shown.

For a slightly better system, use the relatively new tape dots. These are round and are placed on each corner of the drawing. Their advantage is that they will not snag on the T-square or parallel rule when it slides over them, as regular tape sometimes will. Since the extra cost is slight, the dots are recommended.

Caring For Your Equipment

Just as with other tools, a certain amount of care in use and maintenance is required to keep your drafting instruments accurate and useful. Read the instructions that come with each piece and follow them. Use your tools with care. They are reasonably tough, but are not unbreakable; a fall to a hard floor could knock a T-square out of kilter, changing the angle between the cross member and the body. Even a slight change, especially in the middle of a drawing, can put things out of scale and make your drawings inaccurate.

more efficient than using your hand, but it also keeps the drawing clean since you will not smear the pencil lines.

Vellum. This is a fine grade of paper often chosen for its dimensional stability; it does not shrink. It is designed for pencil work and used for the final, finished drawings. It is sold in rolls or in precut sheets with a border already printed. Since the roll will be much more than you will need and precut sheets save a great deal of time and trouble, precut sheets are recommended. About 12 to 15 sheets should be enough. The size should be a few inches smaller than your drawing board and cost will vary with size and number of sheets purchased.

White or Yellow "Rag" Tracing Paper. This is a lightweight, inexpensive paper used for sketching ideas. One 18 inch wide roll will be sufficient.

Use your tools only as they are intended. If you pick up your triangle and use it as a cutting edge for a utility knife, the plastic can become permanently nicked. This would create a little hump in every line drawn thereafter. Because of the angle of the pencil against the triangle when drawing, a small nick can cause a much larger hump on the drawing.

Keep your equipment clean. When using a wooden pencil,

be sure shavings are completely off the point after sharpening. For mechanical pencils, wipe the lead with a tissue or rag to clean the graphite dust from the point. The T-square, triangles, scale, and templates should be occasionally washed in a mild detergent to remove the graphite film that will develop over them. Nothing gets a drawing dirty as fast as dirty instruments. If you use a vinyl mat on your drawing board, it too will need cleaning with a mild detergent from time to time.

Other Equipment You Will Need

There are a few other items you will need to complete your remodeling plans and set up your work area. First, in order to draw your house as it is now—the first step in planning—you must measure it. A roll-up metal tape at least twelve feet long is necessary, and a longer tape is even better.

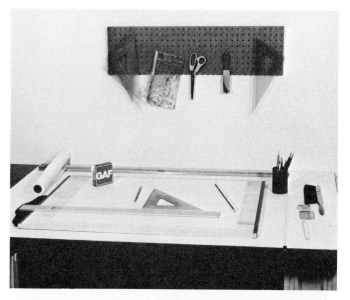

You will also need to keep the drawing instruments in neat arrangement, but close to your fingertips. A piece of pegboard with metal hooks will hold most of the instruments. The pencils, erasers, and other small items can be accommodated in several ways: metal cans, decorated if you like; old sewing trays; even an old fishing tackle box will work fine. Use whatever you have around the house that has different compartments of different sizes and shapes.

You should have about a dozen file folders for keeping track of the various aspects of your remodeling. These folders should be kept convenient to the work area since you will use them often for reference.

Adequate lighting is a crucial factor. You can use any lamp around the house by putting in high wattage bulbs. But, unfortunately, incandescent lights give off heat. The bright light you will need close to the drawing board could raise the temperature of your working area too high for comfortable drawing; perspiration can virtually destroy a pencil drawing. It is strongly recommended that you get a small fluorescent lamp. This, however, could turn into a big expense. Shop the discount department stores first. They could have just what you need for as little as $20.

SETTING UP YOUR WORK AREA

Basically there are two ways of setting up your home office: the "permanent" office and the "temporary" office. The permanent office allows you to set up a working area that will remain intact during the entire planning process. If you can afford the space and the extra materials required, this is preferred. The temporary office is set up only when you are going to work on the drawings, and remains neatly tucked in a closet or storage room at all other times. This is good if you are short on space, which may be your main reason for wanting to remodel.

The "Permanent" Office

The primary requirement for the permanent office is space you can spare. If you have a 4 foot x 8 foot area somewhere in the house that will be available for the few months you will spend in planning, then use this arrangement.

Make a table from an old door, thick piece of plywood, or some other sturdy material with a smooth, flat surface. Use sawhorses or concrete blocks for legs at either end of the table. Be sure to place the table against the wall so you will have a

place for your pegboard or some other device so you can hang the larger tools. Set up the drawing board in the middle of the table so you can use either side for containers holding small equipment, for reference material, and as general-use spaces. Use the sawhorse cross-supports or the concrete block holes for holding rolls of paper or drawings. If you don't have an extra chair or stool, a simple wooden stool will work and will not break your budget.

The "Temporary" Office

If you are cramped for space, you can make use of the dining table, breakfast bar, or existing desk on an "as you need it" basis. You will need some space in a closet or storage room for the drafting tools when not in use, but this will be minimal.

Use an old fishing tackle box, tool box, old brief case, or some other container that can be closed, to store as many tools as possible. When ready to draw, set the drawing board up, arrange the larger instruments near your fingertips, and keep the small items in the container close to your drawing hand.

Whether you use the permanent or the temporary office, the most important factor is ease in reaching your tools. You will find yourself picking up each instrument over and over as you work, so arrange your working area for convenience.

2 Your Home As It Is Now

THE EXISTING FLOOR PLAN

Before you knock out a wall and then regret it, you need a better view of your home as it is. An intimate knowledge of your house will make planning easier. Drawing the existing floor plan is the first step toward remodeling your home. Even if you've lived in your home for many years, certain characteristics will not be noticeable until you look at a floor plan. Having a bird's eye view of the entire house allows you to see important considerations, such as traffic patterns and wasted areas, much more readily.

In most cases the plans your home was built from are unavailable and you will have to begin from scratch. If they could be obtained, however, the work would be a little easier. The procedure for drawing the existing floor plan if you have the original plans will be discussed later in the chapter; continue reading this section because the fundamentals of drawing will be given.

Measuring Your Home

Start by walking around the outside of your house and making a rough sketch of its shape on a note pad. Then, using the roll-up tape, carefully measure each outside wall and mark the dimensions on the sketch. For the floor plan all dimensions should be rounded to the nearest inch. All items near the house, such as air conditioner pads, carports, patios, should be exactly measured for size and location.

In your measurements, include all structural items near the house.

Next, walk through each room and make a separate sketch of the inside of the house. Mark the dimensions for each room, including closets, pantries, and other features on the sketch. You will also need to measure and place on the sketch such items as cabinets, counters, etc. Generally, the bathtub and water closet are standard sizes and can be drawn with the architectural template so they do not have to be measured. (If you have an older home, the fixtures may not be standard.) Their exact locations and the distances between them,

however, are important and should be measured carefully. Lavatories, sinks, and appliances come in a variety of sizes and shapes and will have to be measured accurately for size and placement.

In addition to room sizes, measure all other structural items within your home.

When not in use the rough sketches should be placed in a file folder marked, "No. 1 The Existing House." It is important that you save the sketches since you will need to refer to the dimensions during planning.

THE FIRST DRAWINGS
Exterior Perimeter

Place a sheet of vellum generally in the center of the drawing board, with the long edge of the sheet parallel to the bottom of the board and the long piece of the T-square. Either a vinyl or a paper mat should already be attached to the board as described in Chapter 1. Tape the corners of the vellum to the board. Using the 16 scale, which is a standard twelve-inch ruler, measure the width of the vellum (top to bottom) and put a light mark at the center. Use the T-square and the 2H pencil to draw a very light horizontal line through the mark, from border to border, on the sheet. The pencil should be held against the drawing instrument so that the tip of the lead is pointed slightly away from the instrument. A "very light" line is drawn by using minimum pressure. It should be barely dark enough to register visibly but not dark enough to appear as part of the drawing.

Next, measure the sheet from side to side and draw a very light vertical line through the center by laying the triangle

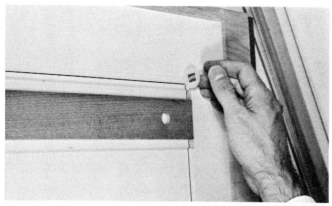

When taping a sheet of vellum to the drawing board, always line up the drawing (the border on a new sheet) with the T-square.

To avoid smearing the drawing with graphite dust hold the pencil so that the tip of the lead is pointed away from the drawing instrument.

along the upper edge of the T-square. Since the triangle is not as wide as the sheet of vellum, the T-square will have to be shifted once or twice to make the line continuous from top to bottom.

Compute the maximum length and width of your home from the rough sketch of the outside. Since the floor plan is usually drawn with the front of the house toward the bottom of the sheet, start with the dimension that represents the maximum size of the house from side to side. If your home is considerably deeper than it is wide you may want to orient the floor plan so that the front of the house faces toward the right side of the sheet instead of the bottom. If so, use the maximum dimension from front to back to begin your drawing.

Assuming that your house is deeper than it is wide, measure from the center of the sheet, where the lines you have drawn intersect, half the length of the house along the horizontal line in both directions using the 1/4 scale (all measurements on the floor plan will be done with the 1/4 scale). If the dimension is in even feet, place the zero on the scale at the center and place a light mark at the proper number of feet (half the total) on the horizontal line. Repeat in the opposite direction. If the dimension is in feet and inches, count back from the zero the distance of the number of inches and place the scale so that this inch line is on the center. Then place a light mark on the horizontal

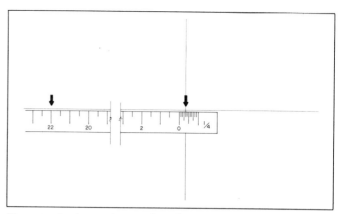

The example shows a house whose longest wall is 44 ft. 8 in. Half this length (22 ft. 4 in.) is marked to right and left of the vertical centerline.

line at the foot mark. Repeat in the opposite direction. Using the triangle draw a very light vertical line through each mark. Now, mark the width of the house in the same manner along the vertical line. Draw very light horizontal lines through each mark using the T-square. The resulting box represents the maximum limits of your home. If your house is a rectangle then the box will represent the actual outside walls. Measure the length and width of the box to be certain it corresponds to the dimensions on the rough sketch.

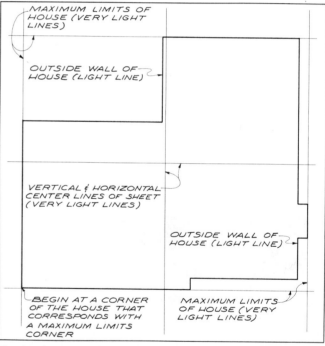

MAXIMUM LIMITS OF HOUSE (VERY LIGHT LINES)

OUTSIDE WALL OF HOUSE (LIGHT LINE)

VERTICAL & HORIZONTAL CENTER LINES OF SHEET (VERY LIGHT LINES)

OUTSIDE WALL OF HOUSE (LIGHT LINE)

BEGIN AT A CORNER OF THE HOUSE THAT CORRESPONDS WITH A MAXIMUM LIMITS CORNER

MAXIMUM LIMITS OF HOUSE (VERY LIGHT LINES)

Drawing the outside of the house. Note that measurement begins in the lower left corner, where the house corner corresponds with the maximum-limits corner; nowhere do the walls extend beyond these maximum limits.

If your house is not a simple rectangle and has jutting walls you will have to measure and draw each wall of the perimeter. Begin by selecting a corner of the house that corresponds to a corner of the maximum-limits box, i.e., a corner that represents the widest and the longest that the house extends. In the rare case where there is no such corner use the rough sketch to compute how far you will have to measure in from the maximum-limits corner vertically, horizontally, or both, to find the actual corner of the house. From this corner move in a clockwise direction as you measure and draw a light line for each wall. A "light" line also is drawn with the 2H pencil, but use medium pressure. The line should be dark enough to be easily visible, but still light enough to be easily erased. Although the clockwise direction is not significant, it is important that you use a consistent system to help avoid confusion.

When you have completed going around the outside the final measurement should fall reasonably close to the corner where you began. An inch or two difference (scaled dimension) is not critical. If, however, there is a substantial difference, or if the house extends far beyond the previously drawn maximum limits at any point, there is an error in measuring the house or in the drawing. Check your work carefully.

A Note Of Encouragement. Since you are just becoming familiar with drafting tools, your chances of making a mistake are high. Don't be discouraged if you have to draw this first work a second or third time before it is correct. Like anything else, a little practice goes a long way and having to redraw now will help you to avoid mistakes further down the road.

The Inside Walls

Drawing the inside of the house will be harder than the outside walls since there is more involved. So make all measurements carefully and check each one as you go. This will help minimize mistakes, saving time in the long run.

First, the thickness of the outside walls must be shown. These will vary according to the type of construction, as shown.

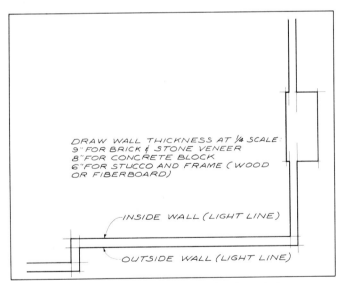

Thickness of the outside walls. These must be shown before you can draw the interior.

For each outside wall measure the proper thickness on the drawing from the outside wall line toward the inside of the house. Draw a light line through your mark parallel to the outside wall line. Continue around the entire perimeter of the house. It isn't necessary to keep lines from overlapping since these are only light lines and the final, darker lines will be drawn later.

Begin the interior walls at the same corner where you began drawing the outside. Find the dimensions of the room at that corner on the rough sketch. From the inside corner of the outside walls measure and mark the horizontal dimensions of

the room, then make a mark representing 4 inches further to represent interior wall thickness. (Older homes have walls that are thicker; you should measure to be sure. Plaster walls are always at least 5 inches thick. The interior wall that contains the plumbing stacks will also be thicker, usually 8 inches.) Repeat for the vertical dimension and draw very light guidelines through your marks. If the room is a bedroom, you may need to draw the closets so that the proper shape of the room is shown. Do not try to draw in windows and doors at this point. Go over the actual wall configuration with light lines so that the room can be easily seen over the very light guidelines (see illustration).

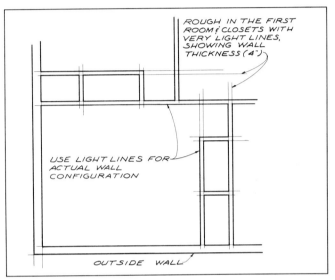

Drawing inside walls. Rough in the lines very lightly until the walls take shape.

Once the first room is drawn, move in a clockwise direction and draw the next room. Coninue until all interior walls are drawn. Once again, if the last room proves to be more than a few inches off you will need to recheck your work carefully. This is the stage where a mistake is most easily made, especially by a nonprofessional, so don't be discouraged if your last room overlaps the first a few feet or if your plan looks like a jigsaw puzzle with a few pieces missing. Find your mistake and correct it, then move on.

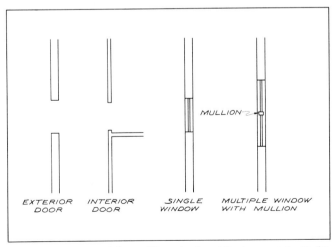

Existing windows and doors. Although all architects may not use the same symbols, the ones shown are easy to understand as well as easy to draw.

Doors And Windows

Working one room at a time, measure the width of each window and door (from inside frame to inside frame) and the distance from the edge of the window or door to a corner of the room. On the floor plan measure the distance from the corner to the inside of the window frame and put a light mark. Then measure the width of the glass of the window or door and put another light mark. Then draw the windows and doors as shown using light lines.

Bathrooms

Use the architectural template to draw the bathtubs and water closets with light lines. Be careful to place all fixtures in their proper positions based upon your measurements. Then measure and draw the lavatories and/or vanities. If your bathroom has a linen closet or any other similar structural feature, this should also be drawn.

Kitchen

On all kitchen walls with cabinets, measure one foot and two feet from the inside face of the wall toward the center of the room, placing a mark at each. Draw very light lines through the marks parallel to the wall, as shown. The one-foot line represents the front face of the wall cabinets and the two-foot line represents the front face of the base cabinets. Draw the ends of the cabinets based on your measurements, then locate and draw the appliances using the architectural template whenever possible.

Other Structural Items

Knowing which walls are supporting (load bearing) walls will be important. An interior wall is load-bearing if it runs at right angles to your ceiling or floor joists. All exterior walls of course are load-bearing. Flues for heating systems also take up space, as well as the systems themselves, and should be identified in the plan.

Other structural features that should be shown on the plan include fireplaces, built-in bookcases or desks, exposed beams, cased openings, etc. Measure and draw each one with light lines. Exposed beams and cased openings (an opening in a wall that stops below the ceiling but contains no door) are represented with dashed lines. Be sure to include features in the immediate vicinity of the outside of the home such as air conditioner pads, stoops, porches, decks, and patios.

DARKENING THE LINES

Once you have drawn all the features of your home and are satisfied with the accuracy of the drawing, you are ready to begin darkening the lines. This will be done with the H pencil and medium-hard pressure, but be careful not to press so hard that you tear the drawing. The dark lines are necessary so that your work will reproduce properly when the tracings are printed.

Begin by darkening the items that are drawn with the architectural template, such as the tubs, water closets, appliances, etc. Then brush the drawing before going further. Pressing hard with the H pencil produces a fine graphite dust which must be constantly removed with the drafting brush so that the drawing will not become smeared. Then use the T-square to

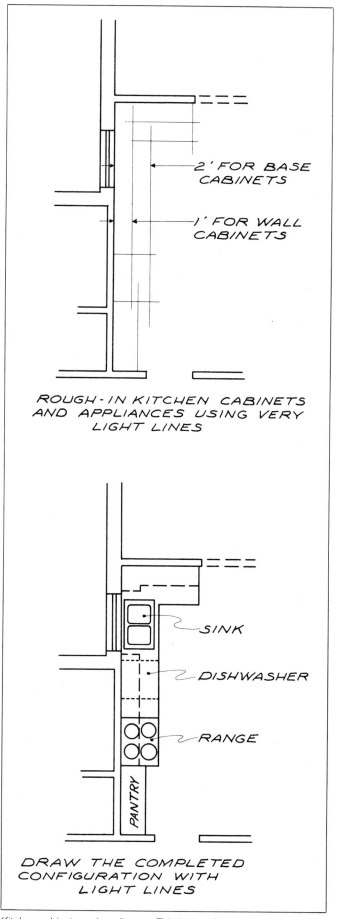

ROUGH-IN KITCHEN CABINETS AND APPLIANCES USING VERY LIGHT LINES

DRAW THE COMPLETED CONFIGURATION WITH LIGHT LINES

Kitchen cabinets and appliances. This is one of the hardest areas of the house to draw, so make all measurements carefully.

darken all horizontal lines. Start at the top of the board and move toward the bottom to avoid smearing the graphite dust. Brush the drawing again. Use the triangle to darken the vertical lines. Begin on the left side if you are right-handed and on the right side if you are left-handed. Brush the drawing again once all lines have been darkened.

LETTERING THE DRAWING

For many professional draftsmen lettering is an art, the major factor that sets their drawings aside as individual from others. But professional lettering takes many hours of practice—sometimes years—to develop. Fortunately there is only one requirement for the lettering on your own remodeling plans: it must be legible.

On the existing floor plan there are a limited number of items to be labeled. The room name must go in the center of each room. When there is more than one of a certain type room, such as baths and bedrooms, designate them by number. You will also need to label items such as the appliances, plumbing fixtures, exposed beams, fireplace, etc.

All notes should be printed exclusively in upper case letters. Make the room names about 3/16 inch high and the other notes 1/8 inch high. For each note draw two very light parallel guidelines the appropriate distance apart. The first few guidelines should be measured until you become accustomed to lettering and can draw them close enough to the proper width without the scale. Draw the guidelines inside the item to be labeled where possible. If not, draw them as close as space will allow.

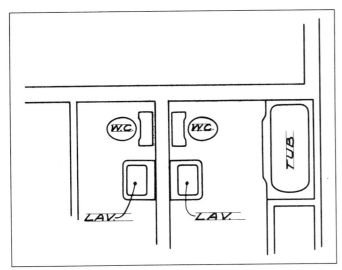

Lettering: Always use very lightly drawn guidelines when lettering. Place any notes inside the item to be labeled when possible. If not, use an arrow, as shown for the lavatory.

Now carefully letter each note making the letters go from the top guideline to the bottom one. Notes written horizontally should read from the bottom of the sheet and notes written vertically should read from the right side of the sheet. When a note is written beside an item draw a freehand line from the note to the item and place a dot on the end (see illustration). Before you begin to letter on the tracing, practice using guidelines on a scrap sheet of paper.

It is traditional to note the north orientation. Also, a title is needed to complete the existing floor plan. An inch or two

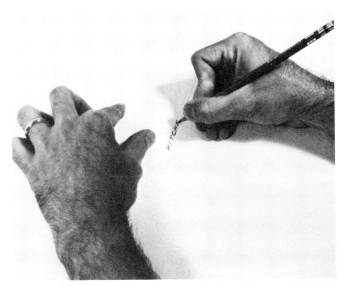

Lettering a drawing neatly requires several steps: (1) use guidelines on all lettering; (2) use all uppercase letters, going from the top guideline to the bottom one; (3) practice your lettering on scrap paper before working on the actual tracing.

under the plan draw two light guidelines about 1/4 inch apart. These should be more or less centered between the sides of the plan. Letter EXISTING FLOOR PLAN between the guidelines and then draw a dark line under the title. Just beneath the dark line draw two guidelines 1/8 inch apart and letter SCALE: 1/4 inch = 1 foot-0 inch. Now you are ready to begin the design process.

TRACING THE ORIGINAL PLANS

If you have the original plans, or prints of them, you may wish to trace what you need in order to save time. For the beginner, however, the longer process is advised. This will give you the experience working with drawing equipment that you will need once you start drawing the new floor plan. It will also avoid the problem of the house being different from the original plans because of changes made during construction. Should you still elect to trace the plans, a quick check of the dimensions is advisable.

Tape the floor plan from the original plans on the drawing board, lining up the longest wall with the T-square. Tape a new sheet of vellum over the floor plan. For remodeling purposes the existing floor plan serves primarily as a base for sketching designs. So most of the material on the original floor plan will not need to be traced. It can clutter the drawing and make design difficult.

With the H pencil and medium-hard pressure trace the plumbing fixtures and appliances first, using the architectural template wherever necessary. Brush the drawing clean of graphite dust. Then trace the walls, cabinets, and other features such as a fireplace and exposed beams, using the procedure previously outlined under "Darkening The Lines." The original floor plan will probably show door swing, material symbols in the walls, and other details. These are not necessary for your existing floor plan and should not be traced. Letter and title the drawing as previously described.

Now that the existing floor plan is drawn, you are ready to study your home more carefully and begin the framework of your new design.

Peeling, cracked, and rotted siding can be replaced with prefinished siding. The newer materials available are long lasting and require less maintenance than the original material (photo courtesy of the Masonite Corporation).

3 Design Ideas

Design, particularly for remodeling, can be taken as a step-by-step process. Using existing ideas and following a few rules, you can develop a unique and functional remodeling plan with little or no direct aid from an architect.

FINDING IDEAS

An architect's original design draws upon his education, experience, professional interaction, and familiarity with professional literature; totally original ideas are rare. Most unique designs, even those that receive widespread publication, are combinations of existing ideas that have been put together in a new manner. The architect works from what he knows; he then tries, to the best of his ability, to suit the design to the needs of his customer. Once you have access to the basic concepts of design, you will be better suited to plan for your needs than anyone else.

You have probably flipped through a magazine or book on homes and had a particular design or setting to catch your eye. Several major periodicals deal exclusively with residential design. To capture this rich source, set up a series of labeled file folders. Mark one for the outside of the home, and another for the outdoor site (patios, decks). Then set up a folder for each type of room already in your house and one for each type of room you would like to add. Clip articles containing ideas or arrangements you like and place them in the proper folders, numbering each clipping so it will be easy to refer to it. Write any notes you may have—such as the particular aspect of the picture that appeals to you, or something that you would like to change—directly onto the clipping. If you do not want to cut up your books, write a reference to the material as well as your notes on a separate sheet of paper. Include appropriate how-to information if you plan on doing some of the work yourself.

Additional Sources

Don't overlook another good source of ideas: homes you have visited. Record these ideas for your files by getting permission to take photographs. The homeowner may also be able to provide you with useful information about how the job was done. Models of new homes also offer an excellent selection of new ideas.

You may also wish to consult architectural periodicals, which should be available in the public library. These, however, tend to contain much more information about large commercial and public buildings than about homes.

There are a number of pamphlets and books available through the Federal Government; check with your FHA or VA office (see address list at back of this book). Also check with building supply dealers; they can give you a variety of brochures that tell you what materials are available and how they

are best used along with the technical data about the products.

SETTING A BUDGET

The first step in design is to establish a budget. Although it is fun and easy to plan a no-limit remodeling, the resulting design would be difficult to build with a moderate pocket book and might not meet actual needs, energy conservation requirements, and easier maintenance levels. At today's construction cost, even for the do-it-yourselfer it is extravagance to build something that will rarely be used. By establishing a firm budget at the onset you will avoid the disappointment of the final design being beyond your means. The latter usually ends up with having nothing at all done to your home, because the cost is discouraging. Your imaginative skills will be tested, but by following the criteria given here for determining realistic needs, you will be able to develop a plan that is attractive, functional, and within your budget.

Funds Available

Discuss your ideas with your banker. He can help you assess your financial condition and arrive at a reasonable budget figure. The budget should allow enough remodeling to increase the usefulness and the pleasure of your home without overextending yourself.

Once you know how much you can spend, you will need an idea of how much work you can do for the money. Talk to several contractors to get a feeling for current cost in your area.

ROOM ADDITION COST COMPARISON

Room	Rank	Remarks
Bath	1	The bath is generally the most expensive room to add due to the high cost of plumbing fixtures and finish materials.
Kitchen	2	Kitchens are also high-cost additions. With all new appliances and new cabinets, they can cost more per sq. ft. than the bathroom.
Great/Family Room	3	This medium-cost addition is the most popular. But with fireplace, exposed beams and quality paneling, the price goes up.
Bedroom	4	Low cost per square foot makes the bedroom a logical choice for an addition. Existing bedrooms can then be converted to other uses.
Living Room	5	The formal living room is placed below the bedroom only because of the extra walls and door required for bedroom closets. But with a fireplace or new carpeting, living room costs rise quickly.

This basement remodeling was an easy do-it-yourself project. The large basement was remodeled into a great room with smaller areas, but keeping the open circulation. Mechanical equipment is hidden behind paneled enclosures (photos courtesy of Armstrong Company).

The construction industry is especially sensitive to inflation—running over 10 percent per year in recent years—and to regional differences. A $20,000 remodeling job in one area could be more than twice that in another area because of differences in labor costs, climate conditions, soil conditions, and accessibility of material suppliers.

The cost of your work will also vary due to the nature of the work. The square foot cost of adding a kitchen or bath will be much higher than the square foot cost of adding a bedroom because of the plumbing fixtures and cabinetry. Work within the existing home can have a wider range for square foot cost since the work can range from simply replacing some finish materials to major surgery; including removing and adding interior walls, new windows and doors, new cabinets, new plumbing and electrical fixtures, etc. Very extensive remodeling on the inside of the home can cost as much per square foot as an addition.

For work of a very expensive nature, square foot figures can become meaningless. For instance, a single sunken bath can cost over $2,000; or, a complete kitchen remodeling with new cabinets and new appliances could run as high as $10,000 and possibly more. For particular items of an expensive nature consult a supplier about cost.

The cost of your work will also be affected by the way it is handled. You can save money by subcontracting the work rather than using a single general contractor, and you can save even more by doing some of the work yourself (see Chapter 10).

Based upon your discussions with contractors and suppliers, determine a reasonable square foot cost for various types of additions and for different levels of work on the inside of your home. Add a 15 to 20 percent cushion to cover increases in cost between planning and construction and to cover other unknown factors which might arise. Then, when planning your new work, keep these figures in mind so that the plans will reflect work that is attainable with the budget you have established.

MAKING LISTS

Go through your home, room by room, and study it closely, carrying the existing floor plan with you. Look for things that annoy you about the home, such as worn carpet or wasted areas, and for good features. Compile two lists as you go, one of the good features of your home that you wish to preserve and one that contains points you would like to change. For later planning purposes, it would be efficient to separate the lists by rooms, leaving one section for overall comments. When you are not using these lists keep them in your first folder, the one set up for the existing home.

FOUR TYPES OF NEEDS

Your remodeling needs can be placed in four categories: aesthetic, space, personal, and, of course, repair. Each of these is of vital inportance in reaching a balanced overall plan.

Aesthetic Needs

Making your home more attractive to you, more appealing to live and entertain in, is the primary objective of planning to meet aesthetic needs. The major considerations, of course, would be decoration and furniture. But there are other aesthetic features which are a part of the actual construction such as exterior styling, type of lighting to be used, bay windows, exposed beams, etc.

You should take into account not only what you see when you look into your home, but also what you see when you look out of it. For instance, you wouldn't want to place a bay window so that the main part of your view was a neighbor's brick wall. Coordinate visual access to the outside with the open natural areas of your yard and any site work you may wish to plan (see Chapter 6).

Space Needs

Designing to meet the family's lifestyle, making your home more comfortable and more useful, is what satisfying space needs is all about. Making rooms large enough for comfortable furniture arrangement and smooth traffic flow, but not so large that they seem cold and empty or become a financial burden is one of the main goals of space planning. Many other factors, however, must enter into consideration, such as the convenient arrangement of electrical outlets and light switches, a large patio complete with cooking center for outdoor-oriented families, keeping general traffic out of a room that requires privacy, a step-saving kitchen arrangement, and adding storage cabinets or spaces without their being too visible or obvious.

Personal Needs

Each individual, even in a very close family, is different and has particular needs. This could range from special lighting around a mirror, or special equipment for the handicapped, to the inclusion of home hobby and craft centers of home offices and studios. By careful space planning, personal needs for things such as hobby centers can be combined with other rooms. This type of double use can be easily disguised and will help keep your remodeling within your budget limitations.

Repair Needs

There are few older homes that do not have a list of headaches throbbing for attention. These repairs, no matter how minor, should also be included in your remodeling. In fact, you can save money on the smaller repair items by making them a part of your overall plans. A plumber, for instance, will charge a considerable fee for traveling to your home just to spend a minute or two fixing a leaky faucet. But when he is bidding on the entire job, the leaky faucet may be included for little or nothing in the interest of securing the contract.

General repairs are not considered as remodeling by most people. But if you added a large family room to your house, and ignored a rotting, leaking roof, you would do little to increase the home's value. And don't overlook unseen repairs such as the replacement of caulking and weatherstripping or the inclusion of sufficient insulation to help keep utility bills down. The savings each month could help pay the overall remodeling cost.

DEFINING YOUR NEEDS

Set up a new folder for remodeling needs. Then provide a sheet for each type of need. The first sheet in the folder, however, should have nothing more than your budget, written in very large numbers. Keep your lists of the home's good and bad points at ready reference as you discuss the aesthetic, space, and repair needs with the entire family. Also keep the idea folders close at hand. As each need is established write it on the proper sheet. Some items may be classified under two different types of needs. A new cabinet, for instance, could be considered as an aesthetic or a space need. You should only write these once, in whichever category you prefer. Do not overload yourself at this point. Make the description of each item brief. Refer to a clipping from the idea folder rather than trying to explain what is in the picture. Do not worry about things such as color selection unless you already have something definite in mind.

Classify by Room
Whenever possible, classify the needs by room. Work with the family as a whole when developing the aesthetic, space, and repair needs. Then discuss the personal needs of each family member individually. The success of the remodeling will be greatly enhanced if everyone is allowed input into the planning.

Write down every need that comes to mind unless it is obviously beyond the budget. Consider all needs equally for the present. Later, as you begin to develop your plan, you and your family may have to establish priorities if meeting all the needs appears to be smashing the budget. Some of the lower priority items may have to be trimmed and some needs can be combined into double-use areas. It would be wise, however, to leave some of each family member's input in the final plan.

Once the needs are established, you must learn a few design concepts and planning principles before you can begin sketching your ideas. Your needs may have to be reassessed once or twice to stay within the budget, but you now have the foundation on which your entire remodeling rests. Extra time and effort spent here can save much more time, trouble, and money during construction and will make the remodeled home more responsive to your needs and your pocketbook.

DESIGN CONCEPTS
One basic theory of architecture, and the one most suited for your remodeling design, is that "form follows function." This means that the use of a room will define its shape, the type of finish materials to be used, and to a large extent its decoration. For instance, a kitchen remodeling must take into account the three basic work areas, as well as appliance arrangement and storage needs. A child's room must be designed for safety and the learning requirements of a youngster; sleep areas, play areas, or perhaps a raised platform are helpful. The walls and floors must be constructed of materials that will stand up to childhood "creativity," as will the furniture, which must also be scaled to child size.

Although certain styles or themes may be used, design cannot be defined in a single context of good taste; it is as varied as human lifestyles and personalities. By choosing to become a self-planner, or at least to understand the planning process even if someone else draws the plans, you are in a much better position to serve your own lifestyle and your own taste.

DESIGN ANALYSIS
Here are general guidelines from which you can compose an individualized plan.

Energy Conservation
As the cost of energy increases at phenomenal rates, and with the threat of limited energy supplies, one prime consideration of any remodeling is energy conservation for both the new work and the existing house. Below is a list of the steps you can take to assure your home is energy efficient.

Insulation. Insulate attics and walls. In cooler climates you should also insulate crawl spaces and slabs-on-grade. Consult with the city building department for the R - value of insulation required in your area.

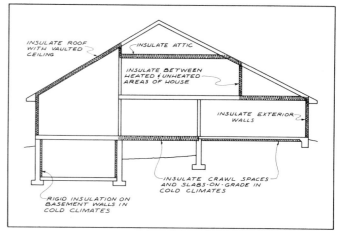

With rapidly increasing energy costs and threatened shortages, home insulation is essential. The required values of the insulation, as shown below, will vary according to your region.

R-VALUES FOR DIFFERENT TYPES OF INSULATION

	Batts or blankets		Loose fill (poured-in)		
R-Values	Glass fiber	Rock wool	Glass fiber	Rock wool	Cellulose fiber
R-11	3½"-4"	3"	5"	4"	3"
R-19	6"-6½"	5¼"	8"-9"	6"-7"	5"
R-22	6½"	6"	10"	7"-8"	6"
R-30	9½"-10½"*	9"*	13"-14"	10"-11"	8"
R-38	12"-13"*	10½"*	17"-18"	13"-14"	10"-11"

*Two batts or blankets required

Weatherstripping. Weatherstripping should be installed, or if necessary replaced, around all windows and doors.

Storm Windows & Doors. Storm windows and doors can be installed over the existing windows and doors.

Insulating Windows & Doors. Double- or triple-pane insulated windows and insulated steel doors are available both to replace the existing and for the new work. Their initial extra cost will be paid back in fuel savings.

Caulking. Caulk all cracks where construction materials meet, such as around windows and door trim, chimneys, etc.

Ventilation. Attics should be properly ventilated with soffit vents in the roof overhang to bring in cooler air and ridge and/or roof vents to allow the hot air to escape. For high ceilings a ventilation system, such as an openable skylight, will let hot air rise out of the house. For capturing summer breezes in the house, place the larger windows on the downwind side of the prevailing summer winds to help pull the wind through. Attic fans or rooftop fans may be necessary in hotter regions. Avoid windows and doors on the winter wind side of the house in colder climates.

Heating & Air Conditioning Equipment. Outdated equipment can be replaced with new energy efficient units that will pay for themselves in a few years through energy savings.

Plants & Trees. Planting around the home is a natural energy saver. Deciduous trees help block the hot summer sun while letting the warm winter sun in through the windows. Evergreen trees and plants help block the cold winds of winter on the north side of the house.

Roof Overhang. A longer roof overhang will help block the more directly overhead rays of the summer sun. The lower sun of winter can shine through the windows.

Exterior Materials. In cold climates darker-colored finish materials will help to absorb heat. In hot climates lighter-colored or reflecting materials are recommended.

Room arrangement. Rooms can be arranged to allow for the maximum use of the sun's warmth. See the section on room arrangement in this chapter.

Solar Energy. Although solar technology is still in its infancy, it is advancing rapidly. In order to make use of solar energy, usually through collectors or heat pumps, consult your local library for up-to-date information from periodicals and books. Be wary of anything on solar technology that is more than a year old.

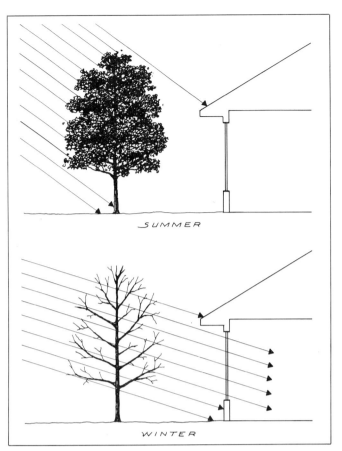

Deciduous trees help by screening the sun's heat in summer and allowing the warmth to enter the house in winter.

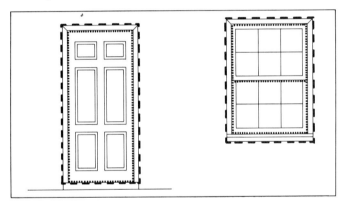

Caulk around window and door trim (dashed line) and along all edges where construction materials meet. Weatherstripping on windows and doors (dotted line) should be checked and replaced as necessary.

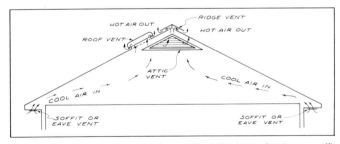

Proper attic ventilation can help keep utility bills down. As shown, soffit or eave vents bring in cooler air while hot air rises out through either roof vents, gable vents, or ridge vents. Electric powered fans are available for most vents to help pull the hot air out.

Light

Light, both natural and artificial, can turn a good remodeling into an outstanding remodeling when planned and used properly. But the use of both requires careful thought and the understanding of some basic principles.

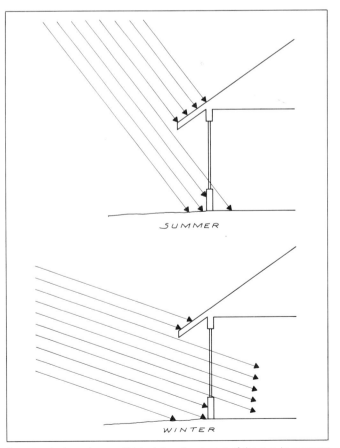

An extended overhang will block the direct rays of the sun in summer while letting them in during winter.

Natural light (sunlight) has the advantage of not only costing less, but it also has a profound effect upon the human spirit. There are two ways to capture natural light in the home: through windows and through skylights. And it can be further enjoyed by planning a livable patio area that extends the use of the home into the outside.

Windows, of course, are the most common method of allowing natural light to enter the home. But some windows and window arrangements are more effective than others. Large windows will obviously let in more light than small ones, which have the double hazard of also causing glare problems. Windows that are placed high on a wall will illuminate better than low windows, even if the lower windows are quite large. This is because the lower a window is placed on a wall the less reflection there will be in a room; the ceiling, particularly, will remain dark. Windows should be placed so that they can "wash" an interior wall, increasing light reflection in a room. Where possible, putting windows on two sides of a room will allow the maximum use of natural light and reduce the possibility of glare. Lighter colored walls will reflect more light, causing a room to be brighter, while dark walls will require more artificial light and, consequently, more energy.

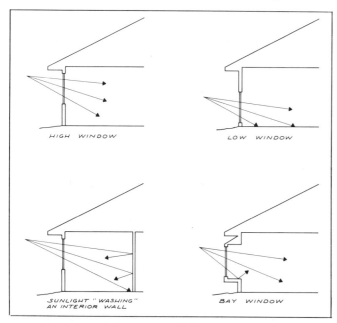

There are many ways that natural light can come in through a window. A high window will keep a room brighter than a low window. Allowing the light to "wash" a wall also makes a room brighter. A bay (oriel) window causes additional reflection, letting in more light and reducing glare.

Skylights can also be used in a variety of ways to capture natural light, as shown in the illustration. This type of lighting has a different effect than windows, and is often more dramatic. Glass, however, should not be used indiscriminately. There is a direct relation between the amount of natural light coming into the house and the cost of heating and air conditioning. Larger areas of glass will have a welcoming warmth in the winter (except on the cold north side), but should be double-paned as well as screened with deciduous trees, heavy drapes, and long roof overhangs for the hot summer months.

There are two main types of artificial lighting: incandescent and fluorescent. Incandescent lights, by far the most common, are warmer both in color and in temperature. Fluorescent

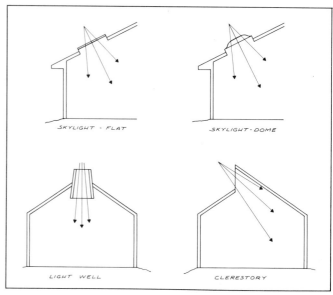

Skylights are available in styles other than the flat and domed lights shown, which all diffuse the sunlight in many directions. Light wells can be used to direct light, especially over indoor gardens; a dramatic lighting effect can be achieved by the use of a clerestory window.

lights put out four to five times as much light per watt and are more useful for high work areas such as over the sink or at hobby and craft centers.

The basic ways in which artificial lighting can be used are:
- Spots (ceiling recessed or on tracks)
- Lamps that diffuse light through shades
- Task lighting from desk lamps, etc.
- General fixtures that spread the light through glass covers or lenses
- Valance lighting, usually hidden, that uses the ceiling as a reflector.

Lighting can be used in certain areas to make double use of rooms possible. It can also be used to close off a larger room and make a corner warm and cozy. Lights can be used in conjunction with dimmer switches to create dramatic effects in a room, setting the desired mood. Since the ways in which artificial lighting can be used are so diverse, chapter 4 suggests you browse through the products available and then consult a lighting dealer prior to drawing the new electrical work onto the floor plan.

The amount of light you will need will vary according to room size and type of room. The table below shows how many lumens are required per square foot in each room. A lumen is a commonly used measure of light. To convert this to your needs, multiply the square footage of the room by the number of lumens for that room in the table. Then divide the total number by 16 to find out how many watts of incandescent lights are required; divide by 70 for fluorescent lights.

Room	Lumens Per Sq. Ft.
Bedroom	35
Hallway	30
Bathroom	50
Kitchen	80
Dining Room	40
Living Room	40
Family Room	50

Color	% of Light Reflected
Pure white	90
Ivory & off-white	80
Pale yellow & cream	75
Orchid, light gray, sky blue, and buff	65
Pale green	60
Shell pink	55
Bright green	50
Olive tan	45
Forest green	20
Dark brown	15
Black	1

These are general figures and will vary depending on the shape of the room (a square room is the most efficient for lighting purposes) and by the reflective quality of the color of the room (see the table above). Other factors should be considered, such as special lighting needs for task areas and special lighting in the bath for cosmetic purposes. Usually the most desirable lighting for any room—artificial, natural, or both—is achieved when the light comes from several directions and is not extremely intense from any of them.

As stated previously, the color of the room is important in helping to diffuse the light. A pure white wall will reflect about 90 percent of the light, but this is too much for visual comfort and can cause glare. A flat finish with a color that reflects 75 percent to 80 percent of the light is the most desirable. The table shows the reflective capacity of several different colors.

Room Arrangement

In order to make more efficient use of your home's square footage, eliminating wasted areas and minimizing the cost of remodeling, you may wish to rearrange the use of your rooms. A clever arrangement could solve a variety of problems, such as a lack of privacy, and save the high cost of an addition; or, at least, give you a more useful home while staying within the budget. Although no layout can be made perfect and compromises will have to be made, a series of suggestions for proper room placement follow. These, however, should be observed keeping your individual taste and life style in mind. For instance, west is the direction of the extremely hot afternoon sun and a patio on the west side could be uncomforatable. But west is also the direction of the most beautiful natural phenomenon on earth, the sunset. If watching the sunset makes the labor of the day worthwhile for you, then you may want to endure the heat of a west side patio, using some sort of overhead screen to help control the heat.

The first, and perhaps the most important thing to consider for room arrangement is the path of the sun. You can take advantage of or exclude the sun's warmth, as well as making the best use of natural light, by using the proper arrangement. The list below discusses the best placement for each type of room. This is an ideal situation and may not be possible in your personal remodeling because of budget considerations, personal needs, or restrictions of codes or existing site features. It would be wise, however, to follow these guidelines whenever possible in considering additions and rearrangement of existing rooms.

Kitchen. By facing east or southeast the brightness and warmth of the morning sun will be brought into the kitchen while avoiding the afternoon heat in the west. This is important for a room which is warmer than the rest of the house during meal preparation. The second choice would be to the south or southwest.

Dining Room or Area. Place this room close to the kitchen by necessity; because it needs the natural light of the sun, the dining room should face east, south, or southeast. West is a reasonable second choice, especially for dinnertime sunsets during summer's daylight savings season.

Bathroom. Since it is sparingly used the bathroom can be placed in any direction, though plumbing connections should be considered. In order to keep cost down the bathroom should be adjacent to the plumbing of the kitchen or another bath.

Great/Family/Recreation Room. With the exception of north, the family room can be located in any direction. South and west are more desirable for capturing natural light since this room is generally used more often in the afternoon than morning. When facing the hot west, strong consideration should be given to the energy conservation measures previously discussed such as extended roof overhangs and careful placement of deciduous trees and plants.

Living Room. Again south and west are the best directions for this type of room. However, if your living room is only rarely and formally used, as many now are, east, and even north, can be considered if necessary.

Bedroom. Since the bedroom is occupied most often in the morning part of the daylight hours, east and southeast are preferable. The morning sun will help warm the cool of night. A good second choice would be either south or northeast.

Storage/Utility Rooms & Garage/Carports. For the cooler climates these areas are good on the north side to provide a buffer between the cold north and the living areas of the house. In hotter climates where the heat of summer is more of a problem, the reverse would be true except for laundry centers which create their own heat and would be better placed on the north, northeast, or northwest.

Room Relationships

Careful layout will make the best use of the sun, but the rooms must be coordinated to work together. The dining room and/or area, for instance, should adjoin the kitchen, with the family room nearby. Even modest outdoor usage by the family will require an access from the family room to the outside. If you have a large attic begging to be finished (or a garage/carport) and need to add a family room, be careful not to make the home inconvenient by placing a popular room in an out-of-the-way area. Perhaps the best solution would be to put the family room in an existing area, move a wall if necessary, and use the attic for children's bedrooms, a master bedroom suite, hobby and work areas, or even an adult retreat. If planning a bath in the newly finished attic, place it over a downstairs bath or the kitchen to assure that plumbing hookups can be made.

From the kitchen you should be able to control the living areas of the house such as the family room, family entrance to the house (though not necessarily in the kitchen), and children's play areas. A good way to keep the house cleaner is to provide a small storage or "mud" room at the family entrance.

Private rooms should be kept private. A person should not have to go through a bedroom to get to another room. The bathrooms, while needing to be convenient to the entire house, should be located on secondary paths; and neither the bath nor the path from the bedroom to the bath should be visible from the major living areas of the home. Children's bedrooms should be placed so as not to be bothered by night traffic.

Bedroom Considerations

When considering any room for reassignment as a bedroom, first take into account the position of the room and windows for privacy. Bedrooms may be clustered for privacy, with rooms such as closets and baths used as buffers between them and the noisier areas of the home. Or you may wish to separate the master bedroom from the guest and children's bedrooms. While this is desirable for many families, controlling the transmission of sound is difficult since the number of buffer areas required almost doubles. Sound insulation is the simplest solution.

Additions

If you are planning an addition that will require plumbing facilities, check with the city building department that the plumbing connections can be made. This is especially necessary for new rooms that are lower than the existing house. If you are not able to get plumbing facilities into an addition without an extremely high cost, consider making the add-on room one that does not need plumbing and then reassign the existing rooms to meet all plumbing needs. If you keep kitchens and baths in the same areas, the cost will be lower because of the accessibility of plumbing facilities. Also, second floor additions should be designed so that the new upstairs plumbing is above a bath or the kitchen. The upstairs wall with plumbing should be exactly on top of the downstairs wall that contains plumbing.

Shape and Size

Room size and shape are also important factors to be considered. A square or rectangular room is cheaper to heat and air condition, but has poorer acoustical qualities than an odd-shaped room. Long, narrow rooms should be avoided for energy reasons. Additions will be cheaper per square foot if there are fewer outside corners, since each corner represents additional material and labor requirements, especially in the roof.

Since most finish materials come in standard sizes, this should be considered in designing room dimensions. For instance, most carpets and other sheet flooring materials come in 12 foot widths (15 foot widths are often available). A room that is 12 x 14 has almost the same area as a room that is 13 x 13, but will be cheaper to carpet because of the waste resulting in the 13 x 13 room when the carpet is cut and seamed to fit. The same is true for walls. Wood or simulated wood paneling usually comes in 4 x 8 sheets. Gypsum wallboard (also called plaster board, drywall, and by the trade name Sheet Rock) is available in 4 x 8 and 4 x 12 sheets. With the twelve foot side placed horizontally, both the 12 x 14 room and the 13 x 13 room will require the same amount of wallboard, but the 13 x 13 room will require additional seaming and labor.

Foot Traffic Flow

Windows and doors should be placed to allow for a variety of furniture layouts and for proper traffic flow. Circulation should be along the edge of major rooms, not through the center. Rooms often used for entertaining should allow thorough circulation and multiple "conversation" areas, whether seating or standing. Rooms requiring privacy should have more "dead-end" situations in the traffic flow. No room should be more than fifty feet from an exit for fire protection purposes.

SOUND INSULATION

The consideration of sound insulation is important during your remodeling because it will be more difficult and much more expensive to correct sound problems once the remodeling has been completed. Since sound is vibrational energy which travels through solids even faster than through air, the standard stud wall does little to stop the transmission of sound from one room to another. Placing insulation between the studs, contrary to popular thought, does not effectively inhibit the flow of sound since the studs are rigidly attached to the walls.

Specialty Items

There are a number of special items or special constructions you may want to consider. These could include skylights, fireplaces and hearths, vaulted ceilings, bay or bow windows, or greenhouses. Some, such as a vaulted ceiling, can be designed to your specifications and will be reflected in the plans you develop in the remaining chapters. Others, however, such as skylights, will necessitate a visit to a building material dealer to determine the type and design requirements for each item.

Alternatives

There are several good ways to insulate the walls for sound; however, some are practical and some are not.

Heavy masonry wall. The heavier a wall is, provided it is not porous, the better it insulates against sound. A double brick wall, an 8 inch concrete block wall or an 8 inch reinforced concrete wall, with the surfaces covered with heavy coats of dense paint, prove very effective against sound. But they can be expensive and few homes have a foundation designed to support such walls.

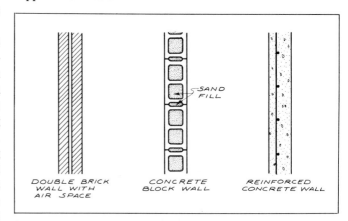

DOUBLE BRICK WALL WITH AIR SPACE   CONCRETE BLOCK WALL   REINFORCED CONCRETE WALL

Generally, the heavier a wall is the more sound resistant it will be. The three walls shown are excellent sound insulators, but are often impractical in terms of cost, size, and weight as interior walls for homes.

Spring mounted wallboard or plaster. There are several types of spring clips available for fastening the wall materials to the studs as in the illustration. The clips absorb the vibrational energy of sound and the system is an effective insulator against sound transmission.

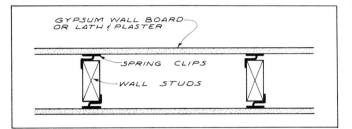

Spring clips between the studs and plaster or plasterboard absorb the vibrational energy of sound.

Staggered stud wall. Another good sound insulator is the staggered stud wall. In this construction, each wall skin has a separate stud wall which does not touch the other. By adding a loosely fitting sound absorbing material, such as a mineral wool blanket, the sound insulation quality of this type of wall is increased.

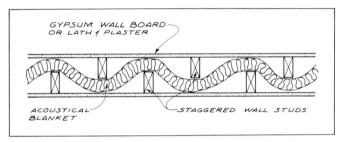

The effectiveness of the staggered stud wall can be further increased by the inclusion of a loosely fitting sound-absorbent material such as a mineral wool blanket.

Split or slotted stud wall. The split or slotted stud wall is almost as effective as the staggered stud wall. The studs are split at the center to within a few inches of each end using a ripsaw. A sound resisting blanket should be placed in the wall cavities, snuggly against the split studs, but should not touch the wall skins.

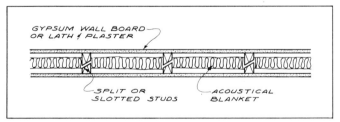

The split or slotted stud wall, though slightly less effective than some of the other designs, is useful when space and money are in short supply.

Resilient damping board. The installation of a resilient damping board layer under the wall surface skins must be carefully applied in accordance with manufacturer's suggested procedures, but when properly constructed it is an effective sound insulator.

Existing walls. Existing walls may be insulated for sound by using a resilient damping board plus a new wall surface as mentioned above, or by adding a single face partition as in the illustration. Although the single face partition may cut down

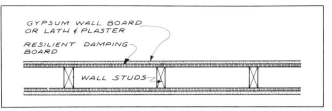

The resilient damping board may be used in conjunction with the other sound-insulating constructions for additional effectiveness.

on room size a few square feet, it is a very effective sound insulator.

All sound-insulated walls should be tightly constructed. Even small cracks can drastically cut down their effectiveness. Doors in sound-insulated walls should either be solid core or special acoustical with all edges stripped with spring-contacting metal weather stripping. Rubber gasketing will be only fair and felt sealing strips work poorly.

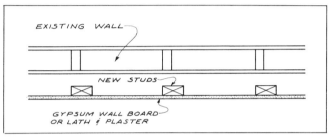

Adding a single-face partition to an existing wall is a simple and inexpensive way to get good sound insulation without removing the existing wall.

Acoustical ceiling tile will lower the reflected sound in a room, but it is not designed to and will not appreciably lower the transmission of sound into a floor above. A dropped or false ceiling is the best approach if there is enough height to allow another set of joists that do not touch the floor joist above. This is not practical in most modern homes where ceilings are already low. In such cases heavy carpet and thick padding on the floor above is the best answer.

One other approach is to use a floating floor. As shown in the illustration, the joists and the finish flooring do not actually touch. This is a very effective but slightly more expensive way to insulate against sound between floor levels.

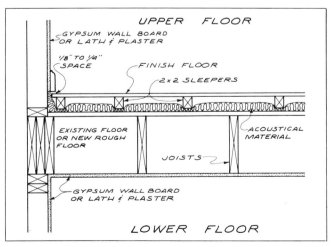

The floating floor has the advantage of being an effective sound insulator between floor levels, but is more expensive than standard construction.

INTERIOR DESIGN

The design analysis of the inside of your home is taken room by room. For ease in designing, a full range of furniture cut-outs is provided at the rear of this chapter and should be used when you begin sketching your design ideas. Develop a design that will allow a number of furniture arrangements in each room. (The cut-outs are found on page 18. Items included are standard sizes; for custom pieces you may have to draw your own template.)

Great/Family/Recreation Room

The family and recreation rooms are mainly the development of the last half century, as lifestyles have become more informal. To further this idea the "Great Room" has been developed in recent years and quite often eliminates the formal living room entirely. This "modern" Great Room is nothing more than the living room of the past, when all the family activities were carried on in a "living" room that was far from the formal reception area it has become.

There are more design variations and possibilities for this type of room than for any other, and consequently there are fewer firm design principles. Since form follows function, plan your space to suit your needs. Consult your idea folder and your own ideas for things you want to include in the room. Frequent entertaining requires more space, plenty of seating area, and access to the outdoors for party overflow. Area lighting and different floor levels can keep the large room from becoming intimidating when the group is small.

The family room should be inviting, with materials and colors that suggest informal living for both family and guests. It is also a great place for double-use areas. A storage room that provides extra seating while entertaining can also double as a dark room. Cabinetry for the TV/music center can double as hobby and craft centers. Built-in seating areas, especially around a sunken conversation area, can be raised for miscellaneous storage. Closets and book shelves may also be necessary in your family room.

Considerations

Important considerations for the informal living area include door and window placement. Take advantage of pleasant views, especially if you plan or already have a nice patio area, by using ample amounts of glass. But keep your furniture in mind when placing windows. Place doors to facilitate traffic within the house and to the outside. Don't let the door arrangement interfere with the use of the room or force someone to constantly dodge furniture to get to the door. Seating that is facing should be no closer than 5 feet apart and no wider than 8 feet. Good conversation areas should have a diameter of 10 feet as measured from the center of the seats. Standing conversation areas should have a diameter of about six feet. There is no maximum size for this type of room, but no wall length should be less than 10-1/2 feet.

A fireplace can be the focal point of the informal living area, or it can be built into a sunken conversation area. Recessed or track lighting with a dimmer switch should be considered in the fireplace area for developing an intimate, cozy space.

With a vaulted ceiling and skylights the sky can virtually be the limit for this room. Let your imagination go, but always be mindful of the budget.

Living Room

Because of the drastic increases in construction cost and today's informal lifestyles the formal living room is passing into extinction. In fact, turning this room back into useful living area can solve many of your needs without adding on to the house.

But if your plans call for a formal living area, the main criteria for planning will be furniture arrangement. Use the furniture cut-outs to help define the size of the room, keeping the seating pieces that are facing each other a minimum of 5 feet apart. Allow 36 inches clearance for main passage through the room and 24 inches for secondary passage. For a moderate three-bedroom home a recommended minimum living room size is 11 x 16, but 12 x 18 is more desirable. The smallest wall should not be less than 11 feet.

Studios

Many leisure time activities and special interests require work areas in the home. These include but are not limited to: photography dark room; hobby and craft centers; home office; sewing center; music center; artist's studio; and, indoor gardening.

These rooms or areas should be designed to meet the needs of the person who will use them. But be careful to keep things that might be harmful to children, such as photographic chemicals or artist's paints, in safe, lockable storage. Usually you will be able to combine a studio area with another room, such as a recreation room or bedroom, which helps to ease the budget. But if the studio area is so extensive it requires a separate room, consider the out-of-the-way attic or storage room; you can even partition off part of the garage. Many of these centers will require bright lighting and/or good ventilation.

Kitchen

The nature of a kitchen makes its planning more technical than most rooms. This is evidenced by the increasing popularity of a new group of professionals: kitchen planners. They work with an architect, or directly with the homeowner, to design an efficient and attractive cooking area. Their rise to prominence emphasizes the age-old adage that the kitchen is the "heart of the home."

By looking at the cooking process as a series of work areas, or centers, the kitchen can be designed to save time and effort. These centers are the refrigeration and mixing center, the preparation and clean-up center, and the cooking and serving center.

The refrigeration and mixing center includes the refrigerator and about 3 to 4 linear feet of counter space for mixing. Cabinets in this area would contain mixing bowls and the dry ingredients used in food preparation. The refrigerator door should open on the side with the counter space.

The preparation and clean-up center is, of course, the sink; and it is also the area for washing fruits and vegetables, preparing foods to be cooked, and cleaning up afterward. Other appliances which would go in this center include the dish washer, disposal, and trash compactor. Provide 2 to 3 linear feet of counter space on either side of the sink for food preparation, dish rack, etc.

Kitchen Floor Plans.

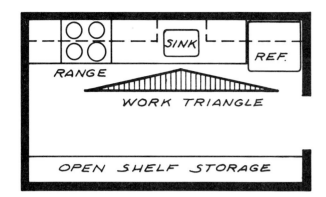

Single-Wall. The single-wall kitchen is ideal as a second kitchen, or as the main kitchen when space is a prime concern. Place the sink near the center of the cabinet wall and keep the range and refrigerator close together. Consider a shallow pantry or open storage shelves on the opposite wall.

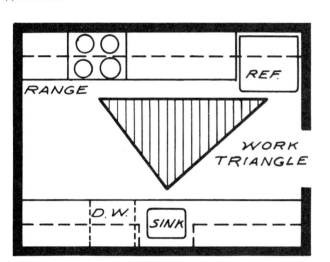

Parallel Wall or Galley. This design works well in narrow areas, but not too narrow, or the work space becomes cramped. About 4 ft. between the cabinets will provide ample space. Be wary of doors at both ends of the galley, which can turn the kitchen into a hallway and break down good working conditions.

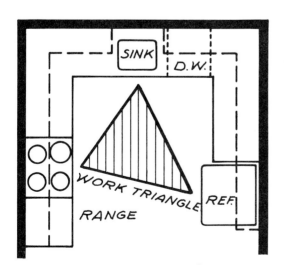

"U" Shape. This is an extremely efficient and convenient kitchen design when one leg of the work triangle is on each wall. Often, one leg forms a divider between the kitchen and a dining or family room. For the best use of a "U" shape kitchen, place the sink in the center leg.

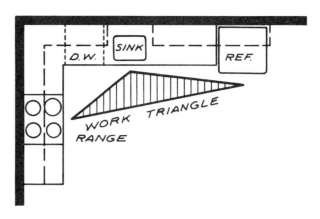

"L" Shape. The "L" Shape is usually built into the corner of a room, especially when the kitchen includes a dining area. This design should not be broken by a door or passage.

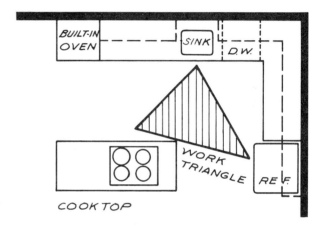

Island. The island is a variation of the "L" or "U" shape and helps make an extremely large kitchen more efficient. By building an overhang and placing stools at the island, it can also be used as an informal eating area.

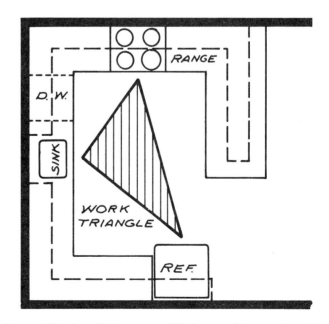

Surround. The four-sided or surround kitchen usually has one leg, often an eating bar, as a divider between the kitchen and another room. It may be broken twice for doors and passageways, but be careful not to funnel general traffic through the area of the work triangle.

The cooking and serving area consists of the range or cooktop and about 2 linear feet of counter space for final preparation before the food is served.

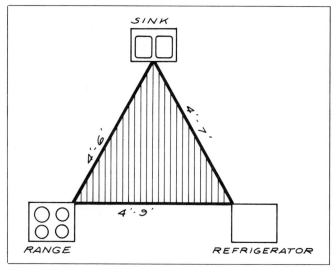

For a work-efficient kitchen, observe the maximum and minimum dimensions shown on the work triangle. A larger work triangle will require too much walking; a smaller triangle, while work-efficient, will create a cramped kitchen with insufficient counter space.

Together these three centers comprise a "work triangle" which will help define your kitchen arrangement. The perimeter of the triangle should be between 12 and 22 feet for maximum working efficiency and should be divided as in the illustration. If you use a cooktop and separate oven, keep the oven convenient but outside the work triangle. You should also avoid having general traffic flow through the work triangle or, for that matter, through the kitchen.

Since a sink is often desirable under a window, this may dictate, to a large extent, the kitchen layout. If your kitchen has only one exterior wall, the sink would go there (the usual size of a window over a sink is 30 x 32).

Don't catch yourself short on cabinet space. Design a minimum of 10 linear feet of base cabinets and 10 linear feet of wall cabinets, more if space and budget allow. Open storage shelves in the kitchen are attractive and save money on cabinet work. A pantry also can ease storage problems.

An island or peninsula makes a neat break between a dining area or family room. The island can also serve as an eating

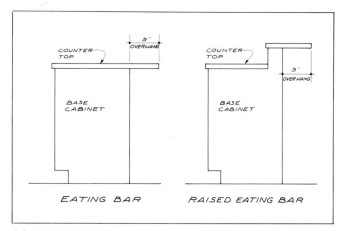

A freestanding counter can double as an eating bar simply by adding an overhang, or raised overhang, to the countertop.

bar. For a little more kitchen privacy, a pass-through with folding doors works well.

Though kitchen design is slightly restricted when adhering to the principle of the work triangle, there is still almost as much room for imagination as in the informal family room. You many wish to combine a breakfast nook with the kitchen, or include a table and chairs for that easy country kitchen look. A desk may also be included for carrying on the family's business. Regardless of what you want in your kitchen, you will find cooking a little easier if the other activities don't interfere with the basic work triangle area.

Dining

Whether the dining area is a cozy little breakfast nook tucked into a bay window or a formal dining room, you should allow unrestricted movement for chair access and for serving. When designing your new dining area use the furniture cut-outs and observe the following minimum clearances between the edge of the table and a wall or other piece of furniture: 32 inches for chairs and access to them; 38 inches for chairs, access, and passage behind the chairs; 42 inches for serving from behind the chairs; 24 inches for passage only.

If the room is a combination kitchen-dining, keep the dining table a minimum of 48 inches from the nearest kitchen base cabinet. For an eating bar at a kitchen island plan a minimum countertop overhang of 8 inches, and 9 inches is even better; or, use a raised overhang as in the illustration.

Bedrooms

At $30 and more a square foot few people can afford the extravagance of a huge bedroom, but generally they should be larger than the FHA minimum of 8 x 10. A size of 11 x 14 is adequate for most bedrooms and a little larger would work for the master bedroom. If your plans include a bedroom addition or a reassignment of an existing room as a new bedroom, use the furniture cut-outs and follow the minimum clearances given to determine the size necessary for the room:

42" at one side or foot of bed for dressing
6" between side of bed and side of dresser or chest
36" in front of dresser, closet, and chest of drawers
24" minimum for major circulation path (door to closet), but 36" preferred
22" on one side of a bed for circulation
12" minimum on the least used side of a double bed, 20" preferred (twin beds may rest against a wall on one side)
24" minimum depth for closets, 30" preferred
60" width for walk-in closets, shelf and rod on each side

When computing bedroom space don't forget to provide an area for other uses, such as a hobby and craft center in a child's bedroom and a home office and/or sewing center in the master bedroom. If the master bedroom is of great importance to your particular lifestyle, you may wish to go considerably beyond these minimum clearances. You could include a small sunken area and fireplace, or a freestanding fireplace in the master bedroom; none of this is out of the question with the modern prefabricated units. Whatever your taste or your lifestyle, remember that form follows function and design the room accordingly.

With a little imagination life can be added to any room; the one shown was built in 1917. The conversion of windows into shelves, combined with the attractive use of hardboard paneling, gives the room an irresistible appeal (photos courtesy of the Masonite Corporation).

Bathrooms

The illustration, adapted from the Department of Housing and Urban Development's Manual of Acceptable Practices, shows minimum clearances for plumbing fixtures. In determining the arrangement and size of a new bath, use the architectural template for plumbing fixtures. The plumbing wall for the bath, usually the one which holds the plumbing for the water closet, will be 8-1/2 inches instead of 4-1/2 inches. The standard tub is 30 inches wide and 5 feet long. Bath vanities are 22 inches deep and as wide as space and money will allow. You may also wish to include a linen closet in the bathroom. This would be 12 inches deep and from 24 inches to 48 inches wide, as room allows, but the normal width is 36 inches.

See the clipping files and use your imagination to add a dash of individuality. This is especially important for the bath off the master bedroom. You may consider separating the vanity area from the rest of the bath, adding a walk-in closet and dressing area, and/or a vanity with seating area.

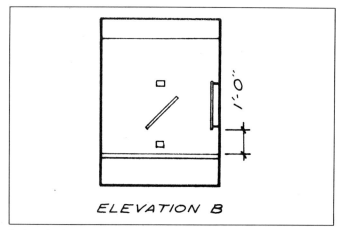

ELEVATION B

Bathrooms for the elderly need a vertical grab bar near the faucets to ease entry, and another grab bar diagonally across the center of the back wall to help when showering and when rising. If a shower is provided, a second soap dish mounted at 4 ft. 6 in. will eliminate the need to stoop.

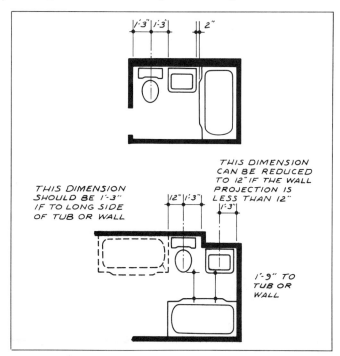

THIS DIMENSION SHOULD BE 1'-3" IF TO LONG SIDE OF TUB OR WALL

THIS DIMENSION CAN BE REDUCED TO 12" IF THE WALL PROJECTION IS LESS THAN 12"

1'-9" TO TUB OR WALL

Here are minimum bathroom clearances, as suggested by the Department of Housing and Urban Development.

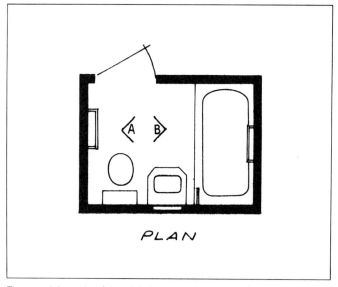

PLAN

The special needs of the elderly can be handled with added features. Note that the bathroom door swings outward and has a flush threshold.

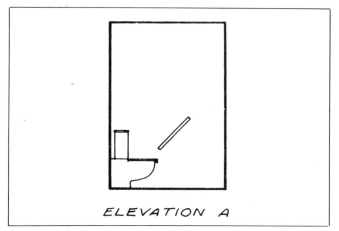

ELEVATION A

To aid the elderly: mount a diagonal grab bar forward of the toilet on the side wall; all grab bars should be about two ft. long and should be set 1½ in. out from the wall.

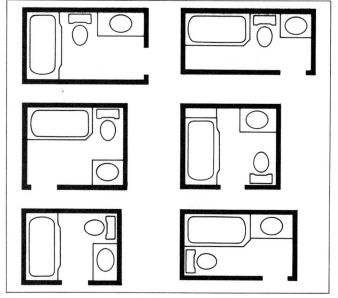

If your bathroom space and/or budget are a little cramped, consider one of these compact arrangements.

A Word Of Caution

There are many outside factors which could affect your remodeling design. Almost all cities have subdivision regulations and building code requirements which must be adhered to. For instance, if you wish to add on a room, you may not be able to add on in a particular area because of lot requirements in your neighborhood. To avoid unnecessary reworking of your plans, be sure you read and understand Chapter 9, "A Word about Codes," before you begin to sketch your designs.

EXTERIOR STYLING

There is such a diversity of materials in today's market that almost any appearance you want can be achieved on the outside of your home, often without an extravagant price. If you would like to have a brick home, for instance, but the roof overhang, doors, and windows will not allow the extra thickness of a standard brick; there is a brick available that is less than 1/2 inch thick which, when applied properly, looks the same. The appearance and feel of real stone can be achieved using stucco or concrete "stones" that look real and are reasonably thin. Wood sidings are available in more styles than ever before. Whatever style you prefer can be accomplished. In the rear of Chapter 5 there is a series of suggested facelifts for different budget levels in a variety of styles. The concepts can be easily adapted to your home.

Style Categories

The following list describes a selection of popular home styles in America. These are "pure" styles, many of which are rarely or are no longer built. Most modern subdivision homes have one or more features of any number of the following styles and fit into a general category only. Your home may fit into one of the style categories, or it may be a cross between two or more. It may also be an example of a style that is indigenous to your local area only.

Cape Cod Colonial. In its more up-to date form this was one of the most commonly built houses in the first half of the twentieth century and is still popular today. It is a small 1 or 1-1/2 story home, symmetrically shaped with a steep, shingled gable roof. The front door is usually in the middle with a central chimney, though these may vary in the newer versions. Windows are double-hung, with shutters; and the siding materials—originally of clapboard, brick, and natural shingles—are of almost any material now. The house is easy to build and is energy efficient, but the interiors are often poorly designed, forcing the inhabitants to go through one room to get to another.

Cape Ann Colonial. This style is essentially the same as the Cape Cod except that it has a gambrel roof and is less commonly used with brick veneer.

New England Colonial. This house is similar to the Cape Cod, but is larger; usually 2 or 2 1/2 stories with side or rear wings. The cornices are more elaborate, being constructed with dentils (alternating small blocks of wood, which gives the appearance of teeth) beneath them. The siding is usually clapboard.

Garrison Colonial. This is a 2 or 2 1/2 story house with the upper floor overhanging the first floor. The gable roof is steep and shingled with a chimney usually at one end. Typical ornamentation consists of four drops just below the second floor overhang. The windows are either small pane casement or double-hung with the upper floor windows being noticably smaller than the first floor. Many Garrison Colonial homes have the roof punctuated with dormers (a projection from the roof that contains a window).

Dutch Colonial. Although this style originated in America, it is so named because it was first built by Dutch settlers in Pennsylvania and New York. The house is a 2 or 2 1/2 story, though usually compact, with a gambrel roof, dormers, and an eave that flares outward. The siding can be of many different materials and the windows are usually double-hung with small panes. A single chimney is most often found at the side of the house.

Salt Box Colonial. This style, also called Catslide, is most noted for the steep roof that extends down to the first floor in the rear though the house is usually 2 or 2 1/2 stories. The windows are double-hung with small panes and shutters. Rarely are windows placed at the rear of the house since it was usually built with the rear facing north. Siding is normally clapboard or shingles and the house usually has a large central chimney.

Southern Colonial. Sporting a number of tall columns, this large symmetrical 2 or 3 story frame house has elaborate cornices, usually with dentils, and often a second story balcony, balustrade, (rail supported by a series of small columns) and belvedere (small glass enclosed room on the top of the house with a commanding view). The roof is either hip or gable and covered with shingles. The windows are double-hung, with small panes and shutters. Usually built with wood siding, this is a derivative of the earlier colonial homes of the north and east.

New England Farm House. These simple clapboard siding houses were commonly built throughout New England during the eighteenth and nineteenth centuries. They are easy and inexpensive to build, box-shaped with a steep roof that doesn't allow heavy snow accumulation. The central chimney is an integral part of the house frame. Built for the needs of the time, the interiors are often awkwardly laid out for today's lifestyles.

Shingle Style. This is a large box-like house with a gable roof. Both roof and walls are shingled and painted or stained a dark color. The windows are double-hung, with shutters, and there are one or more chimneys protruding through the roof.

Western Stick. This is a western derivative of the Shingle Style, but is different in that the structural framing is exposed. It usually has large overhangs, windows with large fixed areas of glass, and sliding glass doors.

Federal. A home built throughout the east in the eighteenth century, the Federal is a 2 or more story box-shaped house that is symmetrically designed and has a flat roof. It can have many forms, but often has a balustrade above the eave, ornamentation that is extravagant by today's standards but modest in its time, small panes of glass in the windows, clapboard or brick walls, chimneys rising high through the roof, and often a belvedere on top of the house.

Elizabethan. Also called Half Timber because the common wall treatment is large timber framing with stone, brick, or stucco between. This style has large, massive chimneys; casement windows with small panes, often diamond-shaped; multilined high peaked roofs; and, 2 or 2 1/2 stories with the second floor often overhanging the first.

Tudor. Similar to the Elizabethan, the Tudor is distinguished by its more fortresslike appearance. The doors and windows have cement or stone trim and the walls are more often stone or brick rather than half timbers and stucco.

Regency. A 2 or 3 story brick house, symmetrically shaped, with a hip roof and usually a small octagonal window over the front door. There is a single chimney on one side, double-hung windows, with shutters, and the brick walls are often painted white.

Eastlake. This is a common style among older areas and is distinguished by the ornamentation that resembles furniture knobs and legs. It is usually rectangular, with a tower or turret, and an open front porch that often carried around to a side of the house. The roof is gable and is shingled.

French Provincial. This formal 1 1/2 to 2 1/2 story house has a very steep hip roof, is perfectly symmetrical, and has curved-headed upper windows that protrude upward through the cornice line. It is usually brick, with french windows, and two symmetrical one-story wings.

American Mansard. This style is also called the Second Empire Style because of its popularity during the reign of Napoleon III (1852-1870). The style has become very popular, again, in recent years, but with less ornamentation than the original. The main feature is the mansard roof which reaches up almost vertically, then appears to be flat on top. Actually, the unseen top of the roof is usually a slightly pitched hip roof. The original style was punctuated with decorative iron and massive decorative cornices. French doors are also commonly used.

Cotswold Cottage. Very popular in the early twentieth century, this style is sometimes called the Hansel and Gretel Cottage. A large brick or stone fireplace decorates the front or side of this asymmetrically designed, small house. The steep gable roofs have complex lines and are often punctuated with shed dormers. The windows are casement, often with diamond-shaped panes, and a variety of materials are used on the walls. The interior layouts are poor with small, oddly shaped rooms and a floor plan that requires walking through one room to get to another.

Swiss Chalet. Very popular in mountain areas, this style is distinguished by decorative woodwork. It is 1 1/2 to 2 1/2 stories, has a steep gable roof with the front of the house usually at the gable, and has curved cornices. Large glass windows are used with sliding glass doors that open onto generous porches.

Spanish Villa. The Spanish Villa is extensively used throughout the southwest and is found in other areas of the country, even in the north. It is distinguished by stucco walls and a red tile roof. It can be from 1 to 3 stories high and often has oval top windows and doors with extensive wrought iron decoration.

Mission. Similar to the Spanish Villa, this style is distinguished by the old mission church appearance caused by repetition of parapet walls. Windows and doors are almost always arched.

Monterey. Commonly found in the west, this asymmetrically shaped 2 story house is distinguished by a balcony across the second floor. The balcony rail is simple iron work or wood and the roof is shingled; walls are usually of adobe brick, stucco, or stone, but can be built with almost any type of siding.

Pueblo. The Pueblo or Adobe style, patterned after the Indian houses, was popular throughout the southwest during the early part of the twentieth century. Derivatives of this style are still being built today. The Pueblo is massive looking, made of adobe brick, or more often now of other materials that give the appearance of adobe brick. The roof is flat and has characteristic projecting beams called viga.

California Ranch. The California Ranch is a compact 1 story home distinguished by a low-pitched roof, often with wood shingles, and large windows, either sliding, double-hung, or picture. It also has sliding glass doors, extensive use of wood, particularly redwood, and is often painted earth tones.

Northwestern. Also called Puget Sound, this style is a 1 story ranch-type house. It is distinguished by its South Sea Island influence, noticeable in the gable and large overhanging roof. Like the ranch it has large windows and, quite often, redwood walls.

California Bungalow. This is a small 1 story house, usually made of wood, with aspects of other styles often found such as South Seas, Japanese, and Spanish. It is often called simply "Bungalow" though this usually denotes a house with an open or closed front porch. This style can and does vary widely throughout the country.

Contemporary. The Contemporary or modern house can be built in a wide variety or shapes and appearances. It will often have extensive use of natural finished or weathered wood with large areas of glass. There is little or no ornamentation of any type.

"A" Frame. A very popular version of the contemporary style, the "A" Frame is most often used as a vacation home. It is unmistakable, with the steeply pitched roof forming the shape of an "A" and the large glass areas in front and back.

Roof Line

When planning a new addition you need to take into consideration how the new roof will tie into the old. With most exterior

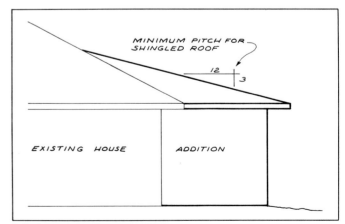

A small addition on the rear can be roofed with a lower slope, but don't go below 3 in 12 if you will be using shingles.

styles you should use the same roof pitch for continuity of design. This is sometimes unnecessary, particularly with a contemporary style which often has more than one roof pitch in the initial design. Nor is it true for small additions in the rear of the house, which can often be handled with a flatter section of roof, as in the illustration. No new roof section, however, should be flatter than 3 in 12. (See Chapter 5 for a discussion of roof pitch.)

Although a flat or "built-up" roof may be used for a rear addition, it is more expensive to build than a conventional roof. In some areas it may be difficult to find a contractor to build a flat roof on a small job. However, if your home already has a flat roof, such as the pueblo style or some variations of the mission and contemporary styles, then the addition will require a flat roof.

There are a number of roof styles, as shown in the illustration. No matter what your style is, if it has a pitched roof (not flat) there are some fundamentals that must be observed to assure proper connection to the existing roof.

When adding on to the length of the house, the width of the addition must be identical to that of the house in order for the new roof to be continuous with the old. If the addition is not as wide as the house, then the ridge line of the new roof will be lower than the existing ridge line. The new roof will then be lower, unless one wall is flush with an existing wall. If the latter is true, one side of the roof will be lower and the side with the flush wall will be continuous (see illustrations). Although it is uneconomical, you may want an addition that is

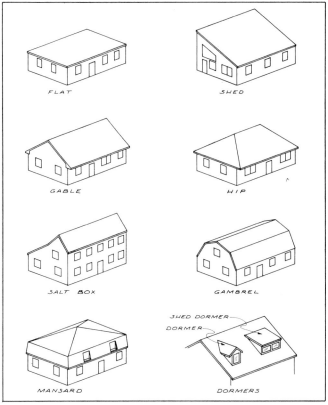

There are a variety of roof types; any of those shown may be used in combination with another when necessary to achieve a particular design.

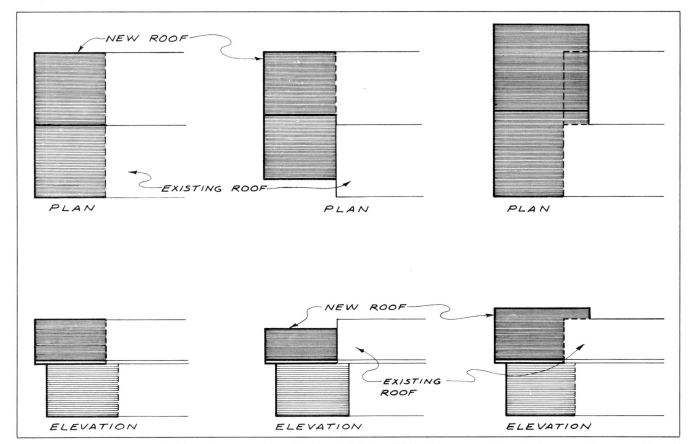

Top row gives bird's-eye view of addition; *lower* row shows elevation. *At left,* the addition is the same width as the house and the new roof is flush with the old. *At center,* addition is narrower than the original, but the back wall is flush; the new roof is flush in back, lower in front, and the ridge line is lower. *At right* is an addition which is wider than the existing house — because of the extra expense, this should be avoided if possible. The front wall and front of the roof are flush. The back of the roof and the ridge line are higher. (Illustrations are drawn using a gable roof.)

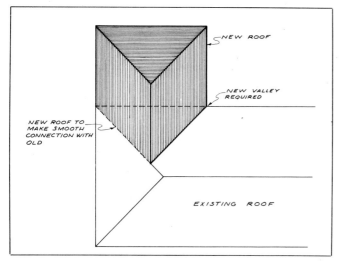

An addition that is perpendicular to the length of the house should be no wider than the house or the new ridge line will show above the existing from any angle. (Illustration is drawn using a hip roof.)

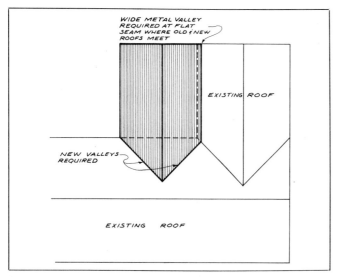

A projecting addition adjacent to an existing projection can be achieved using a wide metal valley in the flat seam. (Illustration is drawn using a gable roof.)

wider than the existing house. The new ridge line would then be higher than the old. A wider addition, however, requires an extra outside corner and more extensive roof construction (especially for a hip roof). It is therefore more expensive, and is not recommended.

An addition perpendicular to the length of the house should also be no wider than the house, otherwise the ridge line of the addition would rise above the ridge line of the house. This makes construction difficult and detracts from the appearance of the house, since even the roof of a rear addition would be plainly visible from the front of the house. If there is already a perpendicular projection to the house, an addition on the side of this projection should be avoided because the flat valley between them would be difficult to drain. However, if this is your only option, it can be handled by the use of a specially constructed wide metal valley, as shown.

Site Design

Any site work you would like to do should coordinate with your home in materials and in style. The patio area can be

made an extension of the house, an outdoor room that coordinates with and continues the living area of the home. Windows should be planned so as to frame attractive views from interior rooms. Because site design is so distinct in design principles, it is covered separately in chapter 6.

SKETCHING YOUR IDEAS

Now you are ready to begin sketching the new floor plan ideas. Tape the existing floor plan to the drawing board. Overlay it with the rag tracing paper. Mark the corners of the house on the sketch so that when you want to overlay the same sketch again it can be easily aligned. Use the HB pencil for sketch work and don't worry about making lines nice and straight. This will be freehand work until you are ready to draw the final plans.

By your side you will need the scale, the architectural template, eraser, the folder on your remodeling needs, your idea folder, and the design analysis section of this chapter. You will also need a calculator or sheet of paper to keep abreast of sizes for design and for budget purposes. Dull the point of the HB pencil a little on a sheet of scratch paper so the sketch will have wide, bold lines. Don't use much pressure, however; the HB pencil will make a dark line without heavy pressure, and tracing paper tears easily. Should you rip through the tracing paper, you might make some unwanted marks on the existing floor plan underneath.

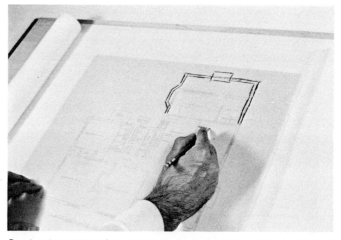

Overlay the existing floor plan with the rag tracing paper and sketch numerous designs before you settle on a final plan.

As you start sketching your ideas, don't try to make the first one perfect. Make a series of sketches incorporating different ideas in each one. The more sketch designing you do the better you will become at design. This is a crucial point in your remodeling plans and should not be rushed. Careful, thoughtful planning now will reap benefits down the road in terms of the livability of your remodeled home, the cost of the work, and the increased value of the home.

Your sketch work and furniture arrangements should take into account the placement of doors and windows. Everything in a room must work together as a comprehensive whole. If you have or will be getting an odd size or shape piece of furniture not covered in the rear of the chapter, measure and draw it at 1/4 scale for use in designing. Don't forget to take into account such things as visibility of the television, indoor plants, views from seating through windows, cabinet and stereo placement, proper traffic flow, views into and out of the room, the relationship of different rooms, or displays and collections. For all your design work try to think in three dimensions even though you are sketching in only two. Consider the heights of each item and try to visualize the three-dimensional appearance of each room.

Don't hesitate to write notes on the sketches about what you want to do, especially for repairs to the existing home. The final design sketch will be developed using the previous sketches so everything from your folders that you wish to use should be noted or drawn on a sketch, with the exception of exterior styling and site work, which will be covered in more detail later.

The Final Design Sketch

Once you have made as many sketch designs as you need, consulting with the family as a whole and with the individuals of the family, prepare a new overlay for the final design sketch. Incorporate the ideas from the previous designs that you wish to use and put a single, comprehensive set of notes on this one sheet. By including all the notes here you will save valuable time when drawing the construction plans. Also mark room sizes for additions or redesigned rooms of the existing home. After the sketch is developed, mark it "Final Design Sketch" to avoid getting it confused with the other sketches. When not in use, keep all your sketches in a folder marked "Design Sketches."

CUTTING COSTS

Should your final computations show your design to be over your budget, here are some ways to cut cost:

- Establish priorities for your needs and consider eliminating low priority items.
- Provide double-use areas wherever possible
- Keep bath and kitchen plumbing facilities in the same locations.
- Reduce the size of additions, but still observe minimum clearances.
- Keep the shape of the addition simple with a minimum of outside wall perimeter and outside wall corners.
- Design room sizes to conform to standard sizes of finish materials.
- Retain the existing cabinet work, refinishing for a new look.
- Consider doing some of the construction yourself, but be realistic about what you can do.
- Keep existing walls in place wherever possible.
- Use existing space, such as attics or garages, for room additions.

CONSULTATION WITH AN ARCHITECT

If you cannot develop a comprehensive design you are satisfied with, or if you simply would like a professional to check your work, set up an appointment with an architect for consultation on an hourly basis. An hour of his/her time may seem expensive, but you could receive some valuable information for your personal design problems. To save time (and money) prepare yourself before you go. Make a list of questions you wish to ask and take the existing floor plan, your design sketch(s), your remodeling needs folder, photographs of your home and the clippings for any ideas you want to incorporate into the plans.

If your plans call for the removal of any walls it is imperative that you consult an architect; or, better, that he make a visit to your home. Certain interior walls may be load carrying or "bearing" walls. It could be that the wall cannot be removed, or that its removal will require the inclusion of a structural beam to carry the load. An architect will be able to direct you as to the size and location of the beam and the steps that will need to be followed when the wall is removed.

If an architect is not available, a reputable contractor, a residential designer, or a city or FHA/VA building inspector may be able to advise you on wall removal.

DRAWING YOUR PLANS

The final design sketch is not the end of the design process, but only the overall concept. As you go through the remaining chapters and draw the construction plans, you will continually refine your design and will develop new elements such as the exterior styling (Chapter 5), site work (Chapter 6), and cabinet design (Chapter 7). Design questions will arise and changes will be made from time to time, even during construction. Don't be loathe to erase a considerable portion of the construction plans and redraw them. Changes on paper are much easier and cheaper than construction alterations.

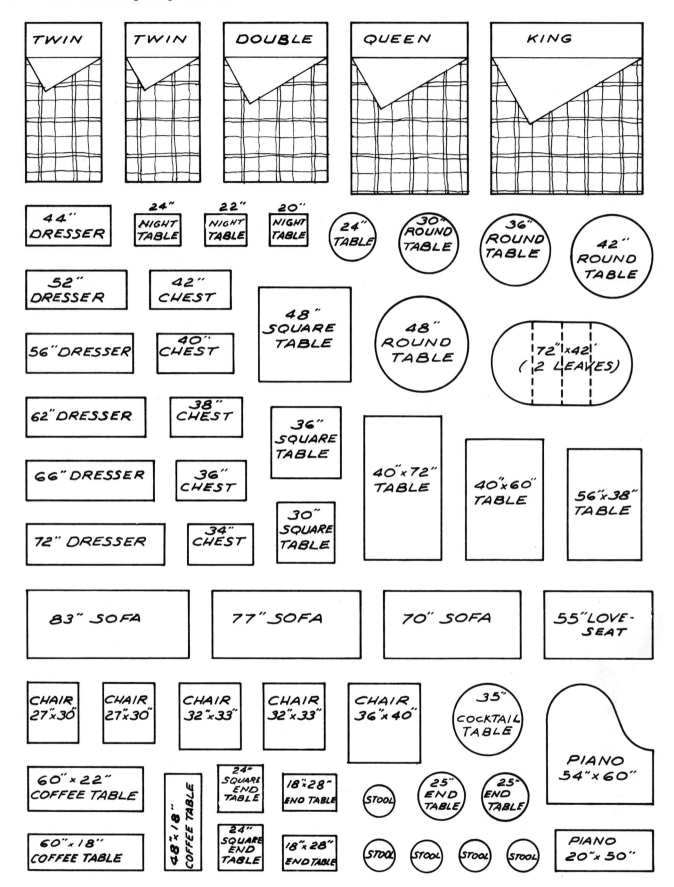

These cut-outs are ¼ scale (¼ in. equals 1 ft.). Use them to simulate various furniture arrangements and to find the one best suited to your needs. For flexibility, make several photocopies of this page and lay out the furniture cut-outs in alternative patterns; for comparison, set up the designs simultaneously.

4   Drawing the New Floor Plan

In every human endeavor the moment of inspiration—recognition of an idea or a need—is only the beginning; the work must follow. Once you have designed a course for your remodeling, you must refine the basic concept and draw the plans. Chapters 4 through 8 will show you how to convert your preliminary sketch into a comprehensive remodeling design and a full set of construction plans.

STARTING THE NEW FLOOR PLAN

Tape the existing floor plan to the drawing board, being sure to align the longest wall with the top edge of the T-square. Overlay the existing floor plan with a new sheet of vellum, aligning the border with the T-square. Since the new floor plan will have additional information on it, you may wish to shift the new sheet so that the floor plan will be near the bottom

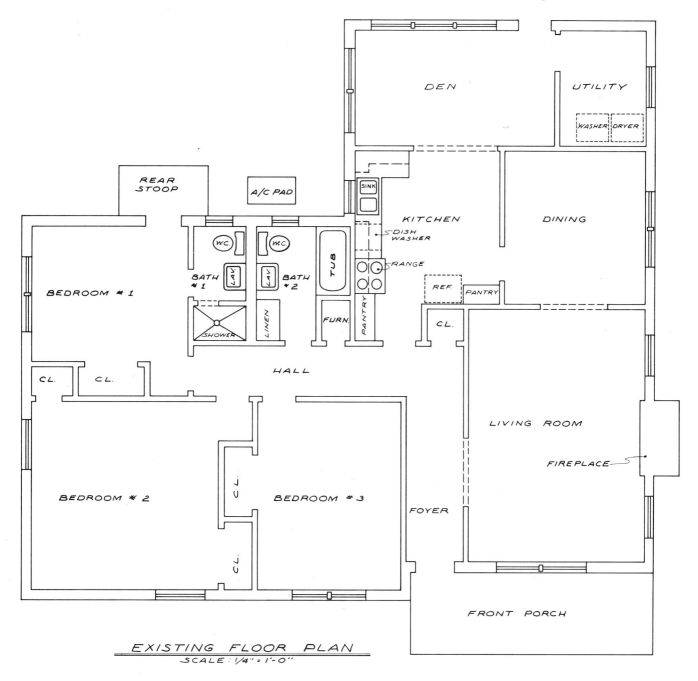

EXISTING FLOOR PLAN
SCALE: 1/4" = 1'-0"

left corner, allowing more room at the top and right of the sheet. Before you tape the new sheet down, however, check the preliminary design sketch you have already made and allow sufficient space for any additions you may have planned.

Now, using the 2H pencil and medium pressure, trace the existing floor plan onto the new sheet. But do not trace any walls, windows, doors, cabinets, or other items that will be removed as a result of your remodeling plans. Coordinate this with your existing design sketch, so that the new sheet will contain only the existing features of the home that are to remain intact.

The lines for this work should be dark enough to reproduce when printed, but should not be as dark as the existing floor plan. This will provide a contrast between the existing and new work, since the new work will be drawn with the H pencil and heavy pressure.

DRAWING THE NEW WORK
Walls, Windows, & Doors

Remove the existing floor plan from beneath the new sheet. From your current final design sketch, measure and draw in any new walls, whether for additions or for new walls within

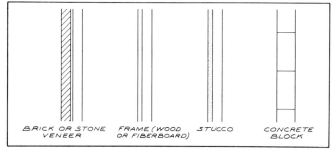

These are accepted methods for drawing the most common types of exterior walls. The outside of each wall is to the left.

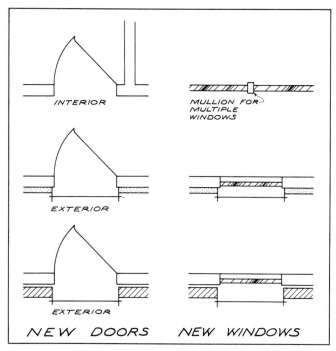

New doors and windows. As is the case with most symbols, the way architects draw windows and doors may vary. The ones shown here are commonly used and contrast well with the existing symbols previously shown.

the existing structure. Indicate the same wall thicknesses you used when drawing the existing floor plan. New outside walls will be drawn with more detail than the existing walls, as shown. Draw all new work with light lines; they will be darkened later. The diagonal lines shown here to represent brick veneer can be drawn with the 45° triangle and should be oriented so their direction is from the lower left to the upper right of the sheet. The distances between them need not be measured, but can be spaced visually.

Next, measure and place the new doors and windows and their dimensions from inside edges on the floor plan (see illustration). When drawing the door swing, use the architectural template and be careful to orient the swing in the proper direction.

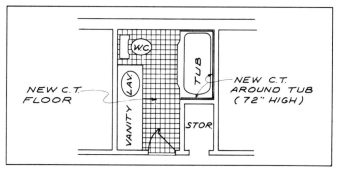

If your bath plans include a new ceramic tile floor, draw in the 4 in. square tiles as shown and use a heavy line for wall tile; state the height of the wall tile in a note (72 in. around tub, 48 in. other walls).

Plumbing Fixtures and Vanities

For new bathrooms and new bathroom fixtures use the architectural template. Then, if the floor will take new ceramic tile, use the 1/4 scale ceramic tile pattern on the architectural template to make guide marks. Draw in the new tile floor as shown. Be sure to place the new plumbing fixtures according to the illustration provided in Chapter 3.

New bath vanities should be drawn 22 inches deep and whatever width your plans require. When placing the lavatory in the vanity remember that the cabinet space beneath the lavatory is needed for plumbing access, so there can be no drawer. If your plans call for a drawer, shift the lavatory to one end of the counter or the other, allowing about a 4-inch clearance from the edge of the vanity top to the edge of the lavatory.

Cost-Saving Note. Unless you require cabinets, vanities, and other features of a particular size in order to match previous items, it may be much cheaper to order from various manufacturers' brochures. These brochures specify cabinets according to size—the first two numbers indicate width and the second two indicate height. For example, ''3032'' for a kitchen cabinet means that it is 30 inches wide and 32 inches high. These prefabricated units will almost always be cheaper than building the cabinet or vanity to suit, and the quality available can be equal to that of fine furniture.

Kitchen Cabinets & Appliances

Begin the new kitchen cabinets as you did for the existing floor plan, by drawing lines one foot and two feet from the wall. Stop the wall cabinets 3 to 4 inches short of either side of any window. The wall cabinets should be drawn with a dashed line. Measure and place the appliances as they are designed on your final sketch plan; use the architectural template to draw these wherever possible.

Other Features

Now add all the remaining items in your remodeling plans such as fireplaces, exposed beams, built-in book cases and desks,

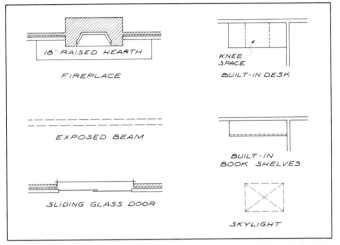

These drawings show some special features you may wish to include in your plans. If there is some special feature or construction that you don't know how to draw, cover it with a detailed note on the plans and in the specifications (also see Chapter 8).

etc. The accompanying illustration shows the proper method for drawing these features.

Once all the features of the remodeled home are drawn, darken the lines of the new work in the same manner as you did on the existing floor plan. There will be some difference, however, since the new work will require two different types of lines. First, with the 2H pencil and medium pressure, darken the diagonal lines used for symbolism, as well as the ceramic tile lines in the bathroom floor. Then with the H pencil and heavy pressure, darken the remaining lines starting with the items drawn using the architectural template, including the doors. Brush the drawing, then darken the horizontal lines from top to bottom and, last, the vertical lines.

ELECTRICAL WORK

All electrical work is drawn using the symbols in the accompanying drawing. But before you begin it would be wise to do some research.

City codes vary in the number and location of electrical outlets required. Consult with your city building department and refer to Chapter 9.

Lighting may be adapted to a room in a variety of ways. Recessed lights, track lights, or rheostats (dimmer switches) can be used to achieve dramatic effects, setting different moods for the room. Visit a lighting dealer and carry your new floor plan with you. Although it is unnecessary to select

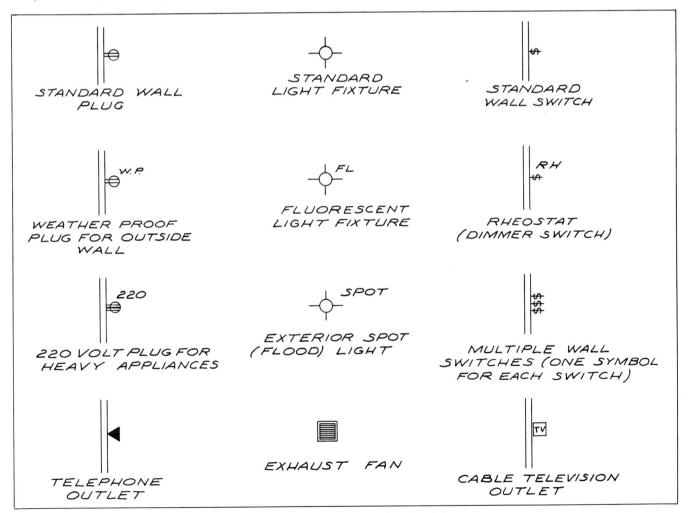

Here are commonly used electrical symbols. Use the architectural template to draw the circles.

specific light fixtures at this time, the dealer can advise you as to what type of lighting is available and how it should be placed. Also discuss with the dealer a reasonable dollar figure, to be included in the specifications as a lighting allowance.

Based on the information you have gathered in your research, draw the electrical work onto the new floor plan. Don't be caught short on electrical plugs; place them wherever you may need one. You may wish to consider placing a floor plug in the center of a very large room. Be sure its location is coordinated with the furniture arrangement as planned in Chapter 3. It would be wise to place at least one plug behind built-in bookshelves and at any built-in desk. Be sure you have a plug for the refrigerator and dishwasher, a 220 plug for an electric stove or clothes dryer, and a plug for each countertop work space 12 inches or wider in the kitchen. When designing light-fixture locations, a recessed light just above a fireplace or book case, switched with a rheostat, adds a lot to a room. This is especially true if your plans call for mirror and/or glass shelves.

Switch connections to lights may be made in a variety of ways, and you may wish to consider double switches for stairs. Older houses often need new service to bring it up to code and to support electrical loads. (See Chapter 9.) Connection lines are drawn freehand with the 2H pencil and consist of a long dash followed by a dot. Note in the illustration how the connection lines should look and the different ways you can design them.

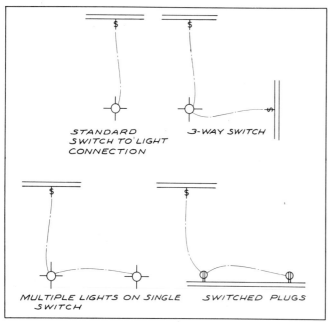

Shown are switch connections to lights and plugs; connection lines may be drawn freehand.

DIMENSIONS

All new work must be carefully and thoroughly dimensioned. Begin by giving the overall dimensions of an addition if one is designed. These will go on the outside of the floor plan as shown. Dimensions for new doors and windows will also go on the outside of the floor plan, between the wall and the overall dimension. Windows and doors are dimensioned to the centerline. Draw the dimension lines with a 2H pencil and medium pressure. Where a dimension begins or ends, use a

dot or slash. Arrowheads are rarely used for architectural work. For exterior walls dimensions are computed from the outside face of the wall, so add the wall thicknesses to the interior room sizes. Start at a house corner and place a dimension to the centerline of the first new window or door, then move from centerline to centerline for additional windows and doors. On existing walls a dimension is not required if a new window simply replaces an old one. But if the new window is installed in a different location, or where there was no window before, then dimensions will be needed. (See also "Window and Door Schedule" in following pages.)

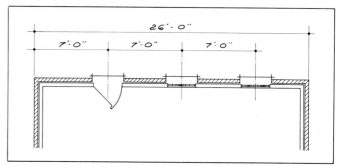

This is the proper method of exterior dimensioning, including windows and doors, and overall dimensions.

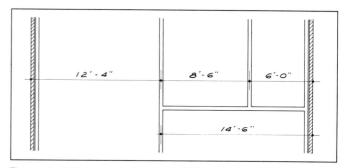

The most widely accepted method of dimensioning the inside of your remodeling is to measure to the center of interior walls as shown. To find the thickness of an exterior wall, measure the inside of the window frame. For an interior wall, measure a door opening. Although some architects measure to the face of interior walls, this method causes difficulty for the nonprofessional when checking dimension accuracy against an overall dimension.

For interior walls the dimensions are drawn to the center of the wall (see illustration) and the wall thicknesses must be taken into account when computing dimensions. Existing walls do not need to be dimensioned.

Be sure a string of dimensions along the interior rooms adds up to the corresponding exterior dimension. A very careful check of your dimension figures can avoid problems and delays during construction.

ADDITIONAL HEATING & AIR CONDITIONING

A sizable addition may require more heating and air conditioning capacity than your home has, or your plans may call for the installation of central heating and/or air conditioning to replace your present system. While at an early stage in drawing the floor plan consult with the city building department or a heating and air conditioning dealer. In the case of a large addition, you will need to know the capacity of your present arrangement before the size of the booster system can be determined. Should you need a new system, a small area of the floor plan must be provided for it. Either the city building inspector or the dealer can advise you as to the size of the area required and the best location for it. You should also consult with them as to sizes and locations of registers, ducts, vertical riser, etc.

LABELING THE NEW FLOOR PLAN

All new structural items and fixtures must be labeled on the drawing. Use the lettering method described in Chapter 2, always being sure to use guidelines. Try to place the notes so as not to interfere with other aspects of the drawing. For an example of what and how to label the new floor plan see the sample floor plan at the end of the chapter. As on the existing floor plan, room names will be larger than other notes, and a title and scale will be required under the new floor plan.

Be clear and concise with your notes, but don't leave anything to chance. Each note is a permanent record of what you want done in your remodeling. During construction a contractor or subcontractor cannot legally ignore a written note on the plans for which he has signed a contract.

Notes are also helpful for calling attention to specialty items that you may not know how to draw. If you are unsure of how to graphically represent an unusual aspect of your remodeling plans, place a note under "GENERAL NOTES" (see below) fully describing what the contractor should do.

For longer notes, such as those designating repairs to be made, place the title "GENERAL NOTES" to the right of the floor plan. For clarity, number each note you place in this area. Then if a general note refers to a particular spot on the drawing you may simply refer to the number of that note by placing a reference on the spot such as "SEE NOTE NO. 3."

WINDOW AND DOOR SCHEDULE

At the top left side of the sheet, or wherever there is room, you will need a window and door schedule which describes each new door and window. If you have not already done so, consult with a building materials supplier about the types of new windows and doors you wish to use, keeping in mind the style of the outside of your home. He can provide brochures and prices for various types of windows and doors and can also provide you with their elevation drawings, which you will need in Chapter 5 when you draw the exterior elevations.

Using the architectural template draw a circle near each window and door on the floor plan. Inside the circles you will place letters for the windows—A, B, C, etc.—and numbers for the doors—1, 2, 3, etc. If there is more than one of a particular type and size of window or door use the same designation. Then draw a box like the one on the sample floor plan that is shown on page 47, allowing a space for each letter and each number. The first column contains the designation. The second column contains the size of the window or door. Sizes are written as four numbers, the first two representing the width in feet and inches and the last two the height. So a 3044 window would be 3 feet 0 inches wide and 4 feet 4 inches high. A 2668 door would be 2 feet 6 inches wide and 6 feet 8 inches high (standard height for all premanufactured doors). The third column contains the description of the type of window or door.

Many older homes will have sizes of windows and doors that cannot be matched without custom-built units. If you wish to replace these, you may order custom units or buy the closest

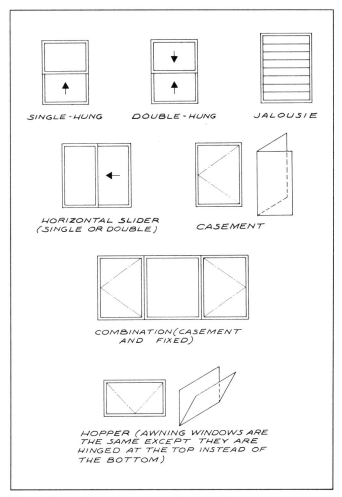

Window Types. For hinged windows the point of the triangle is drawn to the center of the hinged side.

size in a standard unit and reframe around the window or door. The latter will usually be the least expensive method, especially if the exterior walls are scheduled for new work in your plant. For each window or door that must be reframed, letter a note on the new floor plan.

The window description should include the type of material such as wood (WD.), aluminum (AL.), etc. It should include the type of opening in the window such as single hung (S.H.) when only the bottom panel is movable, double hung (D.H.) when both panels move, casement when the window opens to the side, and fixed glass for a window that does not open. It should also include the number of panes of glass in each panel, such as 6/6 for a window with six panes in the top panel and six in the bottom.

The door description also contains several parts. First, designate whether the door is exterior or interior. Then note the material such as wood or steel. For wood doors, designate whether it will be solid or hollow core (H.C.). Finally, designate the style of the door such as "flush" for a smooth door, six-panel colonial, louvered, or other. If the door will contain one or more panes of glass, note this as 1 lite, 3 lite, etc.

If you have chosen a particular style or brand of window or door that you wish to use, simply put the brand name and serial number. A description is not necessary. Whenever a size or description is a repeat of the one above write D.O., which means ditto.

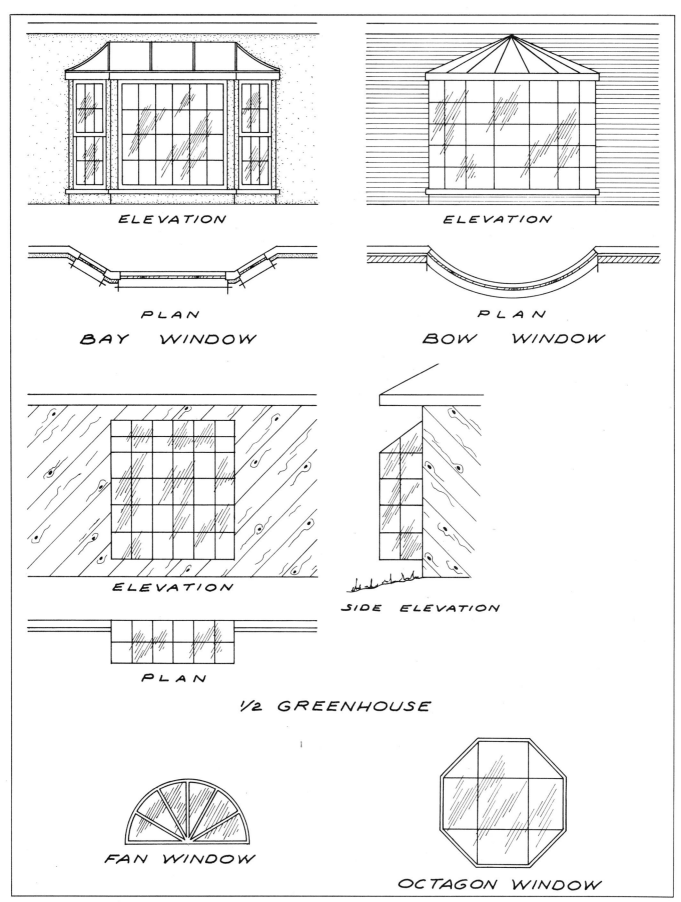

ELEVATION

PLAN

BAY WINDOW

ELEVATION

PLAN

BOW WINDOW

ELEVATION

PLAN

SIDE ELEVATION

1/2 GREENHOUSE

FAN WINDOW

OCTAGON WINDOW

Window Styles. Shown are some typical window treatments. Bow window is the usual name for a curved bay window, but the individual panes of glass are actually flat. An oriel window is a bay or bow window which is not directly supported by the foundation of the house (usually on an upper floor). The fan window can be used above a door or, more typically, on top of windows, — especially in Spanish and Mediterranean styles. The octagon window is used for decorative purposes either above a door, or on one or both sides of the door.

Interior doors. Given is a sampling of the different types of interior doors available, by far the most commonly used is the "flush," or smooth-finished hollow-core door.

Exterior doors. Again, these are only some of the more popular of the many types of doors available. Many of the glass panels shown are available in divided lites, and can also be purchased with wood panels rather than glass.

The original square footage for this house was 1,676. An extension off the kitchen of 180 square feet plus an expansion of the master bedroom of 106 square feet brought the new square footage to 1,962. The family/"Great" room addition frees the existing home for better space arrangements. The home's improved usability gives the impression of a larger, more expensive expansion.

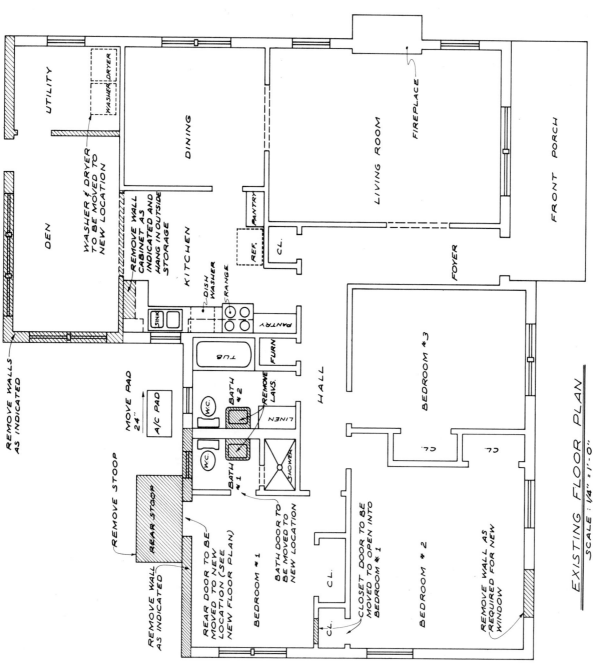

EXISTING FLOOR PLAN

SCALE : 1/4" = 1'-0"

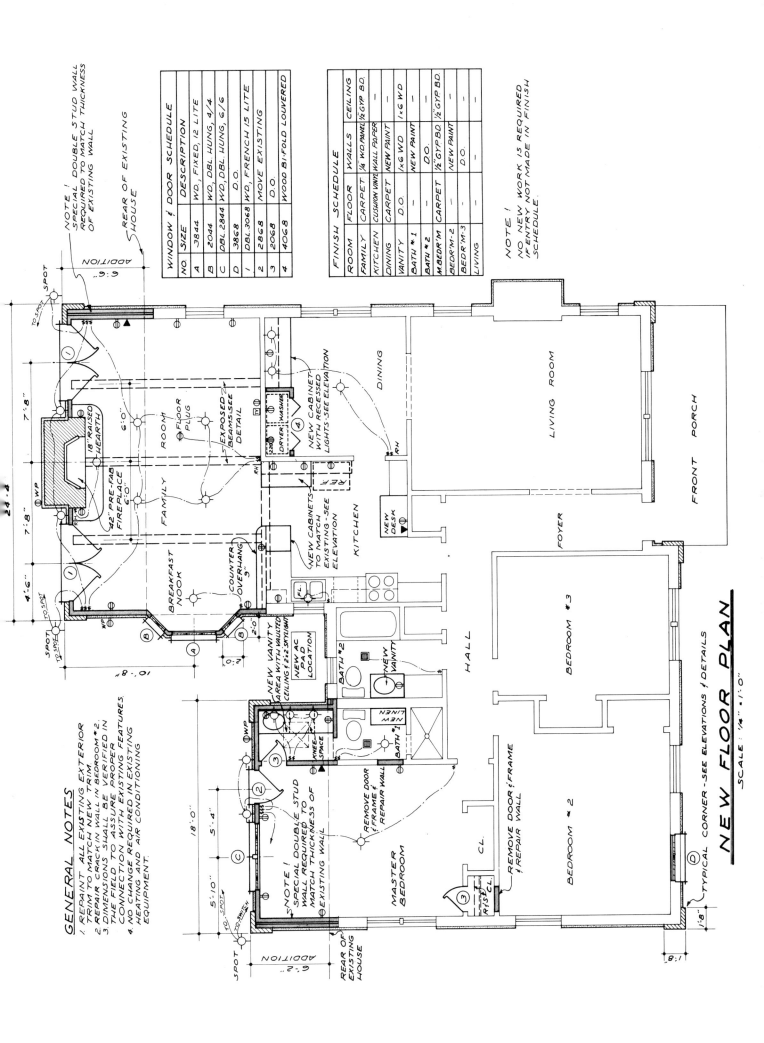

NEW FLOOR PLAN

SCALE : 1/4" = 1'-0"

FINISH SCHEDULE

The finish schedule designates the type of materials to be used in finishing each new and each remodeled room. Draw the finish-schedule box as on the sample floor plan on the preceeding page.

Provide a space for each room that will receive new work based on your remodeling plans. Then fill in the room name and the type of finish material to be used for floors, walls, and ceiling.

LAST STEPS
Shading New Walls

The new stud (wood) walls on your floor plan are designated by shading them with the HB pencil. This should be done on the back of the tracing so that the loose graphite will not smear your other work.

Removing Existing Features

Now overlay the new floor plan with the existing floor plan. Determine exactly what existing walls and other structural features must be removed to allow for the new work. Then shade these areas with diagonal lines using the H pencil and medium pressure (see the existing floor plan in the front of this chapter). For clarity, letter a note for each item to be removed.

Second Floors

For two-story homes that require remodeling work on the second floor or for second floor additions, a separate floor plan must be drawn. Place it on the same sheet if there is ample room, and on a new sheet if there is not. Then use the same procedure as you did for the ground floor to draw your "New Floor Plan—Second Floor."

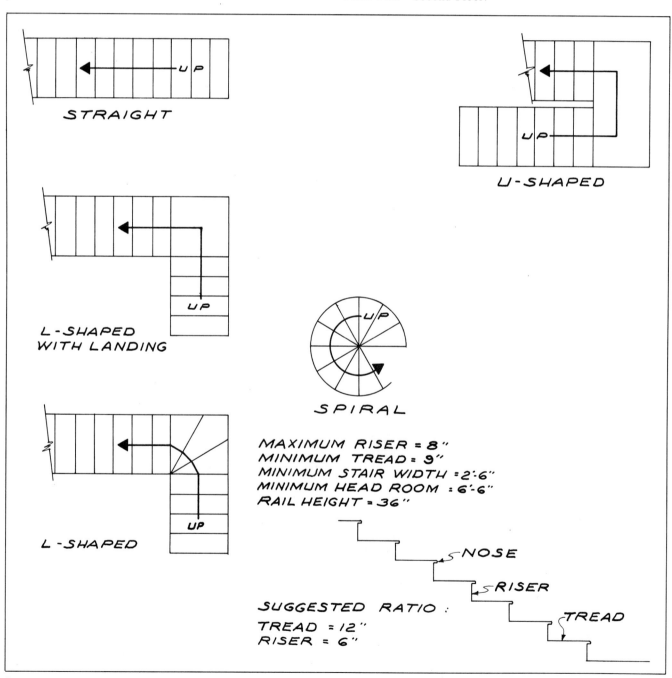

STRAIGHT

U-SHAPED

L-SHAPED
WITH LANDING

SPIRAL

L-SHAPED

MAXIMUM RISER = 8"
MINIMUM TREAD = 9"
MINIMUM STAIR WIDTH = 2'-6"
MINIMUM HEAD ROOM = 6'-6"
RAIL HEIGHT = 36"

NOSE

RISER

TREAD

SUGGESTED RATIO:
TREAD = 12"
RISER = 6"

Stairs may be constructed in several ways as need and space require. Begin the steps from the floor plan — whether first floor, second, basement, — and show any turns involved, then break as shown. Mark an arrow for either up or down.

5 The Exterior Elevations

If your remodeling plans include a room addition, or a facelift for the outside of the house, you may need to draw one or more exterior elevations. Elevations are straight line drawings, without perspective, of the front, back, and sides of your house. Since perspective is not needed the exterior elevations are easy for the nonartist to draw using only drafting tools.

WHICH ELEVATIONS ARE NEEDED

To determine which of the elevations you need to draw, look at your new floor plan. The accompanying illustration shows the direction of view for each elevation. If you are adding a room, an elevation will be needed from each direction in which the addition can be seen. You will also need an elevation when you are planning to facelift the outside of the home. Since the plans for the sample home in this book include additions that can be seen from the rear and both sides, and the front will get an extensive workover, all four elevations must be drawn.

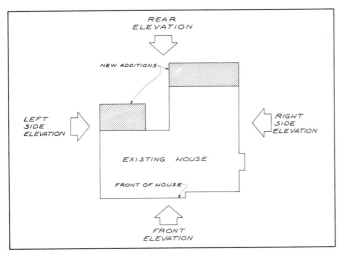

Directions of exterior elevations. In each direction where a new addition can be seen and where the outside of the existing house will be facelifted, an elevation needs to be drawn.

PRELIMINARY MEASUREMENTS

Before beginning to draw there are several measurements you must determine. You must know the roof overhang, fascia width, and roof pitch. The drawing at right shows what dimensions to measure. The roof pitch is the slope of the roof, and it is usually written in increments of 12. In other words, if the pitch of your roof is 4 in 12, this would mean that for every twelve horizontal feet the roof would rise four feet. If you do not know what your roof pitch is, you will need a level and a yard or meter stick to measure it. With one end of the level against the roof, adjust the other end until it is level. From the point where the level touches the roof measure horizontally along the level 12 inches. At that point measure vertically

down to the roof. The number of inches you measure will represent your roof pitch, i.e., if the measurement is 6 inches, you roof pitch is 6 in 12.

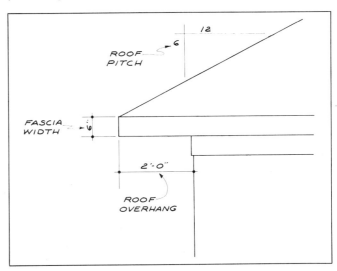

These three measurements of the existing home need to be determined before the exterior elevations can be drawn.

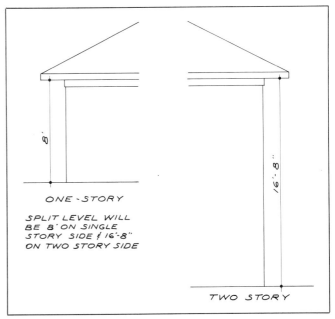

Height from ground to roof overhang. The dimensions are for drawing purposes only and could vary from the actual dimensions; your actual dimensions must be noted.

STARTING THE DRAWING

Tape a new sheet of vellum to the drawing board and measure in two inches (actual size) from the left side and bottom borders; draw very light lines. If the roof overhangs you may want to start the drawing 3 inches (actual size) from the left. Slide the new floor plan under the sheet and align the wall of the elevation you are drawing with the horizontal line. The extreme left wall of the new floor plan should align with the vertical line. If you need to draw a front elevation, this is the one you should begin with, so align the front wall of your house with the horizontal line on the new sheet. Place a light mark on the new sheet to indicate inside frames of each window and door and at the extreme wall on the right side of the floor plan. If there are wall corners other than the sides of the house, place light marks at these also. Now remove the new floor plan and draw very light vertical lines through each mark.

If your house is one-story, draw a very light horizontal line about 8 feet (using the 1/4 scale) above the horizontal base line. Measure exactly since your home may not have a standard height. This will represent the bottom of the roof overhang. If your home is a split-level or two-story, draw the line 16 feet 8 inches high (see illustration). Measure the height of the fascia from this line and draw a parallel line. Then measure the roof overhang from the sides of the house and draw the vertical ends of the fascia.

Gables And Hips

If the sides of the house are gable construction, the end of the fascia will extend vertically to the ridge line of the roof, as shown. The height of the ridge line is computed by dividing half the width of the roof by twelve and multiplying the result by the roof pitch. For example, if the roof is 32 feet wide from front to back (including overhang), divide 12 into 16. Then, for a roof pitch of 4 in 12, multiply 1.33 times 4, which gives a ridge height of 5.32 feet or about 5 feet 4 inches.

Hip roofs are drawn using the architectural template. The roof pitch index on the template should be placed so that the point of intersection for all pitch lines on the template is on the top end of the fascia and the 0 line runs along the top of the

fascia. Then place a light mark at the proper pitch number. Draw a very light line from the top end of the fascia through the mark. Reverse the template and repeat for the other side of the house. Then compute the ridge height as discussed above, measure from the top of the fascia, and draw a horizontal line.

For wall corners other than the sides of the house, you may need to also draw an overhang and hip or gable line. Look at the house to determine if it is necessary; if so, draw as described above. Be sure that when computing the height of the roof ridge line you use the proper width of that area of the roof. In other words, if your house has a wall corner between the sides of the house the ridge lines on either side of the corner may be at different heights (see illustration).

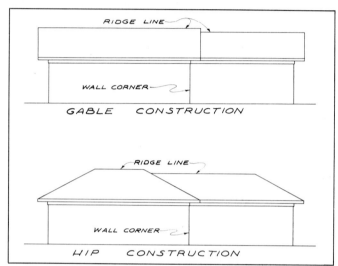

If there are one or more wall corners between the sides of an elevation, the ridge line height could vary. Carefully analyze your home to determine how to draw the roof.

Doors & Windows

Between the vertical lines of any doors on the elevation measure and place a light mark 4 inches above the base or ground line. From this point measure an additional 6 feet 8 inches and

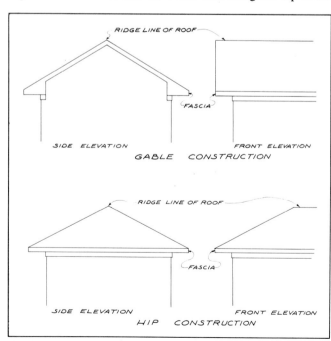

Gable or hip roof. These are the two most common types of roof construction for homes.

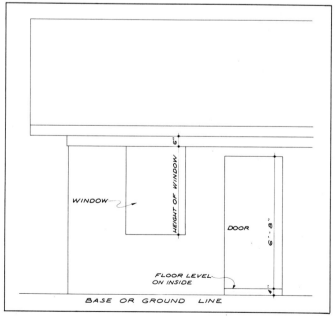

These are the basic layout dimensions for locating the tops and bottoms of doors and windows on the elevations.

place another mark. Draw lines through the marks. These represent the top and bottom of the door.

Measure the actual height of each window that will appear on the elevation. Then from the bottom of the roof overhang measure down 6 inches to indicate the top of the window. From this point measure down the window height and place another mark for the bottom of the window, as shown. Or you might wish to align the sill with those of existing windows or the head of the window with existing windows. In these cases, measure window heights and interior ceiling heights and specify the height required for the bottom edge of the window above the interior floor.

The Existing Area Of The Elevations

Use the same methods as above to draw porches, columns, and any other features not already shown. Then darken the actual lines of the house. The existing work will remain only schematically boxed in and labeled ''EXISTING STRUCTURE'' (see illustration).

NEW WORK

In order to make the drawing look good and to make the new work stand out, material symbols will be used as in the preceding drawing. For the windows and doors you will use, place the elevation as given by the manufacturer, under the box for the window or door. Then trace all the lines onto the exterior elevation. For a special effect, use the HB pencil to make a dark line on the left and bottom of the window panes or draw a series of diagonal lines with the 2H pencil in the glass areas. Beneath the new windows draw a brick or wood sill to match the construction of the house. For stone, stucco or concrete block, draw a single line two inches to scale below the win-

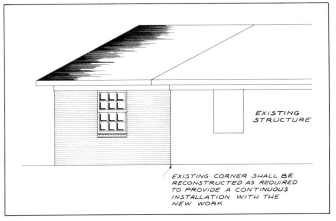

EXISTING STRUCTURE

EXISTING CORNER SHALL BE
RECONSTRUCTED AS REQUIRED
TO PROVIDE A CONTINUOUS
INSTALLATION WITH THE
NEW WORK

Shown is the contrast between an existing area of the elevation, which will remain as it is, and a new addition.

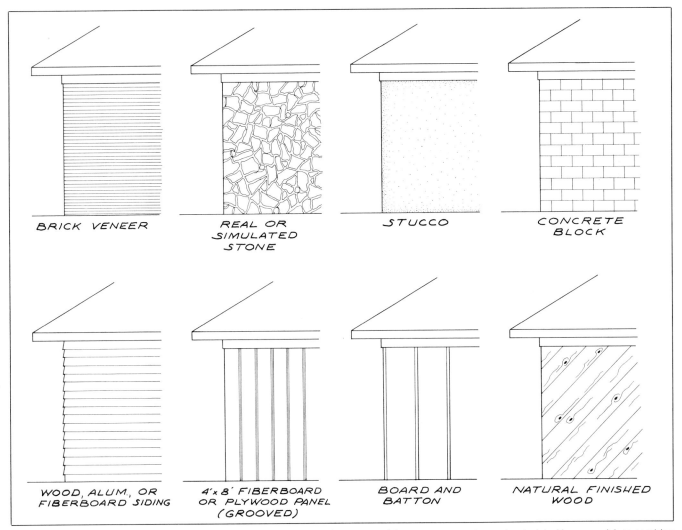

BRICK VENEER

REAL OR
SIMULATED
STONE

STUCCO

CONCRETE
BLOCK

WOOD, ALUM., OR
FIBERBOARD SIDING

4'x 8' FIBERBOARD
OR PLYWOOD PANEL
(GROOVED)

BOARD AND
BATTON

NATURAL FINISHED
WOOD

There are many types of materials for exterior walls. These drawings show some of the more commonly used materials. You may wish to combine materials such as brick and stucco, or stone and natural wood, to achieve the look you want for your remodeled home.

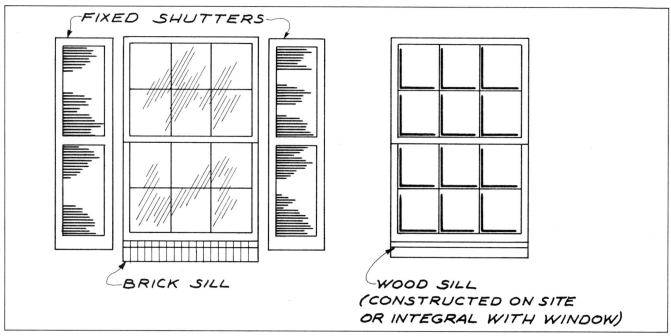

The illustrations show: (1) two different ways to make new windows stand out; (2) how brick or wood sills should look; (3) how to draw shutters. Fixed shutters are two or three inches from the sides of the window, 15 in. wide, and usually go from the top to just below the window.

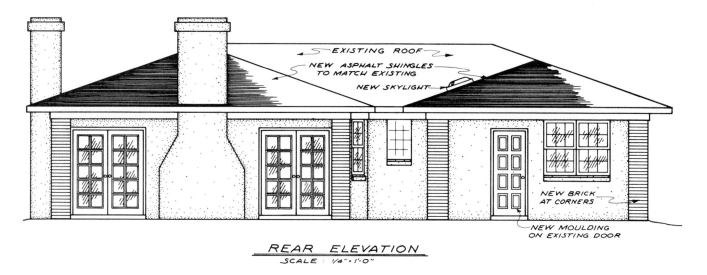

REAR ELEVATION

SCALE : 1/4" = 1'-0"

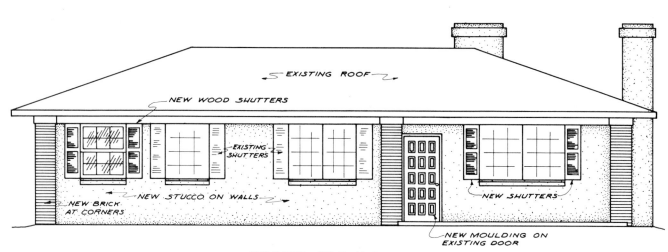

FRONT ELEVATION

SCALE : 1/4" = 1'-0"

dow. This will represent either a masonry or precast stone sill. In conditions where siding is used, or for some stucco finishes, the window is purchased with an integral sill. Complete the new windows with shutters wherever they are to be used.

On the new roof, draw a series of close parallel lines with the H pencil from the left side with a quick, stroking motion so that the lines will fade gradually from dark to light as the pencil moves to the right. This is one of the most common symbols for asphalt shingles; it produces a nice visual effect and is easily done (see drawing at top of p. 51).

For new wall construction there is a series of symbols for distinguishing each type. Use the 2H pencil for these so that the symbol lines will not be as dark as the house lines, as shown. Add a key to the symbols, describing what each symbol represents, to prevent misunderstandings.

LABELING THE ELEVATIONS

The new work on the elevations should be labeled as on elevations for the sample home, shown at the rear of the chapter. On the existing part of the house simply letter EXISTING STRUCTURE and nothing more. Since the new doors and windows are covered in the schedule on the new floor plan, you will not need to label them on the elevations. Draw the remaining elevations you will need on the same sheet if possible, using the outlined procedure. Under each place the title, FRONT ELEVATION, RIGHT SIDE ELEVATION, etc. Just as for the floor plans, draw a heavy line under the title and letter the scale beneath the line.

These elevations are for the sample plan and remodeling shown on the following pages.

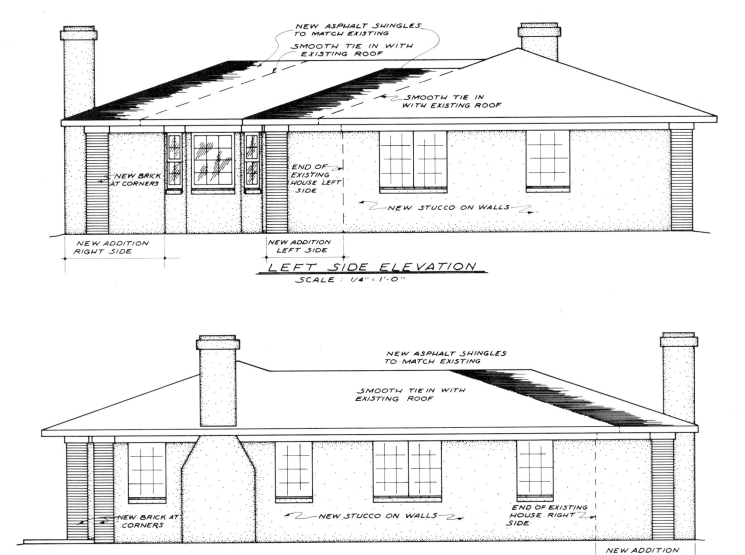

SUGGESTED FACELIFTS: The following illustrations offer suggested facelifts for your home's exterior. Each style has a lower budget and a mid-range budget design. They are drawn here for the sample house below, but can easily be adapted to your own plans.

Colonial — Low Budget. Addition of twin dormers in the existing roof provides the major touch of Colonial styling. A new 6-panel door was also installed and the low budget design was completed by adding round 6-in. columns to the narrow existing porch.

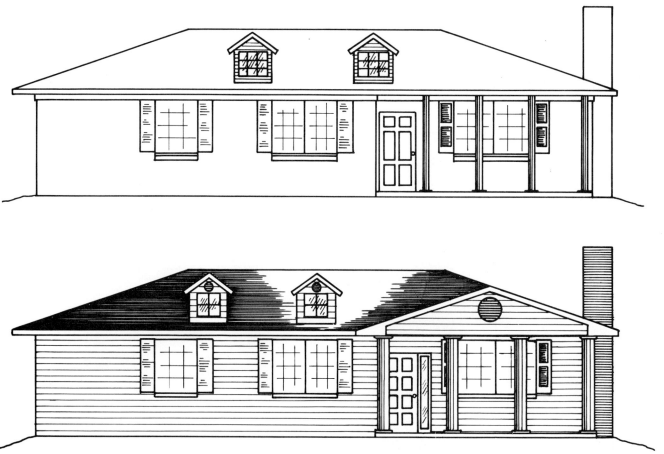

Colonial — Medium Budget. Once again, twin dormers grace the roof of this more extensive Colonial remodeling, but are offset to the left to accommodate the extended gable-end front porch which is supported by four round 12-in. columns. A new asphalt shingle roof, high-low style, gives the appearance of original slate or wood shingles; new shutters have been attached on the right window as well as a new 8-panel door with side-lite. The existing painted brick walls are covered with wood siding by installing wood strips to the brick using masonry set screws, then nailing the siding to the wood strips. The design is finished by removing the paint from the chimney to expose the existing brick.

French — Low Budget. The French feeling is created by the new French door. For additional effect 1/2-in.-thick brick is added to the corners as shown, new shutters are installed on the right windows, and an iron rail separates the porch from the yard.

French — Medium Budget. Since painted brick is common in French styles, the only work on the walls is the full size brick added at the corners. These and the walls get a new coat of paint. Double French doors (which require reworking of the foyer) are the highlight of the remodeling. The new roof is French tile, with the heads of the left side windows curved and extended up through the cornice. The right side windows have new shutters and the chimney has a new brick cap and extended flues.

Spanish — Low Budget. The low budget Spanish has 4 in. by 4 in. rough-finished wood columns added to the existing porch, along with a multi-panel door with fan window above. False beams are cut at an angle to the ends and curved-top shutters are added on the left side to give the appearance of a shuttered window; the existing shutters have been removed.

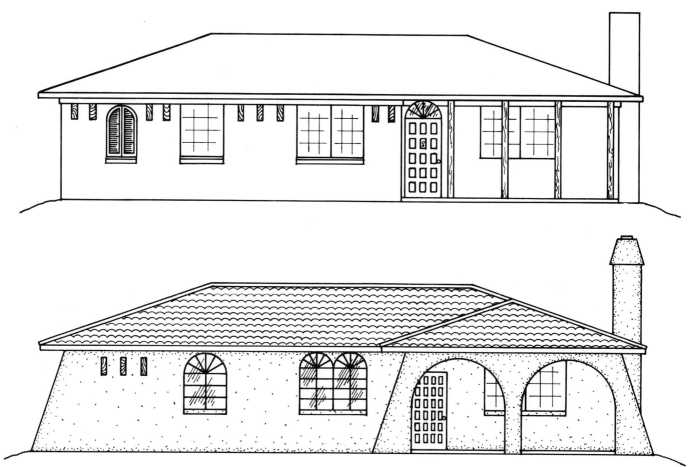

Spanish — Medium Budget. The more elaborate Spanish look is accomplished with stucco over the existing brick walls. Slanted wings are added to the front corners and the front porch is extended and given arched openings. There is a new multi-panel door and false beams, and the left side windows are replaced with shorter windows to allow for the overhead fans. The existing chimney has a new stucco covering and a reworked top. The design is topped off with the traditional Spanish red tile roof.

Ranch — Low Budget. The highlight of this simple remodeling is the inclusion of rough-finished Ranch-style wood columns. There is also a new Ranch-style door and the entire porch area is refinished with cedar plywood.

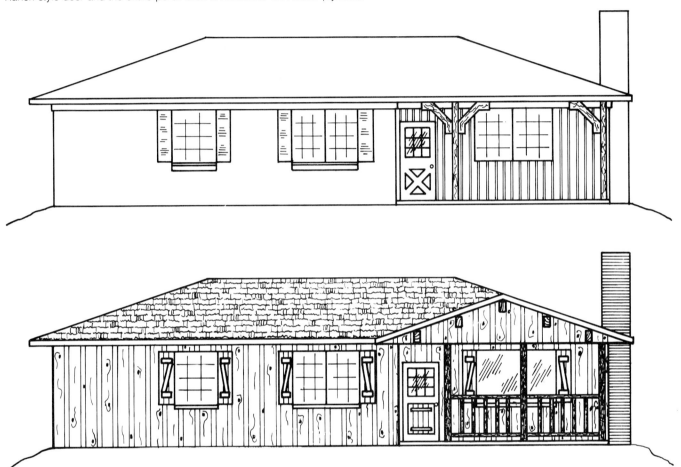

Ranch — Medium Budget. The full spirit of the ranch is captured by covering the existing brick walls with redwood and installing a new wood shingle roof. The front porch is extended, has a gable end and false square-cut beams, and is supported by rough-finished wood columns and rail. The remodeling sports new Ranch-style shutters and doors and the existing chimney is rebricked with 1/2-in. thick bricks.

Contemporary — Low Budget. The existing shutters are removed and rough-finished 2 x 4s placed at the sides of the windows from ground to cornice. Angled 1 x 12s, natural finished, are below the windows. There is a new contemporary door and a portion of the porch has been removed and replaced with exposed rafters that extend beyond the edge of the existing roof.

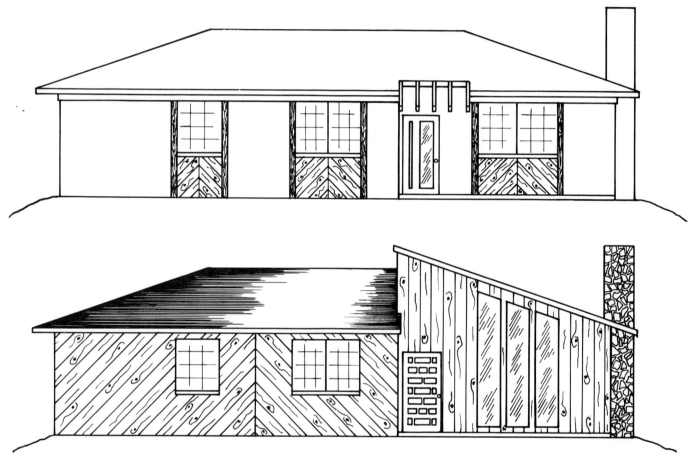

Contemporary — Medium Budget. The heart of this Contemporary styling is the covering of the existing painted brick with natural finished 1 x 12s, both angled and vertical. The roof over the living room and foyer is reworked for a vaulted ceiling and allows for large fixed-glass windows and a new contemporary door. Cement "stones" over the existing brick chimney add the finishing touch.

6 The Site Plan

Though most new homes come equipped with little more than a 12 foot x 12 foot concrete pad or wood deck, there are as many or more design variations for the patio area as there are for the interior. With careful thought and design the patio can become an extension of the house or an outdoor room, which can add a new dimension to living in your remodeled home.

Small porches and patios and door stoops should be shown on the new floor plan. If, however, you enjoy outdoor living and your patio ideas are more elaborate, you will need to draw a site plan. As with home design, you must start by drawing what you have now.

THE EXISTING SITE

Tape the new floor plan on the lower portion of the drawing board. Then tape a new sheet of vellum so that the back walls of your house appear in the lower part of the sheet. This will allow room on the sheet for the expansion of the new patio into the rear yard. If your new patio area is at the sides or even the front of the home, then place the sheets accordingly. But be careful to consult with Chapter 9 and with your city building department, since there may be lot restrictions that could set limits on your design.

Now draw the outside wall of the remodeled home, including doors and windows, but without the detail of the floor plan. Include any existing walks and patios, showing those to be removed with a dashed line, and any trees that are near the area of the new work as in the illustration. Include any other structural features that may be present.

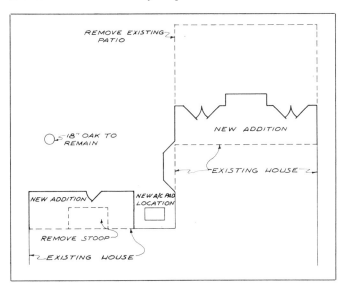

Overlay the New Floor Plan and outline the existing house and addition; on the side(s) where you are planning site work. Show all existing features such as patios and trees. You may need to measure these on the ground to assure their proper location on the plan.

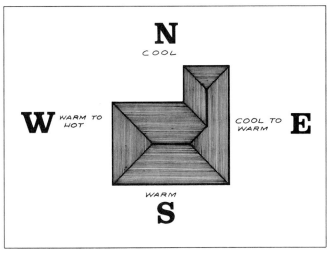

Location of the patio in relation to the sun is an important consideration. Local conditions may affect your choice.

SITE DESIGN
Planning

In addition to the design principles learned in Chapter 3, there are several site design factors that should be taken into account before you begin sketching ideas. Consult your local weather service for conditions of your area you may wish to consider. For instance, if the new patio is exposed to prevailing winds, you may want to design some type of vertical barrier. Extended rainy seasons or extreme heat could be the impetus needed to include a full or partial patio cover.

The location of your patio can also affect your design. A patio area on the south side of your home will remain warm because the sun shines on that side throughout the day. On the west the patio will receive the direct afternoon sun and could get very hot. The north will usually be cool since, in the northern hemisphere, it will receive very little sunlight. The east receives only the cooler morning sun.

This, of course, is only general and will vary due to local weather conditions, amount and type of tree cover near the area, altitude, nearby bodies of water, etc.

The selection of materials for your patio should be restricted to those that complement the design of your home. Some items, such as brick pavers, are versatile and will go with most home designs. Others, such as colorful canvas patio covers, may not fit your home very well.

As with home design the patio area should suit your family's lifestyle. It can be wide, expansive, and designed for play; centered around outdoor cooking; formal and elegant; or close and intimate for a more private outdoor life.

The patio or deck may be a single area, or two or more areas at varying levels, adjoining each other or connected by walks.

You may combine materials, such as wood and brick, but be sure your selections combine well. The patio or portions of it may be enclosed with partial or full vertical screens and/or overhead covers. Your plans could even include a brick walk with redwood lath overhead leading to a gazebo.

The possibilities for site design are nearly limitless. You will need to rely heavily upon your idea folder, keeping the family lifestyle, style of your house, and budget in mind.

Sketching

Overlay the existing site with the rag tracing paper and begin sketching your ideas. Make a number of designs using different approaches. Again, try to think in three dimensions and visualize what the work will look like when it is completed. Many designers adhere to a modular design principle. This means that the size of patios, covers, etc. are based on a dimension module. If your walks were four feet wide, for example, all of the site construction would be designed in multiples of four feet.

If you cannot develp a comprehensive design you are completely satisfied with, or if you need special site design assistance, look in the yellow pages for landscape architects or designers and, armed with your drawing of the existing site, your sketch plans, and any pictures from your idea folder that achieve the effect you want, consult with the professional on an hourly basis. Just as with an architect an hour of his/her time will not be cheap, but you could receive valuable aid in refining your design and on determining cost. If there are no

landscape architects or landscape designers in your area, consult with an architect.

DRAWING THE NEW WORK
Patio & Deck Materials

Concrete is the most commonly used material for patios and walks, and is usually the cheapest. There are several ways, however, to dress up the concrete patio without greatly increasing cost. It may be finished smooth or brushed to achieve different effects, and can be scored on 2 or 3 foot squares. If you choose to use a scored concrete patio, design its size in multiples of the scoring pattern width so that it will work out evenly.

The concrete can be washed to expose the gravel (exposed aggregate) or its surface embedded with attractive pebbles. It can also be sectioned with treated wood joints between the squares. The wood joints can be used in conjunction with exposed aggregate to add a personalized touch to a concrete patio. (An illustration has been provided to show how each is drawn.)

Another popular patio material is brick. Brick pavers come in a variety of sizes and colors and may be set in concrete with mortared joints, or simply laid on a sand bed. Brick may be more expensive than concrete, but is also easier to lay yourself and to coordinate with your home style. The patterns that brick pavers can be laid in are diverse, each lending a different mood to your outside living. Some of the more common patterns are shown.

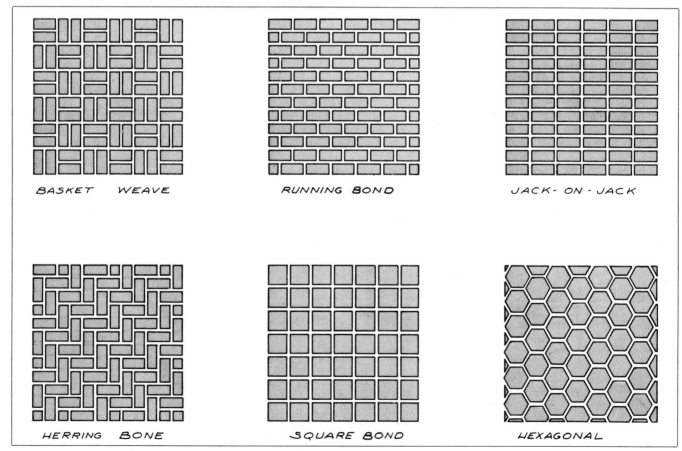

BASKET WEAVE

RUNNING BOND

JACK-ON-JACK

HERRING BONE

SQUARE BOND

HEXAGONAL

These are the more common patterns and types of brick pavers for patios. When drawing the new patio you need only show individual bricks in a corner and note the pattern on the remaining area. But, as it is done on the sample site plan in the rear of this chapter, you may want to draw in the pattern on the entire patio to get a feel for what the design will look like.

CONCRETE PATIO

CONCRETE PATIO SCORED ON 2 FT. SQUARES

CONCRETE PATIO WITH REDWOOD SPACERS

CONCRETE PATIO WITH EXPOSED AGGREGATE

There are several treatments that can be used to dress-up the common concrete patio. The methods shown can also be used in combination such as redwood spacers and exposed aggregate or scored patio with exposed aggregate. Also, there are several types and sizes of pebbles which can be used in an exposed aggregate patio.

Wood patios and decks offer a pleasant natural appearance at a reasonable cost. The wood can be finished in several ways or can be left to weather; they should, however, be treated to prevent pest or fungus problems. The patterns that can be used are as varied as those for brick; the illustration shows some suggestions, but you can let your imagination go and design a pattern as individual as you are. Wood patios also mix well with other materials if your plans call for more than one patio area or for a mixed patio.

For sloping lots wood decks are not only attractive, but highly functional. You can design a large deck for comfortable outdoor entertaining, or a series of smaller decks at different levels to link the garden areas. Decks on sloping sites should have rails for safety.

Other materials you may wish to consider include tile, wood rounds or blocks, Wonder Brix, slate or flagstone. With careful planning each can be an attractive complement to your remodeled home.

All patios and decks should slope away from the home to allow proper drainage. The normal slope is 1/4 inch per foot. For extremely large patio areas you may need drainage structures, in which case consultation with a civil engineer or landscape architect would be advisable.

Vertical Screens

To protect from wind and noise or to create a private, intimate outside patio you may wish to include a partial or full vertical screen on your plans. These can be made of wood, glass, brick, stone, stucco, bamboo, canvas, translucent plastic, or plants and trees. Each of these can be constructed in a number of ways and can be used in combination. Remember that plants and trees may take some time to grow, so if your

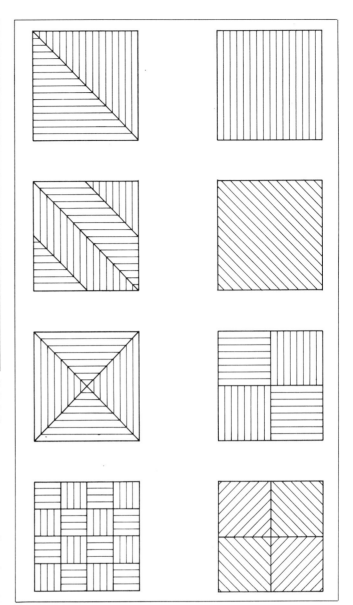

These are a few of the more common patterns of wood decks. If you want something really different, study these, then let your imagination go.

screening needs are immediate you may wish to use a structural device. The illustration shows how to draw several types of screens on the site plan and how each looks in elevation. Whether you use one of these types, a combination, or a design not shown, an elevation should be drawn on the site plan sheet as shown in the example home site plan at the end of this chapter.

Retaining Walls

If there are sharp grade differences in your yard, such as a dirt bank, or if you wish to create them in your design, you will need to construct a retaining wall. These should be shown on the plan and an elevation and section should be drawn as in the illustration. Since strength is important in a retaining wall, the number of designs and the different types of materials are limited. Brick, stone, concrete block, wood posts, and railroad ties are shown here and will all work well. These, however, are designed for grade differences of no more than three feet. Higher walls require much more strength and

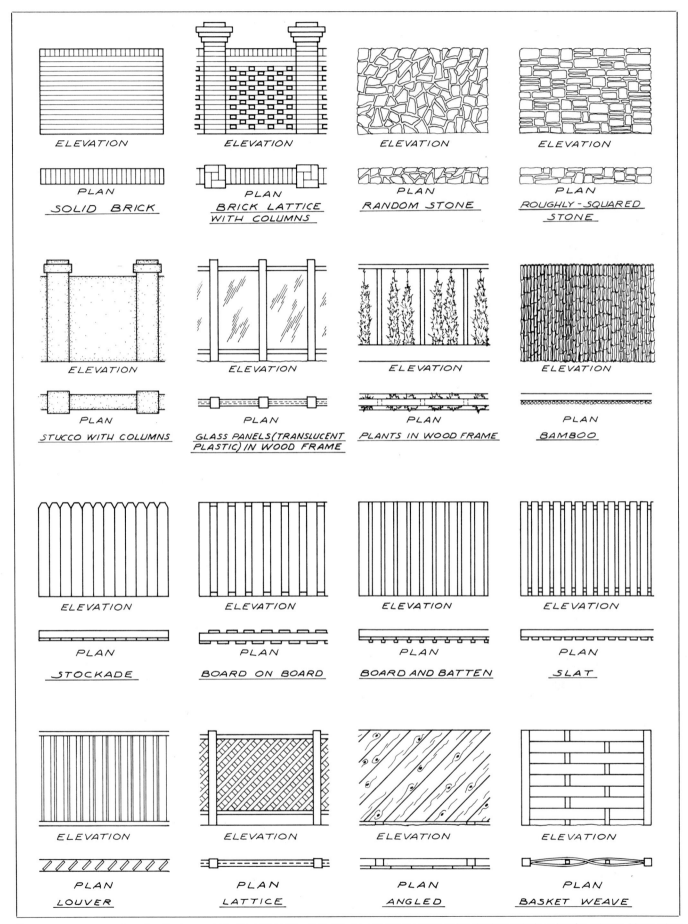

ELEVATION

PLAN

SOLID BRICK

ELEVATION

PLAN

BRICK LATTICE
WITH COLUMNS

ELEVATION

PLAN

RANDOM STONE

ELEVATION

PLAN

ROUGHLY-SQUARED
STONE

ELEVATION

PLAN

STUCCO WITH COLUMNS

ELEVATION

PLAN

GLASS PANELS (TRANSLUCENT
PLASTIC) IN WOOD FRAME

ELEVATION

PLAN

PLANTS IN WOOD FRAME

ELEVATION

PLAN

BAMBOO

ELEVATION

PLAN

STOCKADE

ELEVATION

PLAN

BOARD ON BOARD

ELEVATION

PLAN

BOARD AND BATTEN

ELEVATION

PLAN

SLAT

ELEVATION

PLAN

LOUVER

ELEVATION

PLAN

LATTICE

ELEVATION

PLAN

ANGLED

ELEVATION

PLAN

BASKET WEAVE

These are some examples of vertical screens (walls or fences) which may be used in the patio to block winter winds or just for privacy. Many other patterns can be made; and combinations, such as brick and stucco, can add that extra touch.

should be designed based on consultation with an architect or structural engineer.

Patio Covers

An overhead cover for the patio may be built without openings for protection from rain and sun, or it may be only partially covered to shade and cool the patio. By far the most popular material for cover frames is wood. Even when masonry columns are used, the framework of the cover is usually wood. One alternative is an aluminum frame, especially for canvas covers. The design of the wood framework may be simple—particularly when glass or translucent plastic panels are included—or it may be more elaborate, standing alone as a partial shade or used with plants. A wood lath of redwood, cedar, or cypress makes an attractive, lightweight, and inexpensive cover that does not need finishing. Add vines for a climate-controlled patio; they will block the heat of the summer sun and allow the rays to come through in the winter.

On the site plan you should draw the outside edge of the cover and show all supporting columns. On the same sheet draw a plan of how the cover will be constructed. Refer to the sample site plan at the rear of the chapter. For premanufactured covers note the brand and serial number on the site plan and in the material specifications (see Chapter 8).

Outdoor Cooking

An important consideration for many outdoor lovers is the cooking area. This could range from a simple gas grill, which can be shown on the site plan with a box and a note, to an elaborate barbecue area that will take time to plan, design, and build. If you prefer the more complex system, remember to include a food preparation table near the barbecue pit.

Benches And Tables

If your table and seating needs will be supplied by outdoor furniture, these should be considered when planning size and layout for the patio. But you may also build in wood or brick benches and/or tables as part of the patio construction. They cannot be rearranged as furniture can, but can serve a dual purpose by doubling as storage chests for outdoor toys and

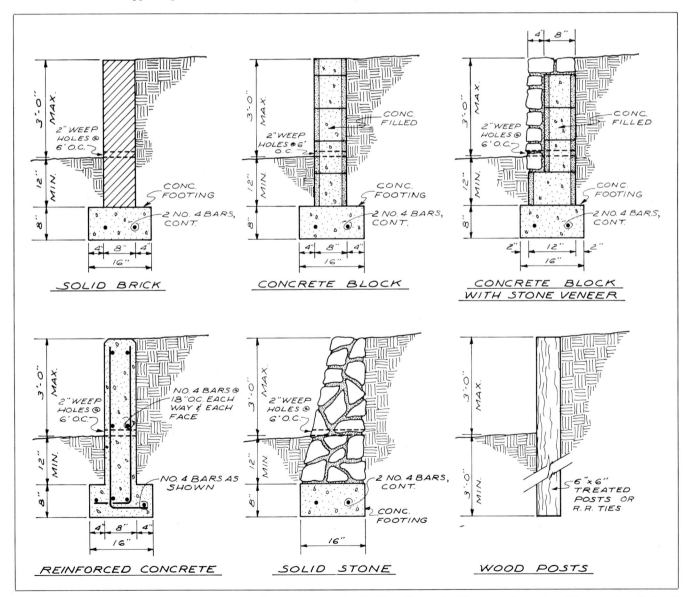

If your plan will include a low retaining wall draw one of these details on the Site Plan. For grade differences of more than 3 ft. professional help will be needed.

equipment. Their location and dimensions should be shown on the site plan as well as a detail or how they are constructed. The illustration on page 65 shows a typical wood bench.

Plants And Gardens

The site plan should designate areas that you wish to have planted, but the types of plants to be used need not be selected until construction is underway. A dollar allowance will be allowed for planting in the material specifications in Chapter 8. It would be wise, however, to consult with a nursery on the general types of plants that would enhance your design and for cost information.

Outdoor Lighting

Lighting is an important consideration for the patio and should be planned carefully. As with the interior lighting you will not need to select fixtures until construction, but you should con-

sult a lighting dealer for the types of lighting available and a reasonable budget.

For cooking at night or for night activity areas you will need to plan sufficiently bright lighting. Other areas may call for subdued lighting. Gardens should be illuminated by unseen fixtures. Show the outside electrical design, including weather plugs, on the site plan using the same symbols that were used on the interior electrical work.

LABELING AND DIMENSIONING THE SITE PLAN

All new items on the site plan should be labeled. For longer notes you may use a "GENERAL NOTES" heading as you did on the floor plan. Be sure to fully describe any repair work, such as correcting drainage problems. Then complete your site plan by dimensioning the patio, walks, length of screens and retaining walls, and supporting columns for patio covers as on the sample site plan.

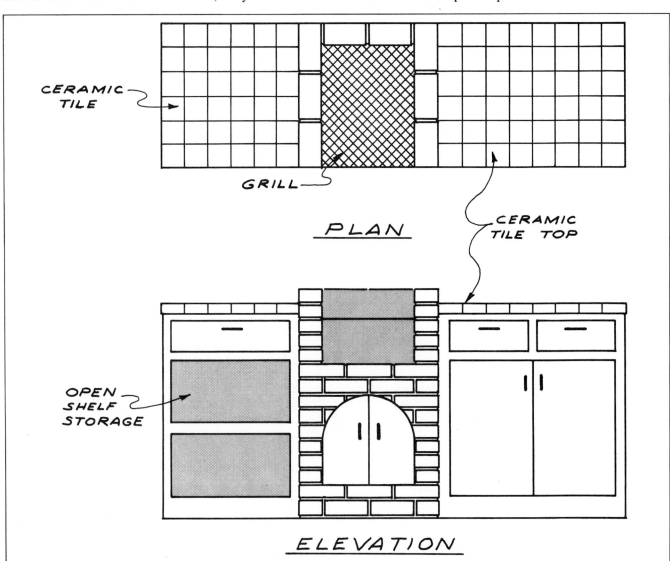

An outdoor cooking center can be even more elaborate than the patio itself, rivaling the kitchen for ease and convenience.

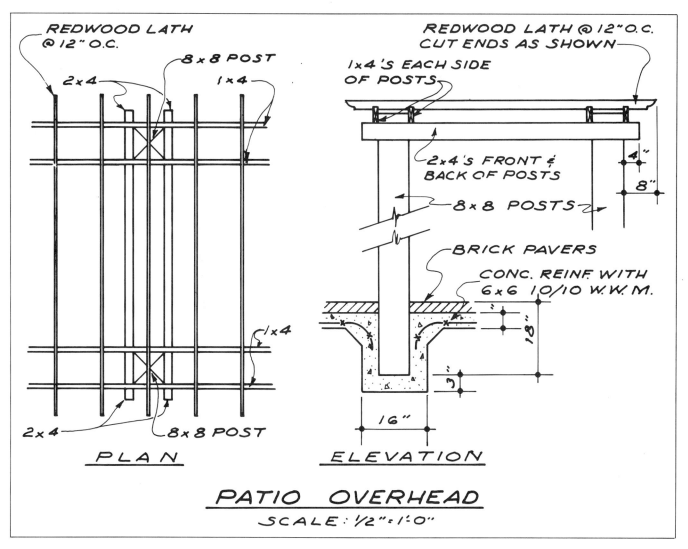

REDWOOD LATH @ 12" O.C.

2×4

8×8 POST

1×4

2×4

8×8 POST

PLAN

REDWOOD LATH @ 12" O.C. CUT ENDS AS SHOWN

1×4'S EACH SIDE OF POSTS

2×4'S FRONT & BACK OF POSTS

8×8 POSTS

4"

8"

BRICK PAVERS

CONC. REINF. WITH 6×6 10/10 W.W.M.

18"

3"

16"

ELEVATION

PATIO OVERHEAD
SCALE: 1/2" = 1'-0"

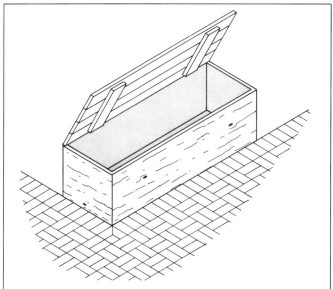

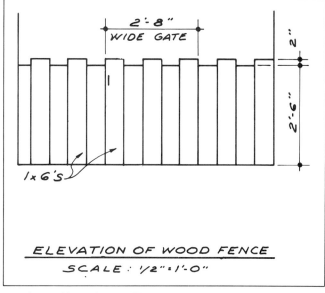

2'-8" WIDE GATE

2"

2'-6"

1×6'S

ELEVATION OF WOOD FENCE
SCALE: 1/2" = 1'-0"

A simple wood bench along the edge of the patio can double as a storage area for outside equipment. The patio overhead and fence plan shown are features of the site plan on the following page.

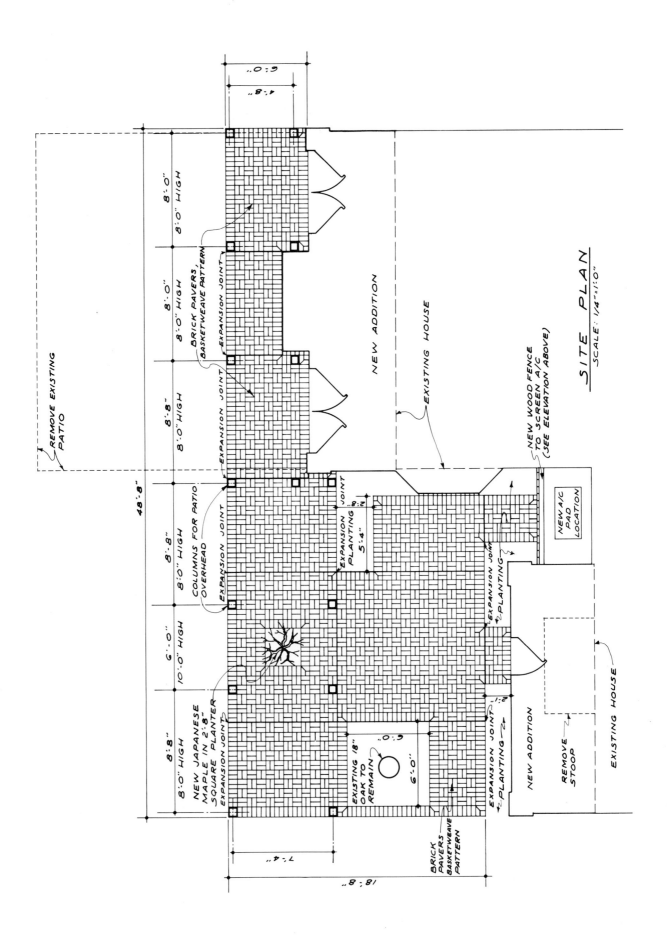

SITE PLAN
SCALE: 1/4"=1'-0"

7 Cabinet Elevations Construction Details Foundation Plans

The final drawing in your remodeling plans will consist of three elements: (1) the cabinet elevations for new kitchen cabinets and/or bath vanities; (2) the construction details to show how the new work will be built; and (3) the foundation plan, which is required only if your remodeling includes an addition. Many commonly used construction details are reproduced in the proper scale at the rear of this chapter. These may be either traced onto the sheet or simply attached to the plans. You will still have to draw the items that are individual to your home and to your remodeling.

NEW CABINETS
Kitchen

If you are replacing the old kitchen cabinets, or simply adding cabinet space, you will need to draw elevations of the new cabinets. On a new sheet of vellum measure in two inches (actual size) from the top and left borders and draw very light lines. The horizontal line will represent the ceiling. Measure the height of your ceiling and then, using the 1/2 scale, mea-

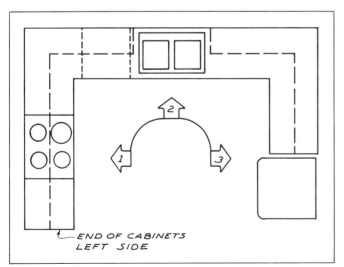

END OF CABINETS
LEFT SIDE

The cabinet wall with the end of the cabinets on the left side should be drawn first. (If there are more than one left side ends any will do.)Then move clockwise and draw the second wall, the third, etc. If there are no new cabinets on a wall an elevation is not necessary.

sure down from the ceiling line and draw the floor line. The 1/2 scale will be used on all cabinet elevations.

If you will be ordering prefabricated cabinets—a less expensive alternative to built-on-site cabinets—work from the manufacturer's brochure as to exact sizes. Some custom-made cabinets can also be ordered this way.

Each wall of cabinets in the kitchen will be drawn as a separate elevation. From the new floor plan find the cabinet end that would be on your left if you were standing in the middle of the remodeled kitchen, as shown in the illustration. This wall of cabinets will be drawn first. Succeeding walls will be drawn by moving in a clockwise direction. Only the new cabinets will need to be drawn if you are adding to existing cabinets.

Measure the length of the cabinets on the first wall from the end on the left side to the end on the right or, if the cabinets turn the corner on the right side, to the wall. (Since the floor plan is drawn at 1/4 scale, be very cautious when measuring from one to the other to ensure that you do not miscalculate.) From the vertical line on the new sheet, which represents the left side of the cabinets, measure the length of the cabinets and draw a vertical line for the right side. Draw a series of horizontal lines using dimensions in the illustration on page 70. Use very light lines until the actual configuration of the cabinets can be darkened. The fur down shown in the illustration is a blocked out space above the cabinets, since a shelf at this height would not be practical. This is optional, however, and will not need to be drawn if you wish to use full ceiling cabinets rather than furred down cabinets.

The 4 inch backsplash is a general standard and is used on premanufactured countertops. If you are not using a premanufactured top you may consider having the backsplash installed to the bottom of the wall cabinets, in which case the line shown will not be necessary. Leave at least 16 inches from the countertop to the bottom of the cabinets when installing new cabinets. For those who are adding on to the present kitchen cabinets, you will need to check these measurements since there could be some differences. Use fur down or ceiling cabinets to match your existing cabinets.

Transformations — in terms of both usability and aesthetics — are possible. Here are before and after photographs of a contemporary remodeling of a midwest Victorian house built in 1889. These pictures show the view looking south. The wainscoting remains, but has been painted dark to match the new cabinets; the door has been replaced. The area above the cabinets has been furred down with a slight overhang.

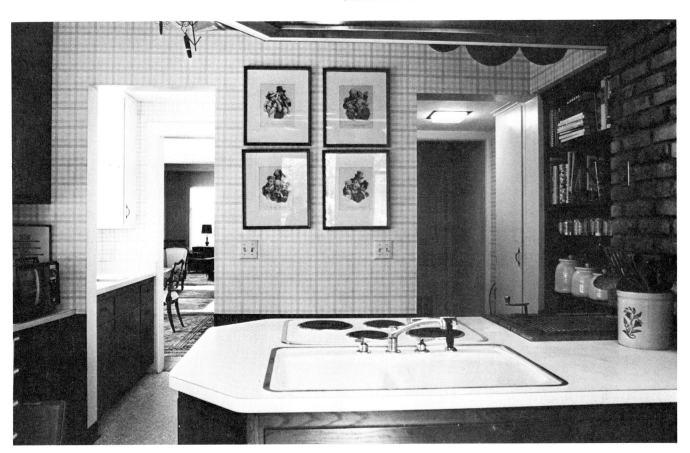

This is the north view of the before and after sequence. The old sink has been replaced with a peninsula extending from the last wall. It now offers a ample counter and storage space. The peninsula has a built-in range, grill, and useful double sink. The overhead task lighting provides needed illumination, and serves as a storage area for attractive copper pans and other utensils.

If the cabinets turn the corner on the right side, block out as shown in the illustration, shading with diagonal lines. On the next elevation the block out will occur reversed on the left side.

Any doors or windows in the wall of the elevation you are drawing must be measured from the floor plan and located on the elevation with vertical lines. The wall cabinets should stop at 3 to 4 inches from each side of a window, and both wall and base cabinets should stop 3 to 4 inches from each side of a door. Now measure and place two vertical lines for the range, refrigerator, or dishwasher. Wall cabinets above the refrigerator should go no lower than 72 inches off the floor and no closer than 30 inches above a range or cooktop. Keep the range a minimum of 12 inches from the edge of the window so that the curtains will not be near the cooktop.

In the usable cabinet areas that remain draw in very light lines for the tops and bottoms of drawers and doors using the dimensions in the illustration. Measure and draw in the sink as shown. Since this area is needed for plumbing access there is a ''dummy'' drawer and double doors which extend about 2 inches beyond either edge of the sink. On the remaining areas

you may divide the doors and drawers to suit your needs. For smaller areas, such as between a wall and the range, you may be restricted in your design. For instance, if this width is only 30 inches, you can have a single door that is 26 inches wide or double doors that are 13 inches wide. When designing in larger areas you will have more freedom in the door and

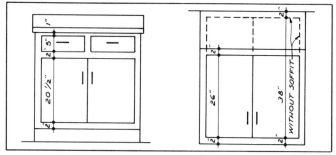

This illustration shows the dimensions used to locate the tops and bottoms of drawers and doors on your cabinets. These and the dimensions on the remaining cabinet illustrations are nominal dimensions used for drawing purposes only. The actual dimensions will be worked out to the fraction of an inch by the cabinet shop, or the manufacturer in the case of prefabricated cabinets.

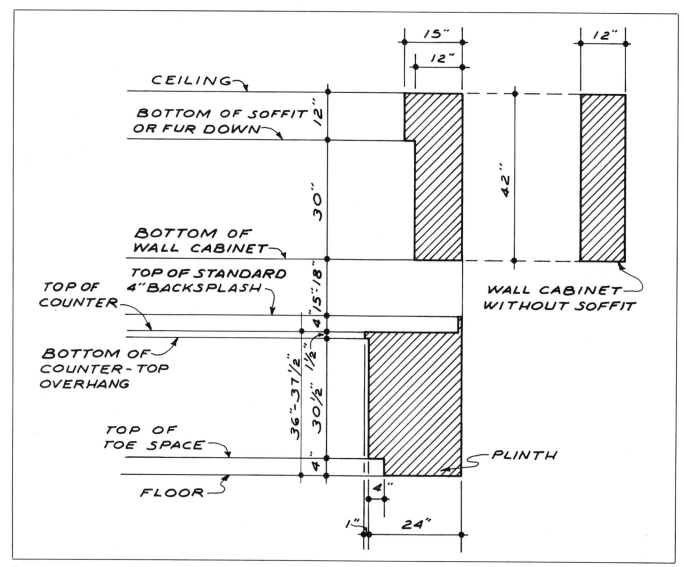

These are standard dimensions for kitchen cabinets with a ceiling height of 8 ft. The normal countertop height is 36 in., but this may be adjusted to as high as 37½ in. for taller people simply by adjusting the height of the plinth (normally 4 in.). Whatever dimensions you use, be sure the distance from floor to ceiling on the drawings is the same as it will be in your kitchen (standard 8 ft.).

drawer arrangement. Try to keep the doors and drawers from becoming too wide; 28 inches is a reasonable maximum width. Leave a two-inch space between the cabinet door or double door and the end of the cabinets or another door, as in the illustration. If you would like a series of drawers in the base cabinets, draw them in by using the dimensions in the illustration, which shows two different arrangements. When the

cabinet design is complete, darken the lines with the H pencil using medium-hard pressure.

Door designs for the cabinets do not need to be drawn in. (These will be covered in the material specifications in Chapter 8.) Label the elevations as in the sample remodeling at the end of this chapter. Since the elevations are only graphic representations of what you want, with the exact dimensions to be worked out by the cabinet builder, a minimum of lettering is required. The title of each elevation is based on the direction you would be facing if you were standing in the center of the kitchen looking at that wall of cabinets. So, if you were facing north the title for that elevation would be "KITCHEN CABINETS—NORTH WALL." You can determine the general direction of north simply by locating the rising or setting sun.

A cross-section is required for the kitchen cabinets as well as through a bath vanity and/or a linen closet. Since these are more or less universal, they have been reproduced at the proper scale in the rear of this chapter. You may either trace them onto your sheet or attach them to the specifications.

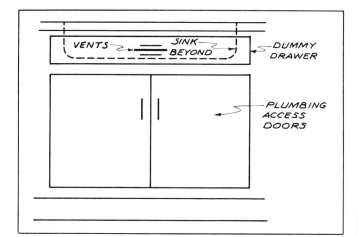

The cabinet below the kitchen sink will have a "dummy" drawer, usually vented, and wide doors for access to the plumbing.

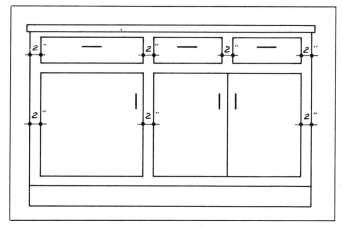

For drawing purposes a two inch space should be left on the sides of drawers and doors as shown.

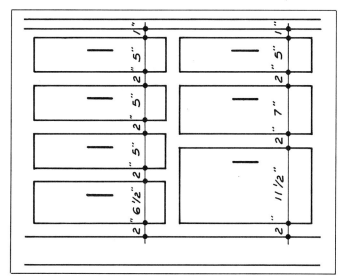

These are two typical arrangements for tiers of drawers.

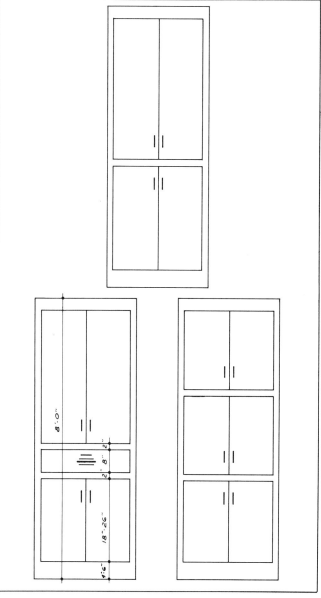

This illustration shows three different types of linen closets. The one on the left has a vented clothes hamper.

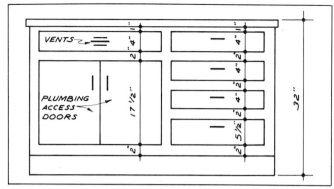

A bath vanity wide enough for plumbing access and a tier of drawers is not only attractive in a bath, but is also functional.

Bath

Vanities and linen closets are drawn in generally the same manner as the kitchen cabinets. The vanity, however, is 32 inches high instead of 36 inches. The illustration shows a sample layout for a vanity with a plumbing access and adjacent tier of drawers. You may use two shallow drawers and one deep drawer if you prefer, or a single drawer and a cabinet door. You may also wish to consider an open "kneespace" (minimum 24 inches wide) as a seating area for applying makeup.

Begin the new vanities where the kitchen cabinets ended, using the same floor line. If there is a new vanity for Bath No. 1, draw it first, then draw the new vanity for Bath No. 2, etc.

Continue beside the vanities with any new linen closets you may have planned. Although the design of the linen closet can be worked out to your needs, the illustration gives general dimensions that can be followed for linen closets with or without clothes hampers.

Other Cabinet Work

If you have planned built-in book cases and/or built-in desks, or perhaps a wine rack, elevations should also be drawn for these. Their arrangements may be very specialized; still some suggestions and minimum dimensions are shown in the accompanying illustrations.

CONSTRUCTION DETAILS

Construction details are large-scale drawings that show the builder how the different elements of the remodeling are to be built. They are not required for standard items that are completely regulated by codes, such as how the electrical and plumbing work is done or how to build a stud wall. They are required when there is some question as to how a certain item will be built, such as the exterior wall or foundation. A full range of construction details is provided at the rear of this chapter for your use. Select the ones you need and trace them onto the new sheet or attach them to the specifications. Since one sheet may contain several details, you will need to cross out those which are not required if you are attaching the sheets to your plans. Certain items, such as insulation requirements or dimensions, may vary from one locale to another due to local codes, ground condition, weather, or other factors. In the cases where several alternatives are given to be selected according to regional needs or requirements, you may present them to the contractor and have him point out the correct local

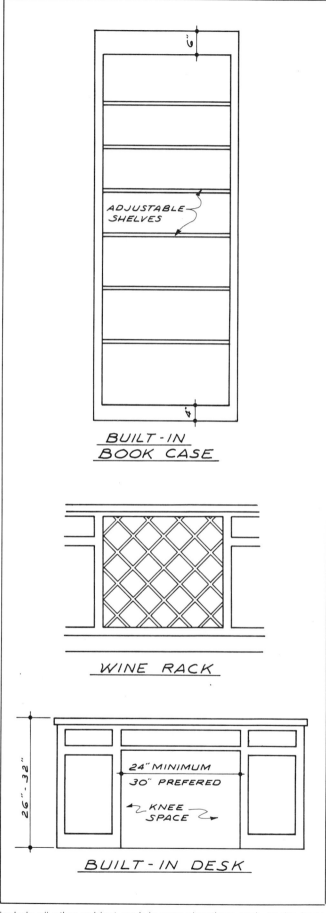

Include all other cabinet work in your elevations such as the items shown.

usage. His selection should be noted as such in the contract you write up in order to ensure his accountability. On each sheet there is an explanation of what figures you must write in and how you can find the information you need.

If your plans include a unique type of construction not covered in the rear of the chapter, consult with your contractor, or with your city building department. If necessary, consult an architect. Either one can make a rough sketch, with dimensions, of what the detail should look like. Using the drafting skills you have learned, draw the detail onto the new sheet, with the rough sketch as a guide.

THE FOUNDATION PLAN

For remodelings that include an addition, a foundation plan is required. In the case of a second floor addition this will be a floor framing plan. Usually the foundation of the addition will be constructed in the same manner as the existing foundation, but this may not always be the case. For instance, if your home is on a conventional foundation and the addition will be at a lower level than the present home, you may wish to make the new foundation a slab on grade. In determining which type of foundation you will use, consult with your contractor or building department, then draw the proper one as outlined.

Slab On Grade

Draw the outside edge of the existing home in the area of the addition. Then draw the outside edge of the new addition using the dimensions on the new floor plan. One foot in from the outside draw a dashed line all around the addition. This represents the inside edge of the footing for the slab. Although the footing may not be exactly 12 inches wide, this is sufficient for graphical representation. You will have to give the exact dimension on the construction detail. Dimension and note the foundation plan as shown in the illustration. Be sure to include a note whether the floor level is the same as the present home or if it is dropped or raised; give the difference as "LOWER NEW FLOOR 8 INCHES" or "RAISE NEW FLOOR 16 INCHES", etc.

Usually a grade beam through the center of the foundation will not be required for an addition. But if you are planning a very large addition or are building over poor soil conditions, it might be necessary. Consult with your city building department as to whether it is needed and, if so, where it should be located.

Then draw the grade beam on the foundation plan as two dashed lines about 18 inches apart. Place a dimension from the outside edge of the foundation to the center of the beam. Since the grade beam should be designed to go under an interior wall, this dimension should equal the corresponding dimension on the new floor plan.

A fireplace constructed on the site will require that the slab be poured the full depth of the footing under the fireplace. Adjust the line of the footing accordingly. It is recommended, however, that a prefabricated fireplace be used since it does not require the additional foundation support and can cost hundreds of dollars less.

Raised Slab

A raised slab will rest on a masonry load-bearing wall and will

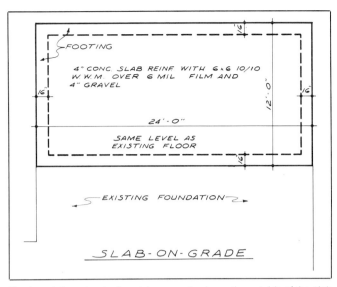

The foundation plan for the slab on grade shows the outside of the slab and the line of the footing as well as dimensions and note on type of construction.

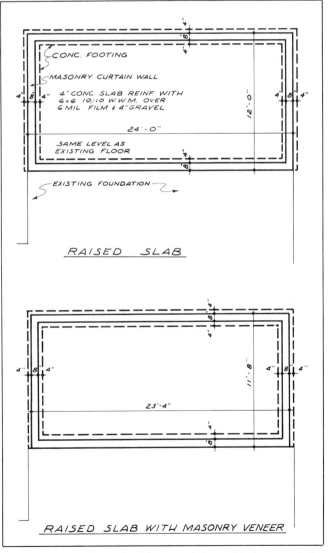

A raised slab is similar to the slab on grade in graphical representation except that the footing shows on both sides of an 8 in. wide curtain or foundation wall. When masonry veneer will be on the outside the dimensions must be adjusted to assure the existing veneer and new veneer will align properly.

be drawn similar to the slab on grade for most types of wall construction, except that the dashed line will be 8 inches inside the outside line and will be drawn solid. The concrete footing will appear on either side of the masonry wall, about 4 inches away, and drawn with dashed lines. If the outside walls will be brick or stone veneer, however, the masonry wall will be 4 inches inside the outer edge of the addition since the veneer will start at the top of the footing. This should be taken into

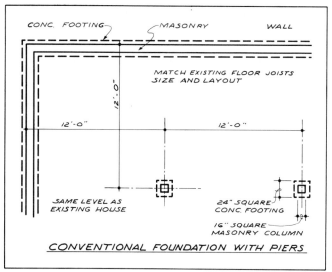

A conventional or wood frame foundation will appear in plan similar to the raised slab. The notes, however, will differ. For a large addition supporting piers will be needed on 12 ft. squares as shown.

account when computing dimensions; i.e., if the dimension is from the existing wall to the outside of the masonry wall, subtract 4 inches from the dimension on the floor plan. If it is from masonry wall to masonry wall, subtract 8 inches. The illustrations show how these should be drawn and dimensioned.

Conventional Foundation

A conventional or wood frame foundation will rest on a masonry wall and will appear on the plan the same as would a raised slab, with the same adjustments for veneer in the dimensions. The difference will be in the notes. Instead of a four-inch concrete slab, the conventional foundation will have a note reading "MATCH EXISTING FLOOR JOIST & PATTERN" or "2 x 10 FLOOR JOIST @ 16 INCHES ON CENTER (OC)." The construction detail in the rear will show all other notes and materials.

For large additions place masonry support piers (see illustration) on 12 foot squares. This means that the floor joists should not span more than 12 feet without support. The use of piers, however, could be regulated by local code, so check with the city building department to determine where they should be located.

Second Floor

For the floor framing plan of the second floor, simply note on the new floor plan that the joists should match the existing size and pattern or use 2 x 10's at 16 inches on center.

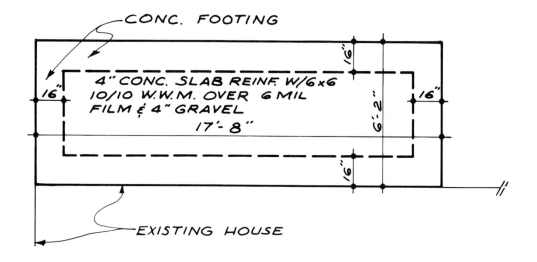

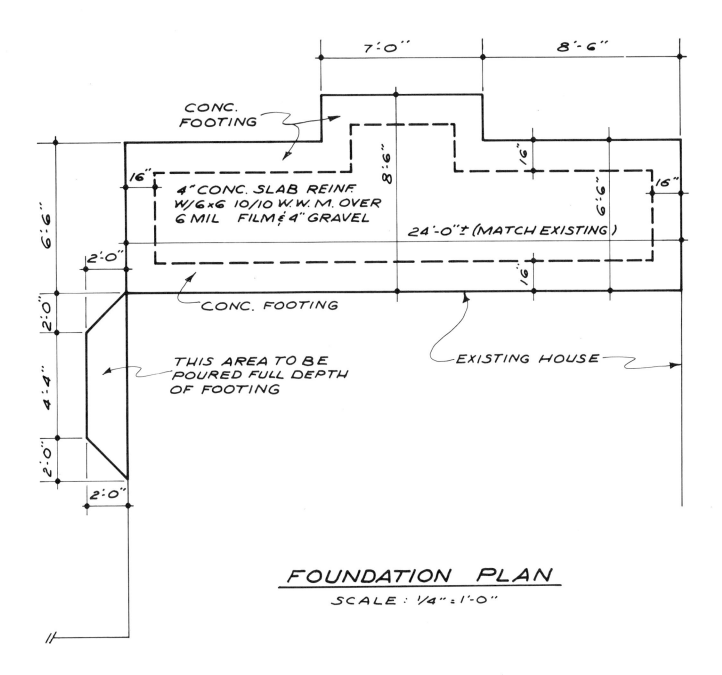

FOUNDATION PLAN
SCALE : 1/4" = 1'-0"

CONC. FOOTING

4" CONC. SLAB REINF. W/6×6 10/10 W.W.M. OVER 6 MIL FILM & 4" GRAVEL

24'-0" ± (MATCH EXISTING)

CONC. FOOTING

THIS AREA TO BE POURED FULL DEPTH OF FOOTING

EXISTING HOUSE

7'-0"

8'-6"

8'-6"

16"

16"

16"

16"

6'-6"

6'-6"

2'-0"

2'-0"

4'-4"

2'-0"

2'-0"

If you will be attaching construction details to the specifications, it should be noted on these drawings.

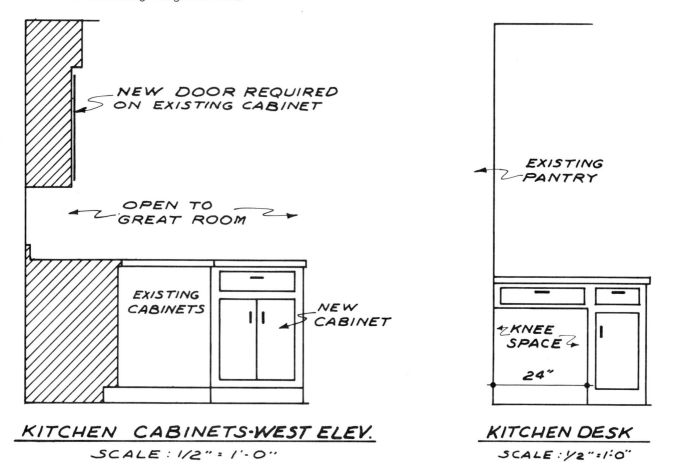

NEW DOOR REQUIRED
ON EXISTING CABINET

OPEN TO
GREAT ROOM

EXISTING
CABINETS

NEW
CABINET

EXISTING
PANTRY

KNEE
SPACE

24"

KITCHEN CABINETS·WEST ELEV.
SCALE : 1/2" = 1'-0"

KITCHEN DESK
SCALE : 1/2" = 1'-0"

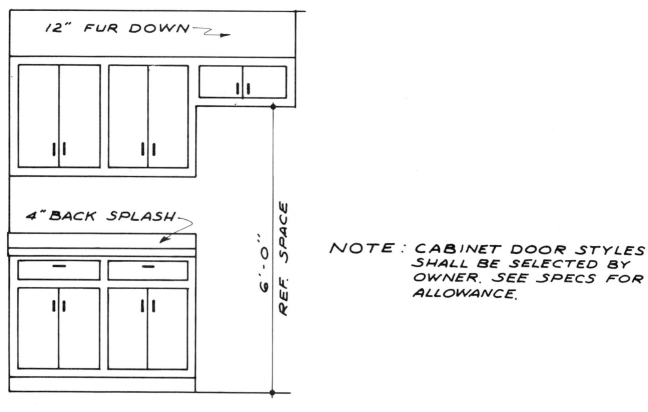

12" FUR DOWN

4" BACK SPLASH

6'-0" REF. SPACE

NOTE : CABINET DOOR STYLES
SHALL BE SELECTED BY
OWNER. SEE SPECS FOR
ALLOWANCE.

KITCHEN CABINETS -NORTH ELEV.
SCALE : 1/2" = 1'-0"

VANITY-BATH No. 1
SCALE : 1/2" = 1'-0"

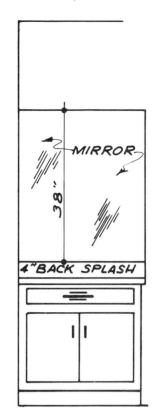

VANITY-BATH No. 2
SCALE : 1/2" = 1'-0"

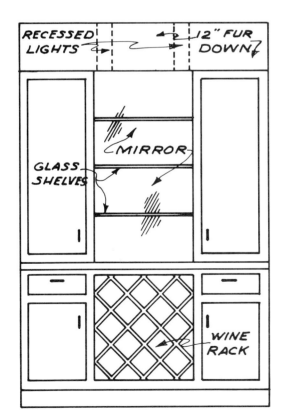

DINING ROOM CABINETS
SCALE : 1/2" = 1'-0"

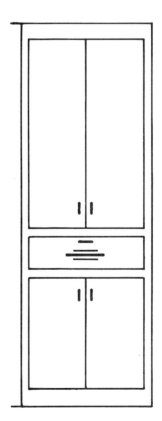

LINEN CLOSET
SCALE : 1/2" = 1'-0"

ALTERNATIVE FOUNDATION DETAILS

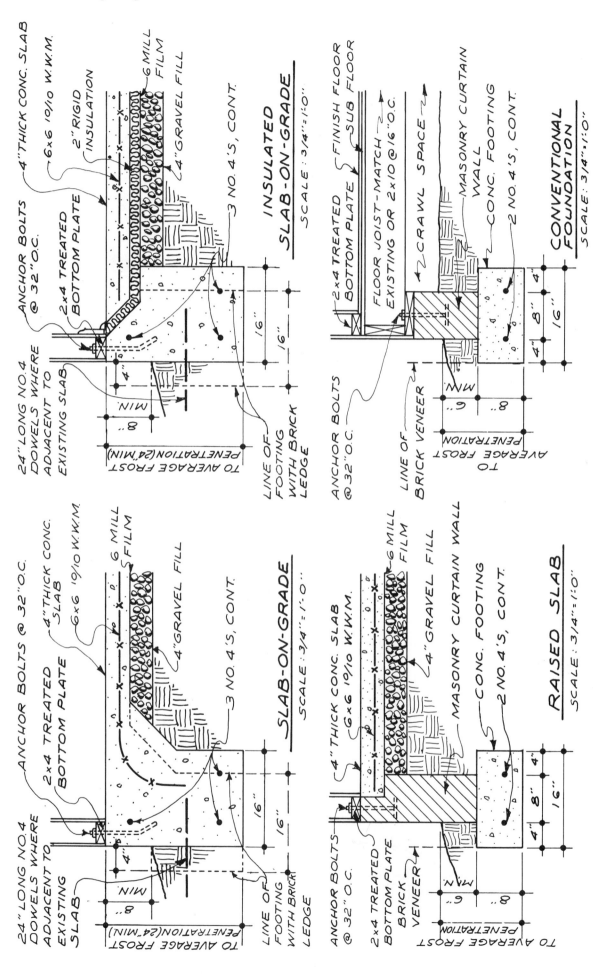

INSULATED SLAB-ON-GRADE
SCALE: 3/4"=1'-0"

24" LONG NO.4 DOWELS WHERE ADJACENT TO EXISTING SLAB
ANCHOR BOLTS @ 32" O.C.
4" THICK CONC. SLAB
6x6 10/10 W.W.M.
2" RIGID INSULATION
6 MILL FILM
4" GRAVEL FILL
2x4 TREATED BOTTOM PLATE
3 NO. 4'S, CONT.
LINE OF FOOTING WITH BRICK LEDGE
TO AVERAGE FROST PENETRATION (24" MIN.)
16"
16"
4"
8" MIN.

CONVENTIONAL FOUNDATION
SCALE: 3/4"=1'-0"

2x4 TREATED BOTTOM PLATE
FINISH FLOOR
SUB FLOOR
FLOOR JOIST - MATCH EXISTING OR 2x10 @ 16" O.C.
CRAWL SPACE
MASONRY CURTAIN WALL
CONC. FOOTING
2 NO. 4'S, CONT.
ANCHOR BOLTS @ 32" O.C.
LINE OF BRICK VENEER
TO AVERAGE FROST PENETRATION
4"
4"
8"
16"
6" MIN.

SLAB-ON-GRADE
SCALE: 3/4"=1'-0"

24" LONG NO.4 DOWELS WHERE ADJACENT TO EXISTING SLAB
ANCHOR BOLTS @ 32" O.C.
2x4 TREATED BOTTOM PLATE
4" THICK CONC. SLAB
6x6 10/10 W.W.M.
6 MILL FILM
4" GRAVEL FILL
3 NO. 4'S, CONT.
LINE OF FOOTING WITH BRICK LEDGE
TO AVERAGE FROST PENETRATION (24" MIN.)
16"
16"
4"
8" MIN.

RAISED SLAB
SCALE: 3/4"=1'-0"

4" THICK CONC. SLAB
6x6 10/10 W.W.M.
6 MILL FILM
4" GRAVEL FILL
MASONRY CURTAIN WALL
CONC. FOOTING
2 NO. 4'S, CONT.
ANCHOR BOLTS @ 32" O.C.
2x4 TREATED BOTTOM PLATE
BRICK VENEER
TO AVERAGE FROST PENETRATION
4"
4"
8"
16"
6" MIN.

These four foundation details are the most commonly used, although there are a number of other ways that foundations are built. You may need to check with a local contractor to determine standard construction in your area. The slab on grade is shown both with and without insulation because of the difference in construction required. For the raised slab and conventional foundation you will need to add a note stating what type of insulation should be used if it is required in your area.

CONSTRUCTION DETAILS

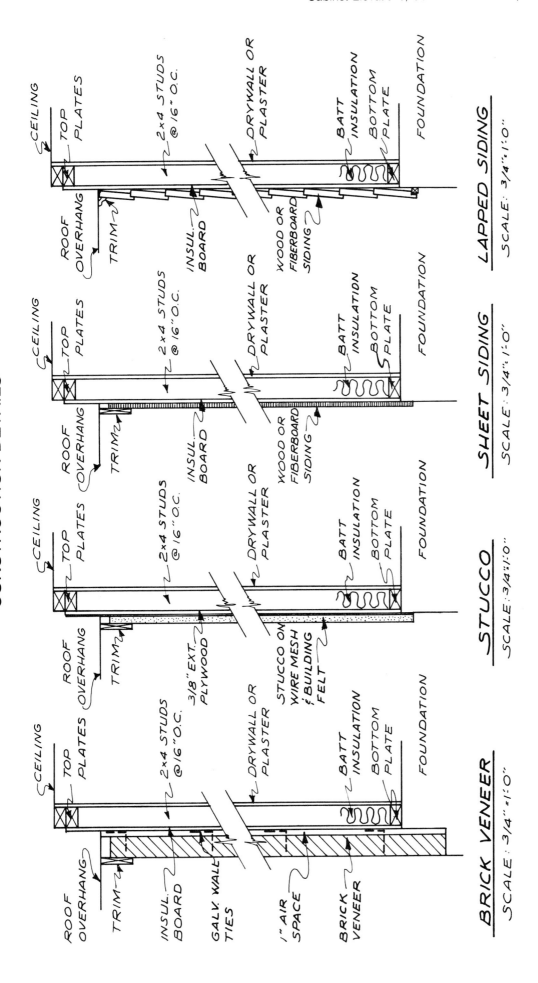

BRICK VENEER
SCALE: 3/4" = 1'-0"

STUCCO
SCALE: 3/4:1'-0"

SHEET SIDING
SCALE: 3/4":1'-0"

LAPPED SIDING
SCALE: 3/4":1'-0"

For new exterior frame walls select the one with the type of material you wish to use. If you have real stone planned you may use the brick veneer detail and change brick to stone. For stuccoed stone use the stucco detail and note the simulated stone finish.

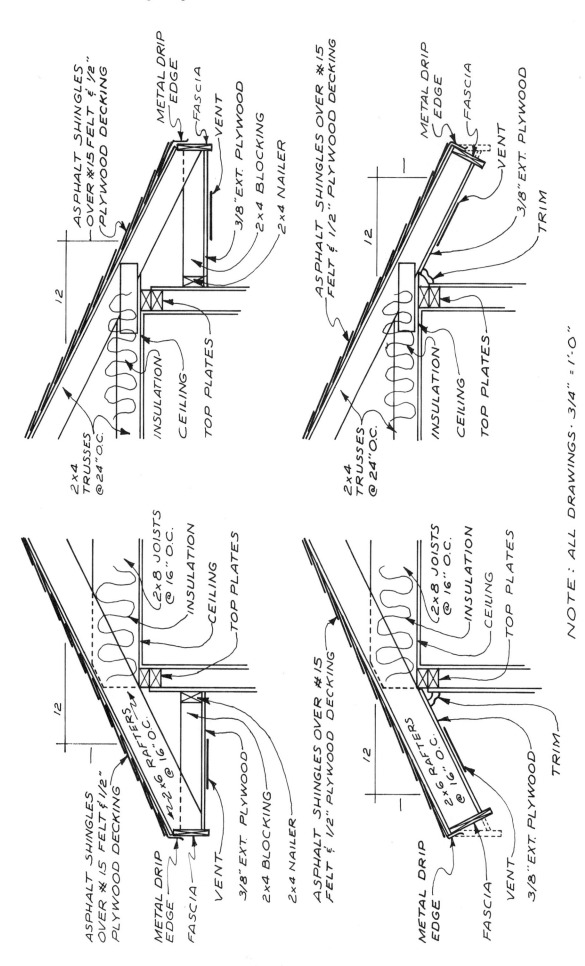

ASPHALT SHINGLES OVER #15 FELT & 1/2" PLYWOOD DECKING

METAL DRIP EDGE

FASCIA

VENT

3/8" EXT. PLYWOOD

2x4 BLOCKING

2x4 NAILER

INSULATION

CEILING

TOP PLATES

2x4 TRUSSES @ 24" O.C.

ASPHALT SHINGLES OVER #15 FELT & 1/2" PLYWOOD DECKING

METAL DRIP EDGE

FASCIA

VENT

3/8" EXT. PLYWOOD

TRIM

INSULATION

CEILING

TOP PLATES

2x4 TRUSSES @ 24" O.C.

2x8 JOISTS @ 16" O.C.

INSULATION

CEILING

TOP PLATES

ASPHALT SHINGLES OVER #15 FELT & 1/2" PLYWOOD DECKING

METAL DRIP EDGE

FASCIA

VENT

3/8" EXT. PLYWOOD

2x4 BLOCKING

2x4 NAILER

2x6 RAFTERS @ 16" O.C.

2x8 JOISTS @ 16" O.C.

INSULATION

CEILING

TOP PLATES

ASPHALT SHINGLES OVER #15 FELT & 1/2" PLYWOOD DECKING

METAL DRIP EDGE

FASCIA

VENT

3/8" EXT. PLYWOOD

TRIM

2x6 RAFTERS @ 16" O.C.

NOTE: ALL DRAWINGS - 3/4" = 1'-0"

The roof sections on the left use an on-site built roof and on the right use roof trusses. Fill in the roof pitch (no less than 3 in 12 for a shingled roof). For roofing material other than asphalt shingles, change the notes accordingly.

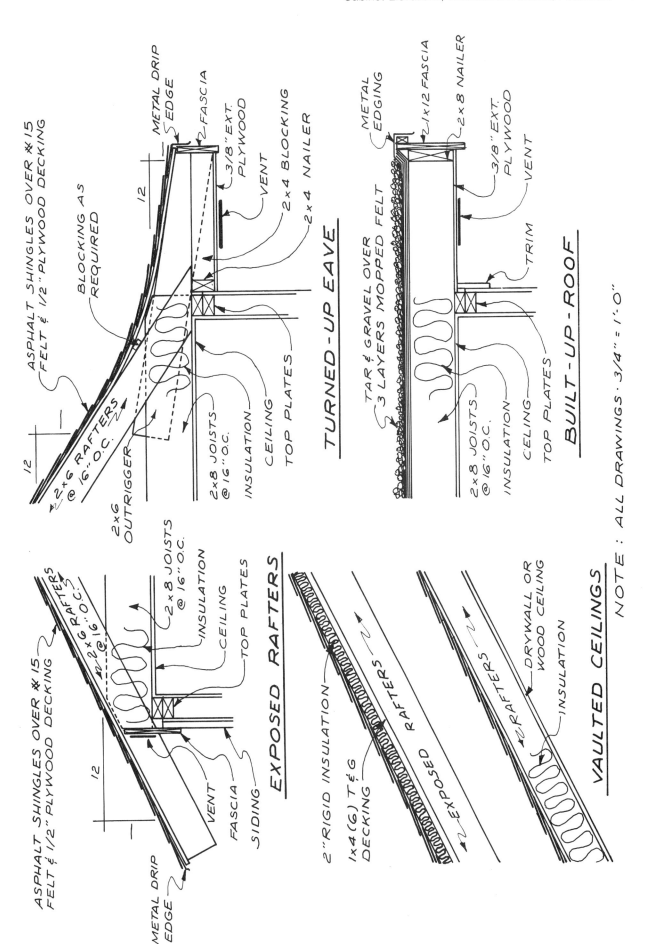

ASPHALT SHINGLES OVER #15 FELT & 1/2" PLYWOOD DECKING

BLOCKING AS REQUIRED

METAL DRIP EDGE

FASCIA

3/8" EXT. PLYWOOD

VENT

2×4 BLOCKING

2×4 NAILER

2×6 RAFTERS @ 16" O.C.

2×6 OUTRIGGER

2×8 JOISTS @ 16" O.C.

INSULATION

CEILING

TOP PLATES

TURNED-UP EAVE

METAL EDGING

1×12 FASCIA

2×8 NAILER

3/8" EXT. PLYWOOD

VENT

TRIM

TAR & GRAVEL OVER 3 LAYERS MOPPED FELT

2×8 JOISTS @ 16" O.C.

INSULATION

CEILING

TOP PLATES

BUILT-UP-ROOF

ASPHALT SHINGLES OVER #15 FELT & 1/2" PLYWOOD DECKING

2×6 RAFTERS @ 16" O.C.

2×8 JOISTS @ 16" O.C.

INSULATION

CEILING

TOP PLATES

METAL DRIP EDGE

VENT

FASCIA

SIDING

EXPOSED RAFTERS

2" RIGID INSULATION

1×4 (G) T & G DECKING

EXPOSED RAFTERS

RAFTERS

DRYWALL OR WOOD CEILING

INSULATION

VAULTED CEILINGS

NOTE : ALL DRAWINGS · 3/4" = 1'-0"

These additional roof treatments may also require that you write in the roof pitch in the blank provided. Vaulted ceilings are shown with and without exposed rafters.

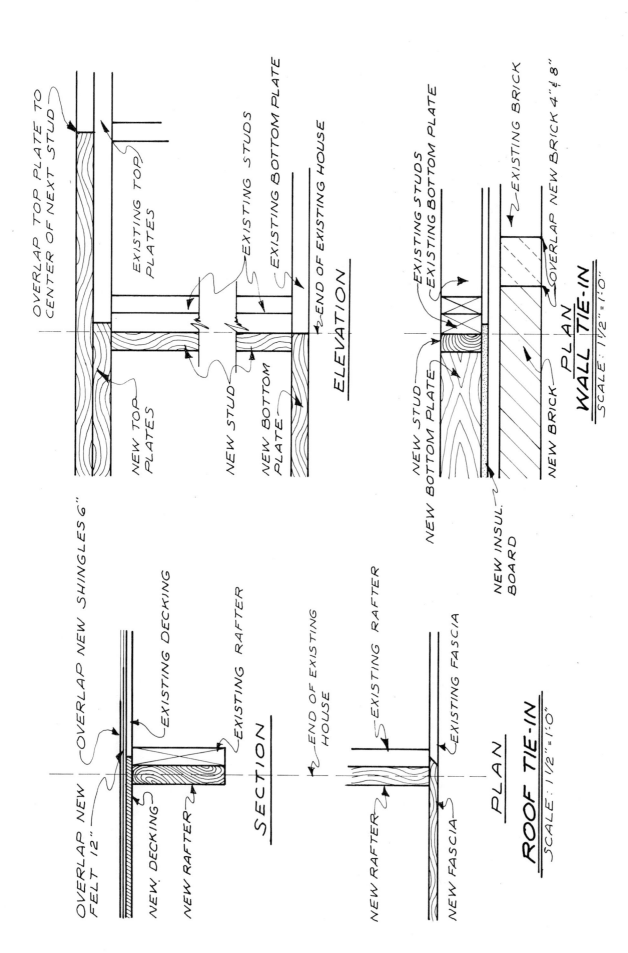

OVERLAP TOP PLATE TO CENTER OF NEXT STUD

EXISTING TOP PLATES

EXISTING STUDS

EXISTING BOTTOM PLATE

END OF EXISTING HOUSE

NEW TOP PLATES

NEW STUD

NEW BOTTOM PLATE

ELEVATION

EXISTING STUDS

EXISTING BOTTOM PLATE

EXISTING BRICK

OVERLAP NEW BRICK 4" & 8"

NEW STUD

NEW BOTTOM PLATE

NEW INSUL. BOARD

NEW BRICK

PLAN
WALL TIE-IN
SCALE: 1 1/2" = 1'-0"

OVERLAP NEW SHINGLES 6"

OVERLAP NEW FELT 12"

EXISTING DECKING

EXISTING RAFTER

NEW DECKING

NEW RAFTER

SECTION

END OF EXISTING HOUSE

EXISTING RAFTER

EXISTING FASCIA

NEW RAFTER

NEW FASCIA

PLAN
ROOF TIE-IN
SCALE: 1 1/2" = 1'-0"

These details show how the roof and walls tie-in where a new addition connects to the existing house.

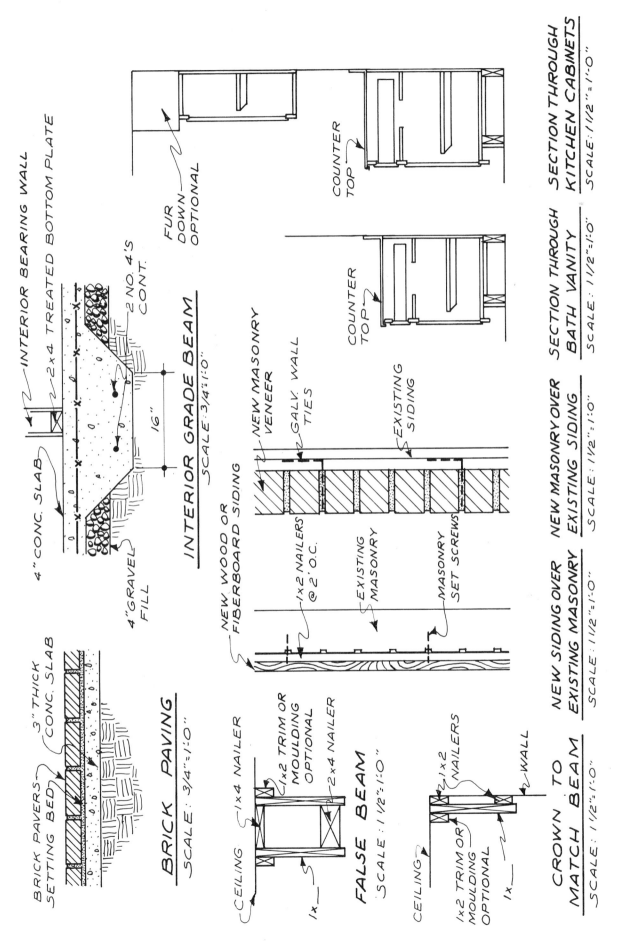

INTERIOR BEARING WALL

4" CONC. SLAB

2x4 TREATED BOTTOM PLATE

2 NO. 4'S CONT.

16"

4" GRAVEL FILL

FUR DOWN OPTIONAL

INTERIOR GRADE BEAM
SCALE: 3/4"=1'-0"

NEW WOOD OR FIBERBOARD SIDING

NEW MASONRY VENEER

GALV. WALL TIES

EXISTING SIDING

1x2 NAILERS @ 2' O.C.

EXISTING MASONRY

MASONRY SET SCREWS

COUNTER TOP

COUNTER TOP

SECTION THROUGH KITCHEN CABINETS
SCALE: 1 1/2"=1'-0"

SECTION THROUGH BATH VANITY
SCALE: 1 1/2"=1'-0"

NEW MASONRY OVER EXISTING SIDING
SCALE: 1 1/2"=1'-0"

BRICK PAVERS

3" THICK CONC. SLAB

SETTING BED

BRICK PAVING
SCALE: 3/4"=1'-0"

CEILING

1x4 NAILER

1x2 TRIM OR MOULDING OPTIONAL

2x4 NAILER

1x

FALSE BEAM
SCALE: 1 1/2"=1'-0"

CEILING

1x2 NAILERS

1x2 TRIM OR MOULDING OPTIONAL

WALL

1x

CROWN TO MATCH BEAM
SCALE: 1 1/2"=1'-0"

NEW SIDING OVER EXISTING MASONRY
SCALE: 1 1/2"=1'-0"

This sheet contains other miscellaneous details you might need. Brick paving is for patios when used. For a large addition with a slab foundation you may need an interior grade beam for extra support. On the false beam and matching crown you will need to fill in the size of the side boards. Use 1 x 6's in an average size room and 1 x 8's in a large room. If you are putting new materials over the existing exterior walls you may need one of the details shown. A detail is not required for new stucco over an existing wall. A cabinet section is necessary if you are planning a new bath vanity and/or new kitchen cabinets.

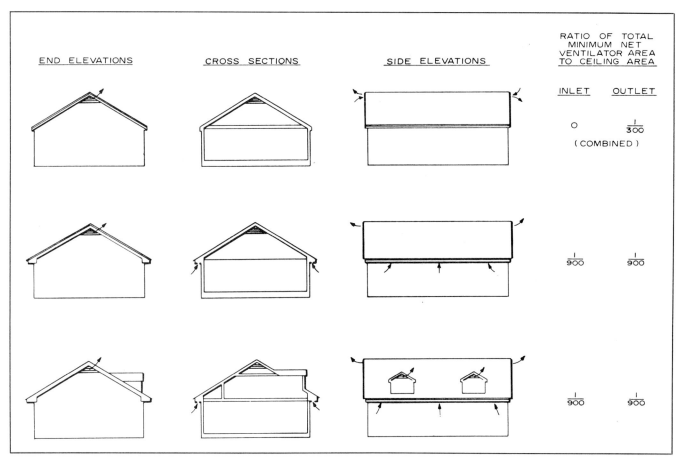

Shown are the various methods of ventilating gable roofs, and the amount of ventilation needed for various types. To find the size of opening required for the vent, multiply the total ceiling area by the ratio indicated. Be sure that the open area is completely unobstructed; if 16-mesh is used to cover the area, double the vent area.

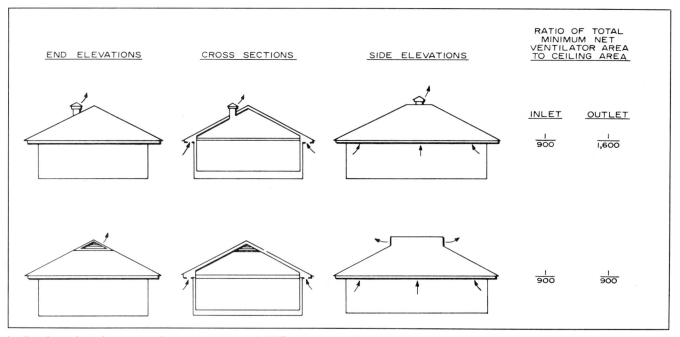

In all regions where the average January temperature is 35°F. or lower, ventilation of attics and crawl spaces is essential, particularly if the home does not have a vapor barrier. Asphalt shingles or built-up roofs sometimes create problems because moisture is prevented from escaping, which again makes ventilation important. The best combination is inlet vents in the soffit area plus outlet vents near the ridge. This gives a natural circulation independent of wind direction. Hip roofs require either a ventilator near the ridge or a special flue in the chimney. The hip roof can also be modified to accept a small gable for a conventional or louvered vent.

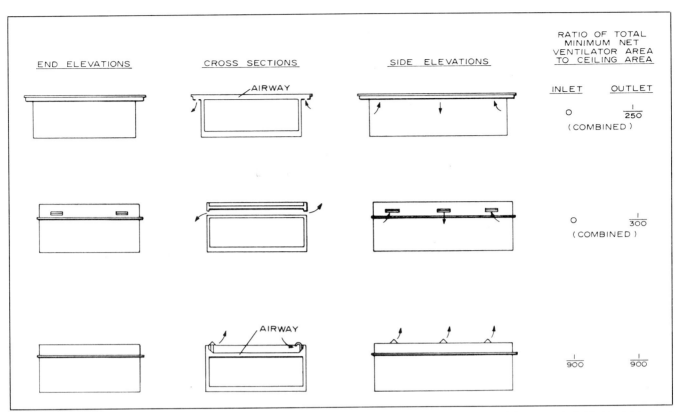

A flat roof — which usually means no attic — requires some type of ventialtion above the ceiling insulation. If the space is divided by joists, each joist space must be ventilated, which can be accomplished by a continuous vent strip in the soffit. Other methods are also shown. Cathedral ceilings take the same type of ventilation as flat roofs, but a continuous ridge vent is also desirable.

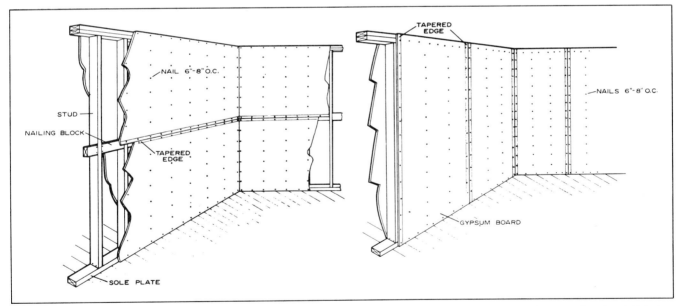

Gypsumboard can be applied horizontally or vertically. If you have designed a room in multiples of eight feet (sheets are four by eight feet or longer) then you can apply the sheets horizontally with no cutting, and have just the one joint midway up the wall.

8 Finished Construction Drawings

In order to finish your set of construction plans you must check your work carefully, fill out the title blocks, and fill out the material specifications. Once you have completed the work in this chapter you will be ready to get your building permit, hire a contractor(s) if necessary, and start construction.

CHECKING YOUR WORK

Go back over the drawings and check for any errors or omissions. Be sure all strings of dimensions add up to the proper overall dimension. If you have made changes along the way, which you probably have, check to see if the change impacted on any other work. For instance, if you shortened a kitchen cabinet on the floor plan or added a new cabinet, the cabinet elevations must be changed accordingly. Or if you changed the size or shape of an addition, you must also change the foundation plan and the exterior elevations. When making changes, always use the erasing shield so that you erase only what must be changed.

Check all your notes carefully to be sure nothing has been left out. All new items should be labeled, and all repairs to be made to the existing structure should be included. Don't give the plans just a cursory check. Sit down and take some time with them; go over them with a fine tooth comb. A mistake is easier to correct on paper than it is during construction. If you feel unsure about anything in the plans, retain an hour's worth of an architect's time or have your city building department review them for you. You may also check with your local FHA/VA office for assistance.

```
A REMODELING OF THE JONES RESIDENCE
2030  MAPLE  STREET

EXISTING  FLOOR  PLAN

DATE: 10-15-79 | REV. DATE: | REV. DATE:
SCALE: 1/4"=1:0" | DRAWN BY: T.M.J. | SHEET 1 OF 6
```

This typical block shows all the necessary information and has two blanks for revised dates.

TITLE BLOCKS

Most precut sheets already contain a title block in which you can write in the appropriate information. If yours has the block, letter in the information. Always use guidelines for your lettering. If there is no box, draw one as in the illustration, and complete the information.

Number each sheet in the same order that they came. Then put the same date on all title blocks — the date when the drawings were completed. If revisions are made on the draw-ings after they have been finished, put the revision date on each sheet and letter in a brief description of the changes made.

MATERIAL SPECIFICATIONS

In the rear of the chapter there is a filled-in set of standard FHA/VA material specifications (specs) for your use. In the back of the book (Appendix 2) there is a blank set that you can fill in or use to make copies. Additional copies can also be obtained through any FHA or VA office. The filled-out copy is based on the sample plans in this book, and can be used as a guide.

Many of the items in the specs are self-explanatory. Others will require that you select certain types or brands of material prior to construction, according to your region and your needs. Only the items that pertain to your remodeling need be completed. If a section does not apply, write "N.A.".

The following is an explanation of when each item should be completed and what must be filled in. You may need to check with building material suppliers or others for some of the necessary technical information for your plans.

1. Excavation

If you are planning an addition, the type of soil you are building on should be noted. Below is a chart of different types of soils and a rating of the soil's quality as a bearing soil for foundations.

If there is any question concerning the bearing capacity of the soil, you may have to get a "boring" (soil test) to determine whether it is suitable for the intended use.

SOIL	QUALITY
Gravel or gravel-sand mixtures, well graded	Excellent
Gravel or gravel-sand mixtures, poorly graded	Good
Silty gravels and gravel-sand-silt mixtures	Good
Clayey-gravels and gravel-sand-clay mixtures	Good
Sands or gravelly sands, well graded	Good
Sands or gravelly sands, poorly graded	Fair
Sand-silt mixtures	Fair
Sand-clay mixtures	Fair
Silty clays, inorganic silts	Fair
Organic silt-clays	Poor
Organic clays or organic silts	Very poor
Highly organic soil	Unusable

Normally your addition will be built upon the same type of soil as your house and there should be no problem with unusable material.

2. Foundations

For a raised slab or conventional foundation, state the type of material to be used in the foundation wall such as brick, concrete block, concrete, etc. Under termite protection, write pressure-treated bottom plates with bonded soil poisoning. Bonded means that the company performing the treatment is liable for termite damage for a specified length of time. This time should be written in, but may vary from one locality to another because of code differences. Call a local pest control service to determine the length of the bonding period you should specify, and whether termite protection is required for your locality. The remaining blanks should be completed as they apply to your individual remodeling. For instance, if you plan a large addition with a conventional foundation, and piers are required, then state the material of which they should be made.

The foundation section should be completed if there is an addition planned. For footings the concrete strength should be 3000 p.s.i., which means the concrete can withstand a pressure of 3000 pounds per square inch after 28 days under normal curing conditions. For a slab-on-grade with an integral footing, the strength of concrete will be the same as the slab, 2500 p.s.i. The lower strength concrete is offset by the larger footing and additional reinforcement bar, as shown in the construction details at the end of Chapter 7.

Concrete is usually ready-mix and is ordered by the strength required; the mix is specified by weight. If, for one reason or another the concrete must be mixed on site, then it should be specified by volume since it will be measured proportionally by shovel loads of each ingredient. However, this should be avoided if ready-mix is available. The chart below shows the mix proportions by weight (pounds) and by volume (cubic feet) to obtain various strengths. It is based on using a coarse sand with a specific gravity of 2.63, 1 inch gravel with a specific gravity of 2.59, and Type I Portland cement. When specifying by volume, the water should be given in gallons.

STRENGTH		Cement	Sand	Gravel	Water
2500 p.s.i.	weight	460	1210	1950	325
	volume	1	3.15	5.15	16.6 gals.
2800 p.s.i.	weight	500	1180	1950	325
	volume	1	2.83	4.75	15.3 gals.
3000 p.s.i.	weight	540	1140	1950	325
	volume	1	2.53	4.39	14.1 gals.

For example, if you are specifying 3000 p.s.i. concrete by volume, it would be written 1:2.53:4.39, 14.1 gals.

Venting for Heater
A new heater or water heater will need to be vented through the roof. The supplier who sells these items will be able to advise you as to the material and size of the vents required.

3. Chimneys
Should your remodeling plans include a fireplace, it is suggested that you use a prefabricated unit; the appearance is the same for most models and the cost is usually much less. In that case simply write in the make and size of the prefabricated chimney. If you choose to have a chimney built on-site, you will have to specify the type of material for the chimney and the flue, including the size of the flue.

Local codes may call for varying types of construction for fireplaces and chimneys, but here are some basic restrictions and requirements.

Foundation. Since the chimney is the heaviest part of a building, it must have a strong, solid foundation to prevent uneven settling. Concrete footings are best. They must be designed to distribute the load over a wide enough area to prevent exceeding the load-bearing limits of the soil. Footings should reach out at least 6 inches further than the chimney on all sides and be 8 inches thick for one-story houses and 12 inches thick for two story houses with basements. If there will be no basement, pour the footings beneath the frostline for an exterior chimney on solid ground.

Walls. Chimneys in frame buildings should be built from the ground up, or they can rest on the building foundation or basement walls — again, assuming that the walls are of solid masonry 12 inches thick. If the addition will have a wall of masonry at least 12 inches thick, the chimney can be built integrally with the wall. This means that instead of carrying it down to the ground, it can be offset from the wall sufficiently to provide flue space by corbelling. This offset should not extend more than 6 inches from the face of the wall, and each course should not project further than 1 inch, and be no less than 12 inches high.

If the walls of the chimney are less than 30 feet high, they should be at least 4 inches thick if made of brick or reinforced concrete, and at least 12 inches thick if made of stone. Brick chimneys that go up through the roof may sway in heavy winds and open up mortar joints at the roof line. It is, therefore, a good practice to make the upper walls 8 inches thick by starting to offset the bricks at least 6 inches below the underside of the roof joist or rafters.

Flue Linings. Flue linings are needed for safe and efficient operation, particularly for brick chimneys. Vitrified fire clay at least ⅝ inch thick is necessary to withstand rapid changes in temperature as well as the action of flue gases. You can choose from round or rectangular linings. Round linings are more efficient, but rectangular is more common and easier to use for brick construction.

The linings will be placed in position with cement mortar, with the joint struck smooth in the inside, and brick laid around it. If you wait to slip the lining in until after several brick courses have been laid, the joints cannot be filled and there will be leakage. In masonry chimneys with walls of less than 8 inches, there should be space between the lining and the chimney walls. This space should not be filled with mortar; the mortar is used only to hold the lining in position and to make good joints. The lower portion of the lining should be supported on at least three sides by brick that extends to the inside surface of the lining. This lining should reach a point at least 8 inches under the smoke pipe thimble or flue ring.

If your chimney contains more than one flue, remember that building codes generally require separate flues for each fireplace, furnace or boiler. If there will be three or more lined flues, each group of two flues must be separated from the other single flue or group of two flues by brick divisions of at least 3¾ inches thick. If two flues are grouped together without a dividing wall, their lining joints should be staggered at least 7 inches and the joints completely filled with mortar.

Consider a soot pocket and cleanout for each flue. If two or more flues use the same cleanout, air drawn from one to another can affect the draft in both.

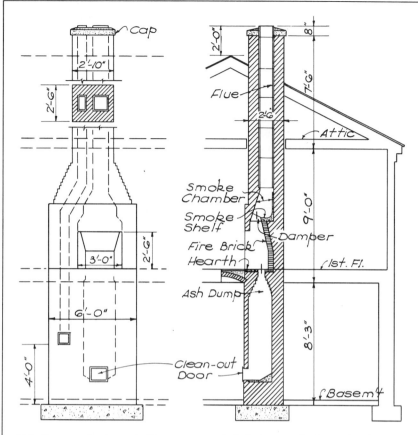

This diagrams the type of chimney commonly built to serve the house-heating unit and one fireplace.

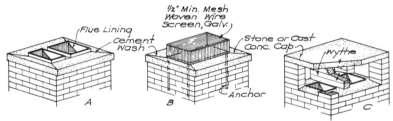

The construction of chimneys ;is shown:
(A) This is a good method for finishing the top of the chimney; the flue lining extends 4 in. above the cap. (B) A spark arrestor or bird screen protects your chimney from the elements, and vice versa. (C) A hood keeps out the rain.

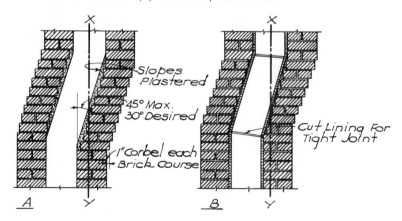

How to offset a chimney: For structural safety there must be a limit to the offset so that the center line, XY, of the upper flue does not fall beyond the center of the wall of the lower flues. Shown at (A): By starting the offset of the left wall of any unlined flue two brick courses higher than the right wall, you avoid reduction of the area of the sloping section due to plastering. (B) This is how to make a tight joint.

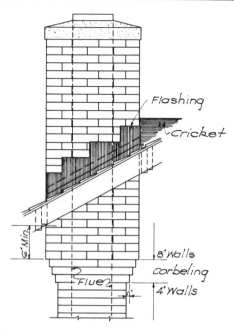

For sections exposed to the weather, corbell the chimney to provide 8 in. walls.

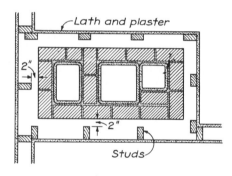

This plan shows proper configuration of three flues. Stagger the joints successive courses to bond the division wall with the sidewalls. Wood framing should be at least 2 in. from any brick work.

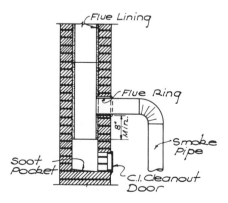

Soot pockets and chimney flue cleanouts make it easy to remove accumulations without expensive repair and heavy construction.

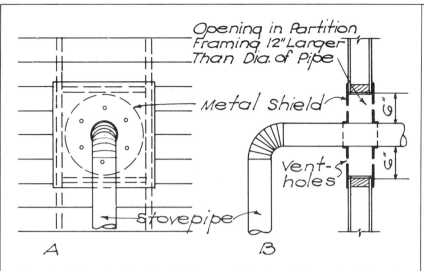

Shown is: (A) an elevation of protection around the pipe; (B) a sectional view, for protection of wood partition when a smoke pipe passes through it.

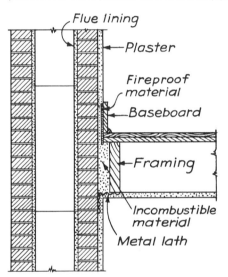

This is one means of insulating wood floor joints and baseboard at a chimney.

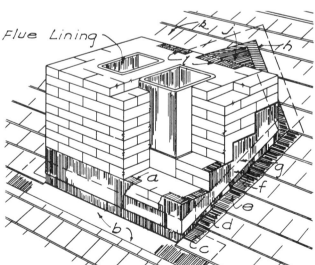

At the point where the chimney passes through the roof, provide a 2 in. clearance between the masonry and wood framing. Flash and counterflash for a watertight juncture. Above: sheet metal (h) over cricket (j), extends at least 4 in. under the shingles and is counterflashed at (1) in joint. Base flashing are b, c, d, e, and cap flashings (a, f, and g) lap over the base flashings to provide watertight construction. Whenever cap flashing is inserted in joints a full bed of mortar is needed.

FLUE AREAS FOR FIREPLACES HAVING TWO OR MORE OPENINGS (FACES)

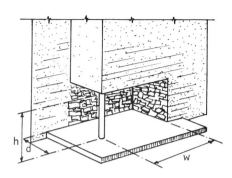

TWO FACES ADJACENT

W	D	H	Flue
30″	30″	36″	16 x 16″
34″	20″	30″	12 x 16″
42″	24″	42″	16 x 20″

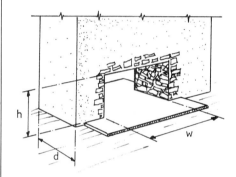

TWO FACES OPPOSITE

W	D	H	Flue
30″	24″	42″	16 x 20″
34″	28″	30″	16 x 16″
38″	28″	36″	16 x 20″

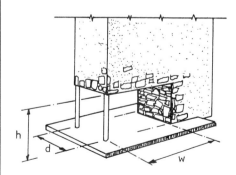

THREE FACES

W	D	H	Flue
34″	24″	24″	16 x 16″
38″	28″	30″	16 x 20″
38″	28″	36″	20 x 24″

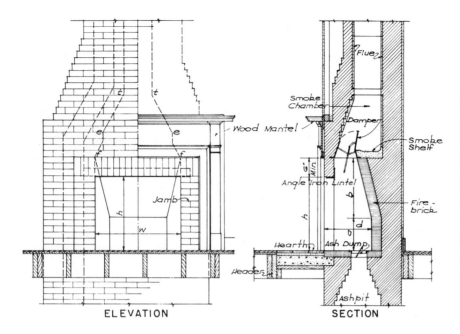

ELEVATION   SECTION

Here are the construction features of a fireplace. The letters correspond to the dimensions in the charts on page 89 and below.

For proper throat area (ff) construction, the side of the fireplace must run vertically up the throat, which should be 6 to 8 in. or more above the bottom of the lintel. The area of the throat must be not less than that of the flue — length should equal the width of the fireplace opening. The width will depend on the width of the damper frame. The sidewalls should start sloping inward to meet the flue (tt) t in. (ee) above the throat.

The section drawing shows an alternate means of hearth support.

The ashpit of a fireplace should be constructed of tight masonry. It should have a tightly fitting iron cleanout door and a frame 10 in. high and 12 in. wide. The drawing at the left also shows a cleanout for a furnace flue.

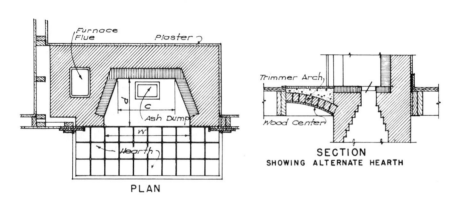

PLAN

SECTION
SHOWING ALTERNATE HEARTH

Dimensions for Fireplaces and Flue Lining Sizes

Size of fireplace opening		Depth	Minimum width of back wall	Height of vertical back wall	Height of inclined back wall	Size of flue lining required	
Width	Height					Standard rectangular (outside dimensions)	Standard round (inside diameter)
w	h	d	c	a	b		
Inches	Inches	Inches	Inches	Inches	Inches	Inches	Inches
24	24	16-18	14	14	16	8½ x 13	10
28	24	16-18	14	14	16	8½ x 13	10
30	28-30	16-18	16	14	18	8½ x 13	10
36	28-30	16-18	22	14	18	8½ x 13	12
42	28-32	16-18	28	14	18	13 x 13	12
48	32	18-20	32	14	24	13 x 13	15
54	36	18-20	36	14	28	13 x 18	15
60	36	18-20	44	14	28	13 x 18	15
54	40	20-22	36	17	29	13 x 18	15
60	40	20-22	42	17	30	18 x 18	18
66	40	20-22	44	17	30	18 x 18	18
72	40	22-28	51	17	30	18 x 18	18

Letters refer to art on pages 89 and above. This chart is produced from Farmers Bul. No. 1889.

4. Fireplaces

Again, a prefabricated fireplace is suggested because of the cost savings. Write in the make and size of the prefabricated unit. Fill in the type of fireplace and note whether it will have an ash dump and clean-out. The instructions for a prefabricated fireplace will also tell you what size hearth is best.

Under facing write in the type of material — brick, stone, or concrete — whether the unit is prefabricated or not. The usual lining is firebrick, though many prefabricated units do not require this. Check with the supplier. The hearth should be written in just as it reflects on the New Floor Plan; for example, 8 inches raised brick, 16 inches raised stone. If you want a mantel on your fireplace, write in the material and the size. Be sure to give the width and thickness of the mantel as well as the length. There are a variety of mantels available at fireplace dealerships; they can also be constructed on-site to your specifications.

On the line for additional information you should write in the style of brick or other facing material to be used, or put in a cost limit. Selection of a particular style will require an advance visit to a dealer, while the cost allowance can be determined over the phone. If you select the style ahead of time, the contractor should agree to absorb cost increases on that material once he submits his bid. This is the advisable step. Write up this part of your contract carefully; since the construction industry has been plagued with overnight price increases in recent years, a good cost allowance could become obsolete by the time you reach that phase of the construction.

5. Exterior Walls

The wood grade and species for framing will depend on what is available and is commonly used in your area. There are many different types of wood, as shown below, and not all are available nationwide. Shipping costs will make certain species cheaper in some areas than in others. The grade can be either No. 1 or 2 for most framing lumber. Number 2 is a slightly lower grade and is usually less expensive. For this reason it is most commonly used in framing. There can, however, be price variations such that a No. 1 grade in a particular species is less expensive than a No. 2 grade in another. It is advisable to call a lumber supplier and discuss the types and prices of wood available locally before specifying.

Soft Woods For Framing

Western Red Cedar	Southern Pine (Yellow)
Bald Cypress	Sugar Pine
Douglas Fir	Redwood
Western Hemlock	Black Spruce
Western Larch	Englemann Spruce
Lodgepole Pine	Red Spruce
Ponderosa Pine	Sitka Spruce
Red Pine	

Sheathing for exterior walls was most commonly 1 x 4 or 1 x 6 T & G (Tongue and Groove) lumber in the past. But because of today's high cost of wood, energy consciousness, and innovative new products, lumber is rarely used. If you would like to use wood sheathing, it is available in the same types of lumber, as mentioned above for framing. Sizes may

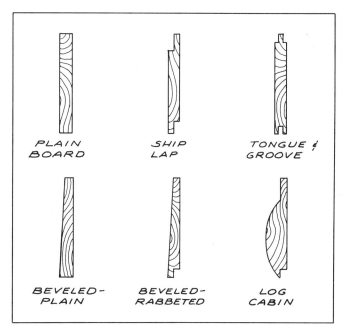

These are the general types of siding available in lumber. Most are available in varying sizes, and four species of woods — cedar, redwood, spruce, and white pine. T & G is not available in cedar and Log Cabin is not available in cedar or redwood. In addition, many of these styles are available in fiberboard. There are also metal and vinyl siding products on the market, some prefinished and not requiring periodic painting.

range from 1 x 4 to 1 x 12 T & G. Although lumber is the only sheathing that may be spaced (usually 50 percent coverage), it is advisable that it be applied solid. Corner bracing is not required for wood sheathing, but it should be covered with 15 lb. asphalt-saturated building paper or felt.

Plywood may also be used for sheathing and should be used under stuccoed exteriors, except where the stucco is being applied over an existing wall. Thickness may be either ⅜ inch or ½ inch, and the standard width is 4 feet. Corner bracing is not required, but 15 lb. felt overlay is.

Of the newer products, the highest insulating value is given by styrofoam or polystyrene. The thicknesses used most often for homes are ¾ inch and 1 inch. These may also be ordered with a foil sheet on one or both sides to increase the insulating value. The edges are available in T & G for a surer joint. Non-T & G edges should be covered with strips of 15 lb. felt. The width is 4 feet. Polystyrene sheathings will melt in a fire while the styrofoam sheathings are noncombustible. Corner bracing is required for the foam sheathings, as it is for all nonwood sheathings. This may be accomplished by using sheets of plywood at the house corners or by using 1 x 4 "let-in" braces across the studs as in the illustration.

Because styrofoam is usually the most expensive of the nonwood sheathings, the most popular type is gypsum exterior sheathing, also called brown board, insulation board, or fiberboard. These boards are usually ½ inch thick and 4 feet wide, and come with an asphalt impregnation so that felt is not required except at the seams. Another popular sheathing, commonly found on prefabricated homes because of its low cost and added strength, is a cardboard sheathing with a foil coating on both sides. This type is only ⅛ inch thick and comes in 4-foot wide sheets.

The finish material for the exterior walls will require a visit

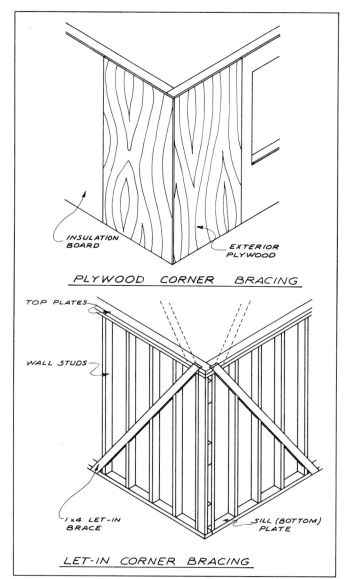

INSULATION BOARD

EXTERIOR PLYWOOD

PLYWOOD CORNER BRACING

TOP PLATES

WALL STUDS

1 x 4 LET-IN BRACE

SILL (BOTTOM) PLATE

LET-IN CORNER BRACING

Corner bracing can be handled in two different ways. The easiest is to use plywood at the house corners. The let-in bracing, shown on the right, is inset into the wall framing and requires more labor for notching the studs and plates. Let-in braces should start at the top plates on the corner and go to the bottom plate at or near a 45° angle. For a second floor the brace starts at the bottom and goes up as shown by the dashed lines.

to a building material supplier and/or brick manufacturer, or consultation with a concrete contractor for stucco. Since these materials will define the appearance of the outside of your home, you should be careful to select what is right for you and your budget.

If you are using a combination of materials, such as brick and cedar siding, complete the proper blanks for each. The necessary information can be obtained from the dealer at the time you make your choice. As discussed in section 4 above, it is strongly advisable that you specify the exact type of material to be used to avoid misunderstandings during construction. The illustrations show the different styles of wood and plywood siding. These are available in many types of wood, and even in nonwood materials. Shingles in this section refers to exterior walls only, not roofs, such as using wood shingles in a gable wall or above a brick wainscot.

Stucco can vary from ¾ inch to 1¼ inch thick and can be

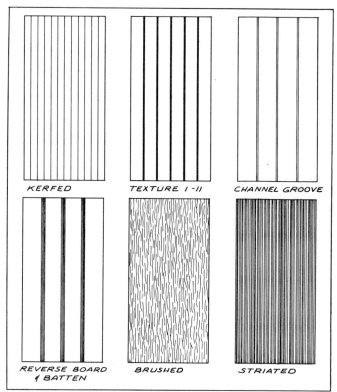

KERFED   TEXTURE 1-11   CHANNEL GROOVE

REVERSE BOARD & BATTEN   BRUSHED   STRIATED

Exterior finish plywood comes in a variety of styles and textures. Kerfed is a series of narrow grooves that are ¼ in. deep and either 2 in. or 4 in. on center. Texture 1-11 and Channel Groove are ⅜ in. wide grooves that are available on 2 in., 4 in., 6 in., 8 in., and 12 in. centers. The difference is that the Texture 1-11 grooves are ¼ in. deep and the Channel Grooves are only 1/16 in. deep. Reverse Board and Batten has grooves that are 1½ in. wide and ¼ in. deep, and are available on 8 in., 12 in., and 16 in. centers. These styles are also available in different textures and in nonwood materials such as fiberboard.

applied in two or three coats depending on such factors as climate, the type of finish you want (smooth or textured) and the material over which it is being applied. The lath is welded wire mesh and the weight will vary. For two coats which total 1 inch thick the weight will be 10 lbs per square foot. It is advisable to consult with a concrete contractor before you attempt to specify a stucco wall.

Masonry veneer can be either a brick or stone veneer wall outside the stud wall. The masonry is for appearance, since the structural bearing wall is the stud wall. Specify the type of masonry and the type of window and door sills (usually the same). The lintels carry the masonry above openings such as for windows and doors and are usually steel. Base flashing is most often 6 mil film.

Masonry walls can be either solid (such as a concrete block or double-brick wall), faced (such as brick over concrete block), or stuccoed. Most of these walls require a stonger foundation than a frame wall and are used more often in commercial structures than in residences. There is a variety of materials and ways in which masonry walls can be constructed. If your plans call for a masonry wall rather than a frame wall, consult with a masonry contractor to determine how this section of the specifications should be completed.

Use the line for additional information to note any styles and/or brands of material to be used. For exterior surfaces to be painted or stained fill in the type of material you wish to use — enamel, exterior latex, exterior stain,   and the number of

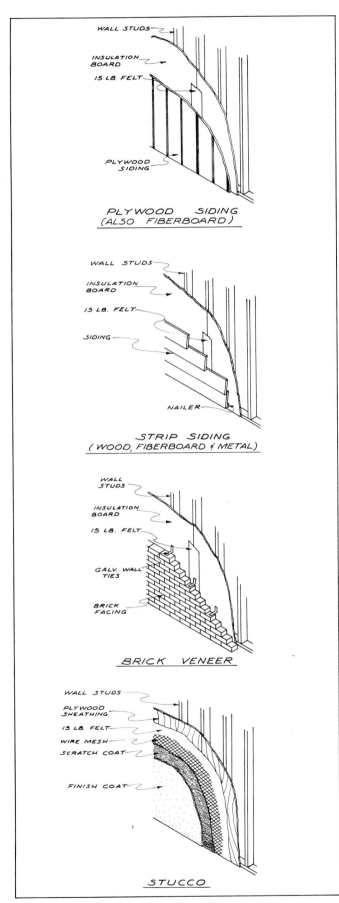

PLYWOOD SIDING
(ALSO FIBERBOARD)

STRIP SIDING
(WOOD, FIBERBOARD & METAL)

BRICK VENEER

STUCCO

These are the typical methods of construction for various types of exterior frame walls. The stucco wall shown is two coat work. Three-coat work would require an intermediate coat of stucco called a "brown coat."

coats, usually two. If there is a new gable wall in your plans, mark if it will be of the same material as the other new exterior walls. If not, specify the type of material to be used. For instance, if a planned addition has a gable roof and brick veneer walls you may wish to carry the brick up into the gable to the bottom of the gable vent. Or you may prefer to stop the brick at the level of the eaves and use siding or wood shingles between the brick and gable vent. See the illustration.

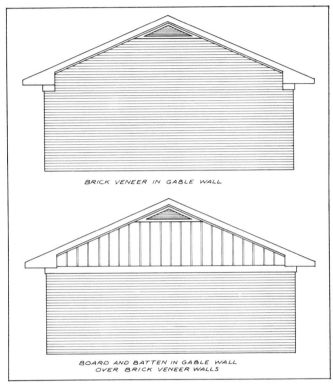

BRICK VENEER IN GABLE WALL

BOARD AND BATTEN IN GABLE WALL
OVER BRICK VENEER WALLS

The gable wall may be constructed of the same material as the main walls or it may be different.

6. Floor Framing

If you are planning an addition this section should be completed. For a conventional or platformed foundation (wood frame) write in the type of wood for the joists and the other framing. This will usually be the same type of wood as the wall framing, but not always. The types mentioned in No. 5 above may all be used. The bridging (between joists for rigidity) can be either wood blocks or metal strips. The floor framing is usually anchored to the foundation wall with anchor bolts at 32 inches O.C.. If your house already has a conventional foundation, you may simply write "Match Existing" in this area.

The common strength for a concrete slab is 2500 p.s.i. with a thickness of 4 inches. The mix may be obtained from the information in section 2 above. Reinforcing is with 6 x 6 10/10 welded wire mesh. The insulation will vary depending on your locale, consult the building department, local FHA/VA office, or local contractors. The usual membrane is 6 mil film and the slab should have 4 inches of washed gravel fill beneath, over compacted earth.

A freestanding slab, one that is not ground-supported, will need to be much stronger. These are rare in single-family residences, but if you have one planned, you will need to consult with a professional.

7. Subflooring

For a new conventional foundation, the subfloor goes directly over the joists; above the subfloor is the finish floor. The most commonly used material for subfloors is plywood, but T & G boards no thinner than ¾ inch and no wider than 8 inches can be used — this is much more expensive. The most economical subfloor is particleboard, which is rapidly increasing in popularity because of its lower price and adequate strength. Plywood and particleboard come in 4 foot by 8 foot sheets and should be no thinner than ¾ inch.

Particleboard is a relatively new product and has not been as fully tested as plywood. Present tests, however, indicate that strengths are comparable to plywood for similar thicknesses. The major drawback to particleboard is its susceptibility to moisture damage; it should not be used in areas where it will be continually exposed to dampness. In areas where the subfloor will not be covered with a finished floor, such as a room to be finished in the future or storage space for the attic, specify that the subfloor be painted with a protective sealent.

Mark the location of the subfloor, whether first or second floor or both. If you wish to floor an area of the attic for access and storage purposes, mark the attic box and compute the square footage to be covered. Plywood and particleboard are usually laid at right angles to the joists. Wood boards may be either at right angles or diagonal, but diagonal is preferred, especially if the finish floor will also be of wood boards.

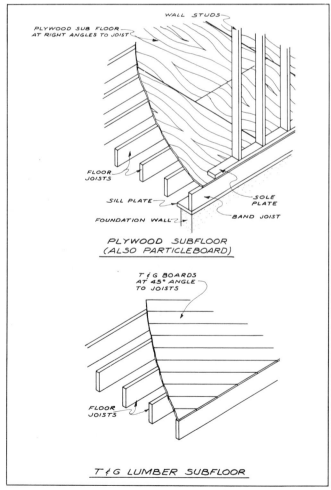

The most commonly used subfloors today are plywood and particleboard. T & G boards, however, maybe used as shown.

8. Finish Flooring

This section is for new finish flooring, whether in an addition or over an existing floor, made of wood. Wood floors are regaining some of the popularity they lost with the introduction of wall-to-wall carpeting, and are now available in more styles and patterns. If you wish to use wood floors in one or more rooms, you will need to shop the building supply dealers and select the style and type you want. The dealer can supply you with the technical information needed to complete this section.

The types of wood used in finish floors are: Yellow Birch; Cherry; Mahogany; Sugar Maple; Red Oak; Teak; Black Walnut; Douglas Fir; Southern Pine.

These wood species are available in standard size T & G boards. Wood floors are also available in a variety of module systems, which are often easier to install and can be developed into a larger number of designs.

9. Partition Framing

Partitions (interior walls) are room dividers. Unless special sound insulating walls are planned (as discussed in Chapter 3) they should be constructed as inexpensively and efficiently as possible.

Nominal size (inches)	Actual Size (seasoned)
Boards	
1 x 4	¾ by 3½
1 x 6	¾ by 5½
1 x 8	¾ by 7¼
1 x 10	¾ by 9¼
1 x 12	¾ by 11¼
Dimension lumber	
2 x 4	1½ by 3½
2 x 6	1¼ by 5½
2 x 8	1½ by 7¼
2 x 10	1½ by 9¼
2 x 12	1½ by 11¼

The studs are exactly the same species and grade as specified for exterior wall framing. By far the most common size and spacing is 2 x 4s at 16 inches O.C. It might be possible to save money by using a larger stud (2 x 6) and spacing them further apart (24 inches O.C.). But if precut studs in larger

Plywood Designations

Area for Use	Interior	Exterior
Surface Quality	A — Smooth paintable surface with no noticeable repairs	
	B — Smooth, repaired surface	
	C — Some knotholes of 1 in. in size (occasionally larger)	
	D — Knots and knotholes up to 1½ in. in size (use on interior side only)	

Plywood may have outside layers of different quality — such as A-C.

Durability	Groups 1 through 5
	Group 1 is made of the most durable wood. Group 5 is very soft and light. Group 5 is most often used as an interior layer in plywood. Group number appearing on plywood stamp will be that of the outside layers.

sizes are not available, any savings in material will be lost because of the additional labor required to cut the larger studs to the exact length needed. The 2 x 4 studs are readily available nationwide in exact lengths that do not need trimming.

Special framing is required at wall intersections, corners, and at openings for windows and doors. These are covered by local codes and by FHA's MPS (Minimum Property Standards), and a contractor is required to observe them. Should you plan on doing any of the framing work yourself, research is essential if you are not familiar with framing techniques.

10. Ceiling Framing and 11. Roof Framing

If you have an addition planned you must specify the type of framing to be used in the roof. Perhaps the simplest way to handle the specification and the construction would be to write "Match Existing" in both spaces. This will work well for small additions. For larger additions it may be more economical to use prefabricated trusses. Trusses are scientifically designed to provide maximum strength with a minimum of material. The method of construction also saves labor. The truss manufacturer will design the truss to fit your job and you need only write "prefabricated trusses" on the specs.

If you do not have local access to trusses and, for some reason, cannot match the existing, specify the species and grade of wood to be used. This will be the same as the other framing lumber (see Section 5). Bridging can be either wood or metal strips. For most additions the size and spacing will be 2 x 8 @ 16 inches O.C. for joists and 2 x 6 @ 16 inches O.C. for rafters, as reflected in the construction details at the end of Chapter 7. But for an extremely large addition with an unusually wide span, you should seek professional help. This can be obtained from the city building department, FHA or VA office, or an architect or structural engineer.

As with wall framing there are special requirements for framing items such as dormers or gable ends. Your contractor will be familiar with code stipulations. Again, if you are doing the framing yourself, consult construction manuals and codes to assure that the work is done properly.

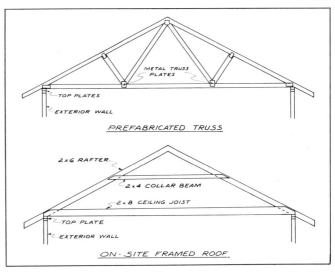

If you have acess to manufactured trusses, they are advised rather than conventional framed roofs. The truss is designed to give maximum strength with less lumber, and is less expensive.

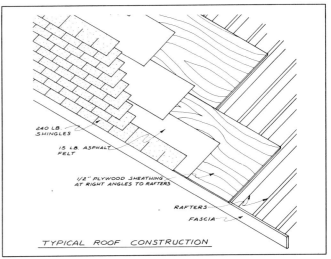

These are the components that make up the most commonly built roof in America. Plywood decking covers the rafters and is covered by 15 lb. felt and 240 lb. asphalt 3 tab square-butt shingles. Be sure to specify seal-down shingles to avoid storm damage.

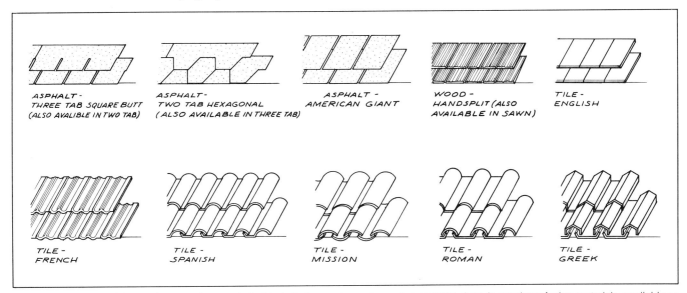

Although the standard three tab square butt asphalt shingle is the most popular roofing material, there is a variety of other materials, available as shown here.

12. Roofing

For an asphalt shingle roof, put in the type of decking — usually ½ inch plywood, solid. Under roofing write "asphalt singles, 20 year roof." The grade will be 240 lb. and the standard shingle size is 12 inch x 36 inch. If you are going to use other than standard shingles, check your dealer for size and grade. The type of shingles should be seal-down, with an underlay of asphalt saturated felt. The felt is 15 lb., 30 inch wide. Fastening is by galvanized nails.

The minimum slope for shingles is 3 in 12, but if you are in a windy area, it is safer to have a steeper pitch. For flatter roof slopes you must use either roll roofing (like asphalt shingles but in continuous rolls) or a built-up roof (discussed below).

Wood and tile roofs come in a variety of sizes, types, and materials. A visit to a supplier must be made to obtain the information you need to specify the individual roof you want to use. The illustration shows different types of roofing materials.

If you need to use a built-up roof, write in "tar and gravel, 20-year roof." This type of roof is not recommended for climates with freezing and thawing cycles. Marble chips can be used in place of gravel, but in most areas these will be much more expensive. For a residential roof the number of plies (layers) will be 3. The surfacing material is gravel or marble chips. Flashing can be of copper (16 oz.), aluminum (.032 inches), or galvanized steel (26 gage). Copper is considered the best, but is the most expensive. Galvanized steel is the most widely used, although aluminum is gaining in popularity. Note the box marked "gravel stop." A gravel stop is a raised flashing at the edge of the roof; it helps keep the gravel on the roof. We would advise you to check this box. Another necessity is adequate drainage. Whether you will need snowguards or not depends on your local conditions; check with a roofer or building material supplier.

13. Gutters and Downspouts

Gutters and downspouts can be used at your discretion. If you have them now you will probably want to include them on any addition.

If you don't have them, you might want to include them on the entire house.

If you live in an area that receives little rainfall, the expense would be wasted. But if your area receives occasional heavy rainfall, as most areas do, gutters and downspouts are a wise investment. Not only do they prevent water run-off from eroding the yard, but they also help keep exterior finish materials from becoming weathered and stained, and they stretch out the length of time before repainting the exterior trim.

Both gutters and downspouts are commonly made of galvanized steel (26 gage) and aluminum (.032 inch for gutters and .019 inches for downspouts). The size will vary according to the size of your roof and the amount of rainfall in your area.

HUD VENT AREAS

Width in Feet

Length	20	22	24	26	28	30	32	34	36	38	40	42	44	46
20	280	308	336	364	392	420	448	476	504	532	560	588	616	644
22	308	339	370	400	431	462	493	524	554	585	616	647	678	708
24	336	370	403	437	470	504	538	571	605	638	672	706	739	773
26	364	400	437	473	510	546	582	619	655	692	728	764	801	837
28	392	431	470	510	549	588	627	666	706	745	784	823	862	902
30	420	462	504	546	588	630	672	714	756	798	840	882	924	966
32	448	493	538	582	627	672	717	761	806	851	896	941	986	1030
34	476	524	571	619	666	714	762	809	857	904	952	1000	1047	1095
36	504	554	604	655	706	756	806	857	907	958	1008	1058	1109	1159
38	532	585	638	692	745	798	851	904	958	1011	1064	1117	1170	1224
40	560	616	672	728	784	840	896	952	1008	1064	1120	1176	1232	1288
42	588	647	706	764	823	882	941	1000	1058	1117	1176	1234	1294	1352
44	616	678	739	801	862	924	986	1047	1109	1170	1232	1294	1355	1417
46	644	708	773	837	902	966	1030	1095	1159	1224	1288	1352	1417	1481
48	672	739	806	874	941	1008	1075	1142	1210	1277	1344	1411	1478	1546
50	700	770	840	910	980	1050	1120	1190	1260	1330	1400	1470	1540	1610
52	728	801	874	946	1019	1092	1165	1238	1310	1383	1456	1529	1602	1674
54	756	832	907	983	1058	1134	1210	1285	1361	1436	1512	1588	1663	1739
56	784	862	941	1019	1098	1176	1254	1333	1411	1490	1568	1646	1725	1803
58	812	893	974	1056	1137	1218	1299	1380	1462	1543	1624	1705	1786	1868
60	840	924	1008	1092	1176	1260	1344	1428	1512	1596	1680	1764	1848	1932
62	868	955	1042	1128	1215	1302	1389	1476	1562	1649	1736	1823	1910	1996
64	896	986	1075	1165	1254	1344	1434	1523	1613	1702	1792	1882	1971	2061
66	924	1016	1108	1201	1294	1386	1478	1571	1663	1756	1848	1940	2033	2125
68	952	1047	1142	1238	1333	1428	1523	1618	1714	1809	1904	1999	2094	2190
70	980	1078	1176	1274	1372	1470	1568	1666	1764	1862	1960	2058	2156	2254

HUD-MPS vent requirements are stated as a ratio. Attics and basementless spaces require one sq. ft. of free area venting for each 150 sq. ft. of floor area, first floor or attic. A vapor barrier over the ground reduces crawl-space vent requirements to 1/1500. The "free area" for each vent type is listed when you buy it. This consistency makes it easier for the homeowner to choose the correct vent size. If vent openings are split so that half are in the upper section of the attic, with the rest in the lower eave, the ratio suggested by HUD is 1/300. For eaves that are closed and unventilated, figure the free area for gable or wall louver vents by doubling the sq. in., for a 1/150 ratio.

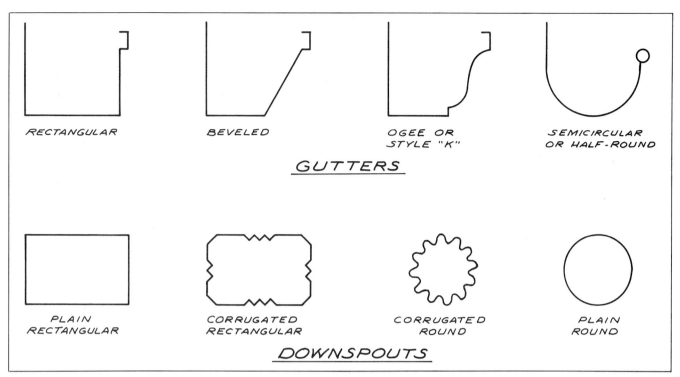

These are the common shapes of metal gutters and downspouts used on residences.

HVI RECOMMENDATIONS

Width in Feet

Length	20	22	24	26	28	30	32	34	36	38	40	42	44	46
20	192	211	230	250	269	288	307	326	346	365	384	403	422	441
22	211	232	253	275	296	317	338	359	380	401	422	444	465	485
24	230	253	276	300	323	346	369	392	415	438	461	484	507	530
26	250	275	300	324	349	374	399	424	449	474	499	524	549	574
28	269	296	323	349	376	403	430	457	484	511	538	564	591	618
30	288	317	346	374	403	432	461	490	518	547	576	605	634	662
32	307	338	369	399	430	461	492	522	553	584	614	645	675	706
34	326	359	392	424	457	490	522	555	588	620	653	685	717	750
36	346	380	415	449	484	518	553	588	622	657	691	726	760	795
38	365	401	438	474	511	547	584	620	657	693	730	766	803	839
40	384	422	461	499	538	576	614	653	691	730	768	806	845	883
42	403	444	484	524	564	605	645	685	726	766	806	847	887	927
44	422	465	507	549	591	634	676	718	760	803	845	887	929	971
46	442	486	530	574	618	662	707	751	795	839	883	927	972	1016
48	461	507	553	599	645	691	737	783	829	876	922	968	1014	1060
50	480	528	576	624	672	720	768	816	864	912	960	1008	1056	1104
52	499	549	599	649	699	749	799	848	898	948	998	1048	1098	1148
54	518	570	622	674	726	778	830	881	933	985	1037	1089	1141	1192
56	538	591	645	699	753	807	860	914	967	1021	1075	1130	1184	1237
58	557	612	668	724	780	835	891	946	1002	1058	1113	1170	1226	1282
60	576	634	691	749	807	864	922	979	1037	1094	1152	1210	1267	1324
62	595	655	714	774	834	893	953	1012	1071	1131	1190	1250	1309	1369
64	614	676	737	799	861	922	893	1045	1106	1168	1229	1291	1352	1413
66	634	697	760	824	888	950	1014	1077	1140	1204	1268	1331	1394	1458
68	653	718	783	849	914	979	1045	1110	1175	1240	1306	1371	1436	1501
70	672	739	806	874	941	1008	1075	1142	1210	1276	1344	1411	1478	1545

If you will be installing a powered roof ventilator, you can use this chart. The Home Ventilating Institute recommends a minimum venting rate of 10 air changes an hour, or .7 cu. ft. per minute per sq. ft. of attic floor space, plus 15% additional for a dark roof.

Shown on the facing page are before and after stages of the remodeling of the Victorian house discussed in Chapter 7. The stairway in the top picture was originally the back stair. The stairway in the bottom picture was removed and replaced with a large closet facing the entryway. The back section of the wall, with the entry to the back stairs, was taken out to open up additional living room space. The pictures on this page show interim and completed stages of the main area of the living room, as well as most of the dining room.

CLOSET

SINK   W.C.

SINK   BATH TUB

Shown are floor plan and final remodeling of a compartmented second-floor bath in the Victorian home previously shown in this chapter. Originally a bedroom (opposite page, above) framing was added to support the plumbing. A pane of translucent glass in the wall separating the shower from the water closet area lets in light, but not image. The result is a sunny and spacious feeling throughout.

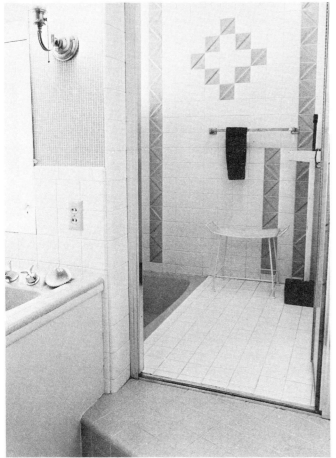

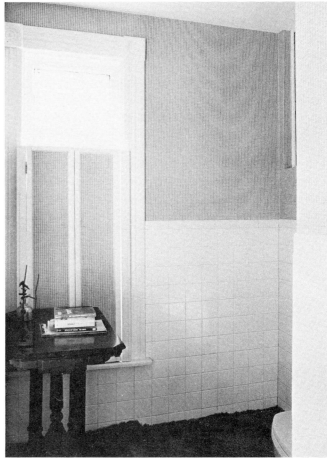

Check with a local supplier. The shape can be selected from the common shapes shown in the illustration. Gutters and downspouts are also available in copper (16 oz.), stainless steel (26 gage), and redwood or fir. (Wood gutters are most commonly found in New York and the New England states.) These types are much more expensive than the common galvanized steel and aluminum.

Downspouts (also called leaders or conductors) may be connected to the sanitary or storm sewer systems, to a drywell, or simply drained onto a 3 inch x 18 inch x 30 inch concrete splash block.

14. Lath and Plaster

The interior walls may be lath and plastered, in which case you will need to consult a contractor for the specifics of how plaster is handled in your area. The more popular finishing for walls and ceilings is drywall. This is because the dry-wall is less expensive. The plaster if more durable and more fire-resistant, but it also must be applied under carefully controlled temperature conditions. The common dry-wall material is gypsum wallboard of ½ inch thickness. Walls are usually smooth finished with two coats of interior latex. Ceilings can be smoothed and painted, sprayed for a stippled finish, or mopped in several designs. Wallboard joints are taped, filled, and sanded smooth.

15. Decorating (Wall Finishes)

This is for interior wall treatments other than interior latex paint. Any rooms that will be newly wallpapered, paneled, or painted with semi-gloss paint should be included here. Also include rooms with new walls and/or ceilings of wood. Rooms which may get wet, such as kitchens and baths, should not be painted with interior latex. You may wish to consider ceramic tile for kitchens or baths.

16. Interior Doors and Trim

For door types, write "see door schedule." The other information may be marked "Match Existing" or you can complete the information based on the individual doors you have already selected. This is for new interior doors only.

17. Windows

Again, under type write "see window schedule." The head flashing should be asphalt felt. All other information will be based on the particular windows you have selected for your home, or can be marked "Match Existing." This section is for new windows only.

18. Entrances and Exterior Detail

Once more, if you have new exterior doors planned, write "see door schedule" and complete the information based on the exterior doors you have selected. Head flashing is asphalt felt. New shutters, attic louvers, wood or iron railings, and storm or screen doors should also be covered here.

19. Cabinets and Interior Detail

Kitchen cabinets are most commonly made of birch plywood or pine. You may also buy prefabricated units, in which case simply write in the brand name and style. Countertops and splashes can be made of a variety of materials, both built on-site and prefabricated. The most common material, and by far the least expensive for countertops and backsplashes, is plastic laminate. It can, however, be scratched, and is easily damaged by hot pans. Butcher block countertops are less susceptible to damage but can become worn and less attractive if used for chopping. Stainless steel is a strong surface, but can be scratched and is very expensive. Ceramic tile, while being much more expensive, provides a durable surface that will stand up well to normal use. Colored grouting with sealant keeps the dirt from lodging and showing in the joints. A synthetic material called methacrylate has the appearance of marble but can be cut like wood. It comes in thicknesses of ¼ inch, ½ inch, and ¾ inch. Scratches can be sanded out, but the cost is high and the color selection is limited. A visit to a building supply dealer is necessary to determine what you wish to use.

Include any new medicine cabinets and/or other built-in cabinetry such as linen closets, book shelves, and built-in desks. Under additional information put a per-door allowance for the style you want on the cabinet doors if you are not using prefabricated cabinets. Or you may visit a cabinet shop and select a particular door trim to write in. The latter is advisable, since there are a number of different types of door treatments — whose cost may vary widely.

20. Stairs

If you are adding a second floor addition, turning an attic or basement into useful rooms, or simply replacing an old set of stairs you may need to fill out this section. Fill out the material (usually wood) and thickness (usually ¾ inch) to be used for the risers and treads (see the illustration). The strings are exact cut pieces which support the treads and risers on the side. They are also usually wood and are ¾ inch thick (see illustration). Handrails and balusters can be built in a wide variety of ways.

For a prefabricated staircase (especially for spiral or disappearing staircases) write in the make and model number.

21. Special Floors and Wainscot

This section is for new floors other than wood or carpet. In the kitchen you may want to use vinyl asbestos tile, cushioned vinyl, ceramic tile, or a host of other materials. There is also a large variety of materials available for bathroom floors, although ceramic tile is the most common. Since the types of materials and cost are so varied, it is advisable to shop for and select the exact floors you wish to use, and then write in the brand name and style.

A wainscot is a wall treatment which does not extend to the ceiling; ceramic tile is most often used for the bathroom. The height of the tile around the tub should be 72 inches; if you want a wainscot on other bath walls the usual height is 48 inches. Ceramic tile is the best treatment for the bath wainscot since it is completely water repellent and very durable. But it is a little more expensive than other materials. Tile can be purchased in both glazed and unglazed, though the glazed is the most common and is easier to clean. You can also get matching colored grout between the individual tiles, but white is the standard.

You may also use a one-piece tub enclosure, available in

many styles and colors, rather than a wainscot. This would be covered in the plumbing section (22) below. For new bath accessories (towel racks, soap dishes) check whether they are to be recessed or attached and fill in the material (most commonly tile or metal) and the number of pieces.

22. Plumbing

Any new plumbing fixtures or a new water heater will require entries to be made in this section. First you must select the exact units you want to use. The dealer can assist you with the technical information needed to complete the blanks.

Most homes that are twenty years or more old were constructed with cast iron sewer pipes and galvanized steel water pipes. Although these are still available, in many areas P.V.C. (polyvinylchloride or plastic) pipe for sewers is acceptable; copper tubing is common for water pipes. P.V.C. pipes cost less than the older cast iron sewers, and copper is a little more expensive than the galvanized steel. The major advantage of these is the savings in labor cost. Because of different installation techniques, they can be assembled much more quickly. Since fittings are available to adapt the newer materials to the old, there is no problem in using the less expensive piping for any plumbing addition you might have planned.

23. Heating

If you determined earlier that new heating and/or air conditioning equipment would be needed either because of a large addition, or as a replacement for the existing system, then this section should be completed. The technical nature of the information will require a discussion with a heating equipment dealer and selection of a unit to fit your personal requirements. Also, if you are planning a new attic fan and/or kitchen exhaust fan, the make and model numbers should be noted in this section.

24. Electrical Wiring

Mark whether your electrical service is overhead or underground. If you are planning only minor electrical revisions, mark in whether the present panel is a fuse box or circuit breaker type. If the panel will be replaced, mark "circuit breaker" since fuse boxes are rapidly becoming obsolete. Even if you are not adding a lot of electrical work you may want to upgrade the panel. Most older homes are equipped with a 60 amp service panel. Today the minimum service is 100 amp for a single-family home with 6 circuits or more, and sometimes 240 amp for a home with a number of heavy appliances. Since a home that meets codes will require at least 6 circuits (preferably 20) you should have a minimum 100 amp service installed if the present service is less. Many cities, in fact, will require that the service be updated when you remodel.

Codes may vary widely from one locale to another, and electricity is one of the items that more often than not is better left to the expert. So before you specify any work in this section, it would be wise to consult with the city building department or, even better, an electrical contractor.

Wiring for most older homes was by a system called knob and tube. This is rarely, if ever, used anymore. The most popular wiring is nonmetallic cable with copper or aluminum wire. Aluminum is more often used because of its much lower price, but some cities may require copper in their codes since it is a higher quality wire. There will be little need to connect new wiring to an old system since most remodeling will require that the new electrical work come directly from the panel. Even if the work is only minor it is advisable that old and new wiring not be connected. This is because newer electrical systems have a built-in ground wire and older systems do not. Extremely old wiring may warrant strong consideration for a complete rewiring job. This can be a fairly

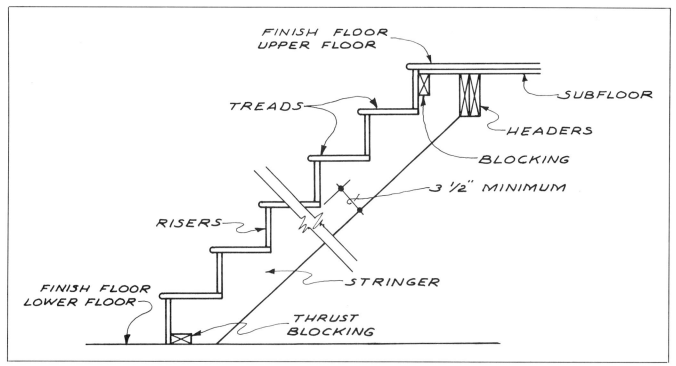

This cross-section shows the main structural components of stairs. The stringers can be tied to an adjacent wall or can rest on studs from the bottom floor.

ELECTRICAL DEMAND FACTORS AND LOAD CALCULATION

Location	Estimated Watts	% of use	Amperes
Dining, Laundry, Living	1250		15
Entry, Kitchen, Bath No. 2	1250		15
Microwave (separate circuit suggested)	650		15
Hall, Den, Bedroom No. 1	1100		15
Bedroom No. 2, Bath No. 1	900		15

NOTE: General lighting circuits total 3 watts per sq. ft. (approx.)

Kitchen, Dining	1000		20
Kitchen, Laundry	1000		20
Dining, Laundry	750		20
Garage-Workshop	1250		20
	9150	3000w @ 100% 6150w @ 40% = 2460	

Range: 12kw model, Max. demand 8kw	8000		20
Water Heater	4000		20
Bathroom Heater	1500		20
Furnace (1/4 & 1/200 HP motors)	600		20
Automatic Washer	450		20
Dishwasher	1000		20
	15,550	15550w @ 75% = 11663	

Service Demand: 3000 + .2460 + 11663 = 17,123. 17,123 watts divided by 230 volts equals 75 amps.

Service Required: 100 ampere service will meet needs.

substantial cost, but is much less of a fire hazard and will greatly improve the value and convenience of the house. It also has the advantage of allowing you to add new receptacles, since many older systems do not meet today's electrical codes.

25. Lighting Fixtures

This section requires only that you put in the number of new light fixtures needed and an allowance for cost, since the exact type of light fixture to be used is usually one of the last selections made and is rarely made prior to construction. Unless you have already chosen specific fixtures, put in a generous allowance based on your prior discussion with a lighting dealer. If you have already selected the fixtures, list the makes and model numbers, using an attached sheet if necessary.

26. Insulation

Since you have already determined what new insulation is needed during the formulation of your plans, simply fill in this section as necessary. If the new insulation shown is for an addition only, state it. This will help the contractor avoid bidding extra work that is not intended.

Hardware. This section is for new door knobs whether on new or existing doors. Write "match existing" if you are adding a few new doors and want to keep your house coordinated. If you are changing your existing knobs or want special knobs on the new doors only, it will be necessary to shop for your choice then write in the make and model of each new knob. State how many doors will require new hardware, as

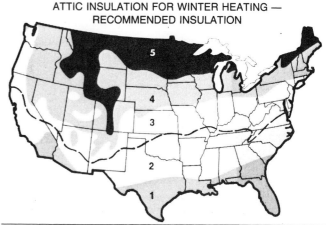

ATTIC INSULATION FOR WINTER HEATING — RECOMMENDED INSULATION

	Minimum	Maximum
Zone 1	None	R19
Zone 2	R-11	R-38
Zone 3	R-11	R-49
Zone 4	R-19	R-57
Zone 5	R-19	R-66

Amount of insulation required depends upon fuel cost savings desired

well as how many are new doors, how many are existing, whether they are interior or exterior, and which will need new locks.

Special Equipment. If your plans include new appliances such as a stove or dishwasher, you will need to make a selection and then include the make and model number and description here. Many of these items may require special wiring, which should be discussed with an electrical contractor.

27. Miscellaneous

This section is for any new work in the house that you have not described elsewhere.

Porches, Terraces, Garages, Walks and Driveways, and Other Onsite Improvements. These sections are for describing new work that is outside the house. All new work shown on your site plan should be described here. If the new work you have planned is limited to the house, then no entries need be made in these areas.

Landscaping, Planting, and Finish Grading. Even if you are not planning any landscaping work, write in that the contractor is responsible for repairing any and all destruction to the existing yard and that he is also responsible for hauling off the site all trash and waste from the construction work.

FINDING ASSISTANCE

The specifications are a very important part of your plans and should be completed carefully, being sure they agree with your drawings. If you need assistance, check with the city building department, your local FHA or VA office, building material suppliers, contractors, or you may retain an architect for a short period of time. The public library is also a valuable source of information. It is important that you make as many material selections as possible prior to letting your plans out for bid. This will save you time and money in the long run and will help to prevent misunderstandings between you and any contractors you use.

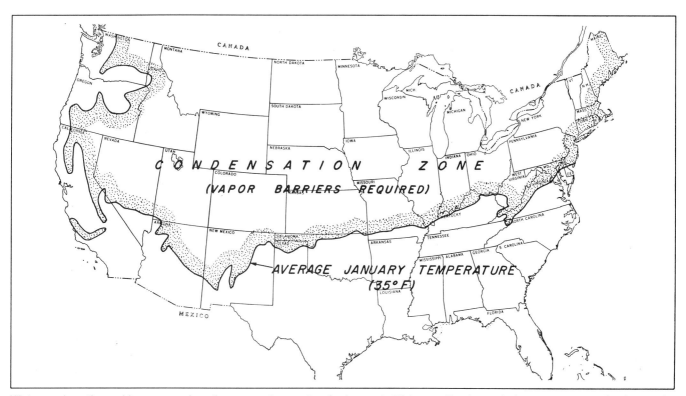

Winter condensation problems occur where the average temperature for January is 35 degrees F. or lower. In these areas, a vapor barrier over the insulation (facing into the room) is essential.

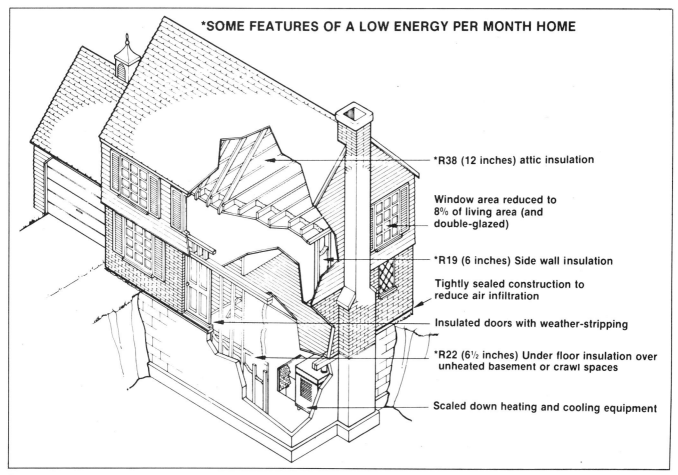

*SOME FEATURES OF A LOW ENERGY PER MONTH HOME

*R38 (12 inches) attic insulation

Window area reduced to 8% of living area (and double-glazed)

*R19 (6 inches) Side wall insulation

Tightly sealed construction to reduce air infiltration

Insulated doors with weather-stripping

*R22 (6½ inches) Under floor insulation over unheated basement or crawl spaces

Scaled down heating and cooling equipment

Shown are changes in construction methods, that cut fuel needs, for both new and remodeled homes. The 2 x 6 studs on 24 in. centers, called "Mod 24", allow use of thicker batts of building insulation. The system also reduces construction costs, since less lumber is needed than for conventional 2 x 4 walls. The vapor barriers prevent condensation and water damage, as well as air penetration and heat loss. (Drawing courtesy Owens-Corning Fiberglass.)

FHA Form 2005
VA Form 26-1852
Rev. 2/74

U. S. DEPARTMENT OF HOUSING AND URBAN DEVELOPMENT
FEDERAL HOUSING ADMINISTRATION
For accurate register of carbon copies, form
may be separated along above fold. Staple
completed sheets together in original order.

Form Approved
OMB No. 63–RO055

☒ **Proposed Construction**
☐ **Under Construction**

DESCRIPTION OF MATERIALS

No. _____
(To be inserted by FHA or VA)

Property address _____ **City** _____ **State** _____

Mortgagor or Sponsor _____
(Name)   (Address)

Contractor or Builder _____
(Name)   (Address)

INSTRUCTIONS

1. For additional information on how this form is to be submitted, number of copies, etc., see the instructions applicable to the FHA Application for Mortgage Insurance or VA Request for Determination of Reasonable Value, as the case may be.
2. Describe all materials and equipment to be used, whether or not shown on the drawings, by marking an X in each appropriate check-box and entering the information called for in each space. If space is inadequate, enter "See misc." and describe under item 27 or on an attached sheet. THE USE OF PAINT CONTAINING MORE THAN FIVE-TENTHS OF ONE PERCENT LEAD BY WEIGHT IS PROHIBITED.
3. Work not specifically described or shown will not be considered

unless required, then the minimum acceptable will be assumed. **Work exceeding minimum requirements cannot be considered unless specifically described.**
4. Include no alternates, "or equal" phrases, or contradictory items. (Consideration of a request for acceptance of substitute materials or equipment is not thereby precluded.)
5. Include signatures required at the end of this form.
6. The construction shall be completed in compliance with the related drawings and specifications, as amended during processing. The specifications include this Description of Materials and applicable Minimum Property Standards.

1. **EXCAVATION:**
Bearing soil, type _____ sand-clay _____

2. **FOUNDATIONS:**
Footings: concrete mix __ 1:3:5 __; strength psi __ 2500 __ Reinforcing __ 2 No. 4's, continuous __
Foundation wall: material __ same __ Reinforcing _____
Interior foundation wall: material _____ Party foundation wall _____
Columns: material and sizes _____ Piers: material and reinforcing _____
Girders: material and sizes _____ Sills: material _____
Basement entrance areaway _____ Window areaways _____
Waterproofing _____ Footing drains _____
Termite protection __ Pressure treated bottom plates and bonded soil poisoning __
Basementless space: ground cover _____; insulation _____; foundation vents _____
Special foundations _____
Additional information: _____

3. **CHIMNEYS:**
Material _____ Prefabricated (make and size) __ Standard Fireplaces, 18" round __
Flue lining: material _____ Heater flue size _____ Fireplace flue size _____
Vents (material and size): gas or oil heater _____; water heater _____
Additional information: _____

4. **FIREPLACES:** __ Standard Fireplaces Model No. 6901, 42" __
Type: ☒ solid fuel; ☐ gas-burning; ☐ circulator (make and size) _____ Ash dump and clean-out _____
Fireplace: facing __ brick __; lining _____; hearth __ 18" raised brick __; mantel __ 4" x 8" x 5' woo __
Additional information: __ Facing brick to be Old Colonial from Johnson Brick Co. __

5. **EXTERIOR WALLS:**
Wood frame: wood grade, and species __ No. 2 Southern Yellow Pine __ ☒ Corner bracing. Building paper or felt __ 15 lb. __
Sheathing __ insulation board __ thickness __ 1/2" __; width __ 4' __; ☒ solid; ☐ spaced _____ " o. c.; ☐ diagonal; _____
Siding _____; grade _____; type _____; size _____; exposure _____ "; fastening _____
Shingles _____; grade _____; type _____; size _____; exposure _____ "; fastening _____
Stucco __ 2 coats, smooth finish __; thickness __ 1 __ "; Lath __ wire mesh __; weight __ 10 __ lb.
Masonry veneer __ finish __ Sills __ stucco __ Lintels __ steel __ Base flashing __ 15 lb. felt __
Masonry: ☐ solid ☐ faced ☐ stuccoed; total wall thickness _____ "; facing thickness _____ "; facing material _____
Backup material _____; thickness _____ "; bonding _____
Door sills _____ Window sills _____ Lintels _____ Base flashing _____
Interior surfaces: dampproofing, _____ coats of _____; furring _____
Additional information: _____
Exterior painting: material __ Exterior latex __; number of coats __ 2 __
Gable wall construction: ☒ same as main walls; ☐ other construction _____

6. FLOOR FRAMING:
Joists: wood, grade, and species _____ ; other _____ ; bridging _____ ; anchors _____
Concrete slab: ☐ basement floor; ☒ first floor; ☒ ground supported; ☐ self-supporting; mix __1:3:5__ ; thickness __4__ ";
reinforcing __6 x 6 10/10 W.W.M.__ ; insulation _____ ; membrane __6 mil film__
Fill under slab: material __washed gravel__ ; thickness __4__ ". Additional information: _____

7. SUBFLOORING: (Describe underflooring for special floors under item 21.) N.A.
Material: grade and species _____ ; size _____ ; type _____
Laid: ☐ first floor; ☐ second floor; ☐ attic _____ sq. ft.; ☐ diagonal; ☐ right angles. Additional information: _____

8. FINISH FLOORING: (Wood only. Describe other finish flooring under item 21.) N.A.

Location	Rooms	Grade	Species	Thickness	Width	Bldg. Paper	Finish
First floor ___							
Second floor ___							
Attic floor ___	___ sq. ft.						

Additional information: _____

9. PARTITION FRAMING:
Studs: wood, grade, and species __No. 2 Southern Yellow Pine__ size and spacing __2 x 4 @ 16" O.C.__ Other _____
Additional information: _____

10. CEILING FRAMING:
Joists: wood, grade, and species __match existing__ Other _____ Bridging _____
Additional information: _____

11. ROOF FRAMING:
Rafters: wood, grade, and species __match existing__ Roof trusses (see detail): grade and species _____
Additional information: _____

12. ROOFING:
Sheathing: wood, grade, and species __1/2" plywood decking with clips.__ ; ☒ solid; ☐ spaced _____ " o.c.
Roofing __asphalt shingles__ ; grade __240__ ; size __12"x36"__ ; type __3-tab square butt__
Underlay __asphalt felt__ ; weight or thickness __15 lb.__ ; size __36"__ ; fastening __galv. nails__
Built-up roofing _____ ; number of plies _____ ; surfacing material _____
Flashing: material _____ ; gage or weight _____ ; ☐ gravel stops; ☐ snow guards
Additional information: _____

13. GUTTERS AND DOWNSPOUTS:
Gutters: material __galvanized steel__ ; gage or weight __26 gage__ ; size __4"x4"__ ; shape __Ogee__
Downspouts: material __galvanized steel__ ; gage or weight __26 gage__ ; size __2"x3"__ ; shape __rectangular__ ; number __4__
Downspouts connected to: ☐ Storm sewer; ☐ sanitary sewer; ☐ dry-well. ☒ Splash blocks: material and size __concrete, 3"x18"x30"__
Additional information: _____

14. LATH AND PLASTER
Lath ☐ walls, ☐ ceilings: material _____ ; weight or thickness _____ Plaster: coats _____ ; finish _____
Dry-wall ☒ walls, ☒ ceilings: material __Gypsum wallboard__ ; thickness __1/2"__ ; finish __blown ceiling, smooth walls__ ;
Joint treatment __tape, fill, and sand smooth__

15. DECORATING: (Paint, wallpaper, etc.)

Rooms	Wall Finish Material and Application	Ceiling Finish Material and Application
Kitchen	Adams Wallcoverings Style K632	see 14 above
Bath #1 & 2	2 cts. semi-gloss enamel	see 14 above
Other Vanity	rough finish 1 x 6, diagonal	rough finish 1 x 6, diagonal
Family Room	1/4" wood paneling	see 14 above

Additional information: __paneling style: Sanders Products Light Walnut, No. 616__

16. INTERIOR DOORS AND TRIM: see Door Schedule
Doors: type _____ ; material _____ ; thickness _____
Door trim: type _____ ; material _____ Base: type _____ ; material _____ ; size _____
Finish: doors _____ ; trim _____
Other trim (item, type and location) _____
Additional information: _____

17. WINDOWS: see Window Schedule

Windows: type _match existing_; make _____ ; material _____ ; sash thickness _____

Glass: grade _____ ; ☐ sash weights; ☐ balances, type _____ ; head flashing _asphalt felt_

Trim: type _____ ; material _____ Paint _____ ; number coats _____

Weatherstripping: type _____ ; material _____ Storm sash, number _____

Screens: ☐ full; ☐ half; type _____ ; number _____ ; screen cloth material _____

Basement windows: type _____ ; material _____ ; screens, number _____ ; Storm sash, number _____

Special windows _____

Additional information: _____

18. ENTRANCES AND EXTERIOR DETAIL: see Door Schedule

Main entrance door: material _____ ; width _____ ; thickness _____ ". Frame: material _____ ; thickness _____ "

Other entrance doors: material _____ ; width _____ ; thickness _____ ". Frame: material _____ ; thickness _____ "

Head flashing _asphalt felt_ Weatherstripping: type _____ ; saddles _____

Screen doors: thickness _____ "; number _____ ; screen cloth material _____ Storm doors: thickness _____ "; number _____

Combination storm and screen doors: thickness _____ "; number _____ ; screen cloth material _____

Shutters: ☐ hinged; ☒ fixed. Railings _____ , Attic louvers _____

Exterior millwork: grade and species _No. 1 White Pine_ Paint _Exterior latex_ ; number coats _2_

Additional information: _____

19. CABINETS AND INTERIOR DETAIL:

Kitchen cabinets, wall units: material _Birch plywood_ ; lineal feet of shelves _11_ ; shelf width _12"_

Base units: material _Birch plywood_ ; counter top _laminated plastic_ ; edging _laminated plastic_

Back and end splash _laminated plastic_ Finish of cabinets _stain & 2 cts. varnish_ ; number coats _____

Medicine cabinets: make _____ ; model _____

Other cabinets and built-in furniture _All new cabinet work to be of birch plywood and stained as noted._

Additional information: _Door style shall be American Cabinet Shop Style 74_

20. STAIRS: N.A.

STAIR	TREADS		RISERS		STRINGS		HANDRAIL		BALUSTERS	
	Material	Thickness	Material	Thickness	Material	Size	Material	Size	Material	Size
Basement										
Main										
Attic										

Disappearing: make and model number _____

Additional information: _____

21. SPECIAL FLOORS AND WAINSCOT:

	LOCATION	MATERIAL, COLOR, BORDER, SIZES, GAGE, ETC.	THRESHOLD MATERIAL	WALL BASE MATERIAL	UNDERFLOOR MATERIAL
FLOORS	Kitchen	Kelly Flooring cushioned vinyl, Style F362	metal	wood	
	Bath				
	Vanity	Carpet – Sims Carpets, Style 8601		wood	1/2" sponge pad

	LOCATION	MATERIAL, COLOR, BORDER, CAP. SIZES, GAGE, ETC.	HEIGHT	HEIGHT OVER TUB	HEIGHT IN SHOWERS (FROM FLOOR)
WAINSCOT	Bath				

Bathroom accessories: ☐ Recessed; material _____ ; number _____ ; ☐ Attached; material _____ ; number _____

Additional information: _____

22. PLUMBING:

FIXTURE	NUMBER	LOCATION	MAKE	MFR'S FIXTURE IDENTIFICATION NO.	SIZE	COLOR
Sink						
Lavatory	2	Baths 1&2	Peters	FN 628301	19"	White
Water closet						
Bathtub						
Shower over tub △						
Stall shower △						
Laundry trays						

△☐ Curtain rod   △☐ Door   ☐ Shower pan: material _____

Water supply: ☒ public; ☐ community system; ☐ individual (private) system.★

Sewage disposal: ☒ public; ☐ community system; ☐ individual (private) system.★

★*Show and describe individual system in complete detail in separate drawings and specifications according to requirements.*

House drain (inside): ☒ cast iron; ☐ tile; ☐ other _____ House sewer (outside): ☒ cast iron; ☐ tile; ☐ other _____

Water piping: ☐ galvanized steel; ☒ copper tubing; ☐ other _____ Sill cocks, number _____

Domestic water heater: type _____; make and model _____; heating capacity _____

_____ gph. 100° rise. Storage tank: material _____; capacity _____ **gallons.**

Gas service: ☐ utility company; ☐ liq. pet. gas; ☐ other _____ Gas piping: ☐ cooking; ☐ house heating.

Footing drains connected to: ☐ storm sewer; ☐ sanitary sewer; ☐ dry well. Sump pump; make and model _____

_____; capacity _____; discharges into _____

23. HEATING: N.A.

☐ Hot water. ☐ Steam. ☐ Vapor. ☐ One-pipe system. ☐ Two-pipe system.

    ☐ Radiators. ☐ Convectors. ☐ Baseboard radiation. Make and model _____

    Radiant panel: ☐ floor; ☐ wall; ☐ ceiling. Panel coil: material _____

    ☐ Circulator. ☐ Return pump. Make and model _____; capacity _____ **gpm.**

    Boiler: make and model _____ Output _____ Btuh.; net rating _____ **Btuh.**

Additional information: _____

Warm air: ☐ Gravity. ☐ Forced. Type of system _____

    Duct material: supply _____; return _____ Insulation _____, thickness _____ ☐ **Outside air intake.**

    Furnace: make and model _____ Input _____ Btuh.; output _____ **Btuh.**

    Additional information: _____

☐ Space heater; ☐ floor furnace; ☐ wall heater. Input _____ Btuh.; output _____ Btuh.; number units _____

    Make, model _____ Additional information: _____

Controls: make and types _____

Additional information: _____

Fuel: ☐ Coal; ☐ oil; ☐ gas; ☐ liq. pet. gas; ☐ electric; ☐ other _____; storage capacity _____

    Additional information: _____

Firing equipment furnished separately: ☐ Gas burner, conversion type. ☐ Stoker: hopper feed ☐; bin feed ☐

    Oil burner: ☐ pressure atomizing; ☐ vaporizing _____

    Make and model _____ Control _____

    Additional information: _____

Electric heating system: type _____ Input _____ watts; @ _____ volts; output _____ **Btuh.**

    Additional information: _____

Ventilating equipment: attic fan, make and model _____; capacity _____ **cfm.**

        kitchen exhaust fan, make and model _____

Other heating, ventilating, or cooling equipment _____

24. ELECTRIC WIRING: Existing service to remain

Service: ☐ overhead; ☐ underground. Panel: ☐ fuse box; ☒ circuit-breaker; make _____ **AMP's** _____ **No. circuits** _____

Wiring: ☐ conduit; ☐ armored cable; ☒ nonmetallic cable; ☐ knob and tube; ☐ other _____

Special outlets: ☐ range; ☐ water heater; ☒ other _____ dryer

☐ Doorbell. ☐ Chimes. Push-button locations _____ Additional information: _____

25. LIGHTING FIXTURES:

Total number of fixtures _____ 18 _____   Total allowance for fixtures, typical installation, $ 500.00

Nontypical installation _____

Additional information: _____

26. INSULATION:

Location	Thickness	Material, Type, and Method of Installation	Vapor Barrier
Roof			
Ceiling	6"	Batts	
Wall	4"	Batts	
Floor			

HARDWARE: *(make, material, and finish.)* Match existing material and finish

_____

SPECIAL EQUIPMENT: *(State material or make, model and quantity.   Include only equipment and appliances which are acceptable by local law, custom and applicable FHA standards.   Do not include items which, by established custom, are supplied by occupant and removed when he vacates premises or chattles prohibited by law from becoming realty.)*_____

N.A.

_____

_____

_____

_____

_____

_____

27. **MISCELLANEOUS:** *(Describe any main dwelling materials, equipment, or construction items not shown elsewhere; or use to provide additional information where the space provided was inadequate.   Always reference by item number to correspond to numbering used on this form.)*

Note: Sod all disturbed yard areas not scheduled for other construction or planting. Clean and remove construction waste from site.

_____

_____

_____

_____

_____

PORCHES: N.A.

_____

TERRACES:

Brick paving (Johnson Brick, Varied French Pavers) basketweave pattern over 3" concrete and 1" grout setting bed.

GARAGES: N.A.

_____

_____

WALKS AND DRIVEWAYS: N.A.

Driveway: width _____ ; base material _____ ; thickness _____ "; surfacing material _____ ; thickness _____ "

Front walk: width _____ ; material _____ ; thickness _____ ". Service walk: width _____ ; material _____ ; thickness _____

Steps: material _____ ; treads _____ "; risers _____ ". Cheek walls _____

OTHER ONSITE IMPROVEMENTS:

(Specify all exterior onsite improvements not described elsewhere, including items such as unusual grading, drainage structures, retaining walls, fence, railings, and accessory structures.)

Patio Overhead: Redwood lath and supports as detailed

Wood Fence: 1 x 6 Redwood, vertical, as detailed

LANDSCAPING, PLANTING, AND FINISH GRADING:

Topsoil _____ " thick: ☐ front yard; ☐ side yards; ☐ rear yard to _____ feet behind main building.

Lawns *(seeded, sodded, or sprigged)*: ☐ front yard _____ ; ☐ side yards _____ ; ☐ rear yard _____

Planting: ☐ as specified and shown on drawings; ☒ as follows:

__1__ Shade trees, deciduous, __2__ " caliper. (Japanese Maple)	_____ Evergreen trees. _____ ' to _____ ', **B & B**
_____ Low flowering trees, deciduous, _____ ' to _____ '	__6__ Evergreen shrubs. __1__ ' to __2__ ', **B & B**
_____ High-growing shrubs, deciduous, _____ ' to _____ '	_____ Vines, 2-year _____
__6__ Medium-growing shrubs, deciduous, __2__ ' to __3__ '	
__8__ Low-growing shrubs, deciduous, __1__ ' to __2__ '	

IDENTIFICATION.—This exhibit shall be identified by the signature of the builder, or sponsor, and/or the proposed mortgagor if the latter is known at the time of application.

Date_____   Signature _____

Signature _____

9 A Word About Codes

Homeownership today falls far short of the simplicity of past times, as we are beset on all sides by a web of legalities and regulations from all levels of government. But the conditions under which many earlier homeowners lived are almost unacceptable in modern society. Restrictive as the regulations may seem at times, most are designed to and will work as a benefit for the homeowner and for the community as a whole. If a regulation does become excessively burdensome or outdated, there are often legal ways to maneuver around it.

FHA/VA REGULATIONS

The Federal Housing Administration, a division of the Department of Housing and Urban Development — and the Veterans Administration, because of their involvement in home mortgages — publish regulations for the design and construction of houses. Although your remodeling will probably not be subject to the requirements of these regulations, it is strongly advisable to incorporate their standards. These are designed to assure a safe, comfortable, and properly constructed home.

The *Minimum Property Standards* (MPS) and HUD's *Manual of Acceptable Practices* (MAP) are available for a reasonable price through your local FHA or VA office. These books are thick and are filled with technical advice and requirements. If you do not wish to try to decipher the information that is applicable to your remodeling from these large books, you don't have to. Remember, this book has been written with the federal regulations in mind and this is reflected throughout. But your local FHA or VA office can often assist you with any specific questions; there is no charge for this assistance. These regulations are accepted as standard in the home construction industry and any licensed contractor should be thoroughly familiar with them. By making the observance of these regulations a prerequisite in any contract for construction, whether dealing with a general contractor or subcontractor, proper construction techniques become the full responsibility of the contractor. (This is discussed more fully in Chapter 10.)

LOCAL BUILDING CODES

Most city and county governments have adopted a building code for homes in their locality. These codes, such as the Uniform Building Code or the Southern Standard Building Code consist of very large, highly technical books. These are further supplemented by other technical codes such as electrical, plumbing, fire protection, etc. Again, it is not necessary that you immerse yourself in the detail that these codes offer. Your local building department is familiar with the codes and with local ordinances that differ from the standard codes, and will inspect your remodeling periodically during construction to assure that regulations are complied with. A licensed contractor or subcontractor in your area, whose work is continually subject to the approval of the building department, will be familiar with the codes. However, if you wish to study one or more of these books, a copy of each should be available in the public library or the building department for your use.

ZONING ORDINANCES

In addition to the regulations controlling the construction of your home, there are restrictions which define the location of your house and other improvements on your lot. These are contained in local zoning ordinances. Their main purpose is to properly regulate the use of the land so that a noisy commercial establishment cannot be built in the middle of a quiet residential neighborhood. But they may also have one or more other restricting features such as: minimum setback from the street, minimum clear side and/or rear yards, maximum building height or number of stories, maximum amount of lot coverage by improvements, and the types of uses to which your home can be put.

It is important that you find out what type of zoning your lot is in, and what the restrictions of that zone are before you begin planning in earnest. This information can be obtained either through your local planning department or board, the public library, or the building department.

Variances

It would be wasted energy to spend hours planning an addition to the front of your home only to find out that the present front of the house was built on the setback line and no addition could be made. On the other hand, if you feel that the zoning restrictions have unduly tied your hands, you may petition your local planning commission for a variance. But before you attempt to circumvent the regulations, try to get the support and approval of your neighbors. Without it, your chances are slim. There may be some technical procedures necessary for presentation of the variance request, for which your building department can be of assistance. But the actual presentation should be made by you, in person, if possible.

Plats

It is likely that a plat of your lot, such as the one shown in the illustration, is recorded in the local court house. Your lot may be only a part of a larger plat, one showing all the lots in an entire subdivision. Get a copy of this plat. It will show the size of your lot, the building setback, any restricting easements such as storm drainage or sanitary sewer easements and, in some cases, will list the zoning restrictions applicable to the subdivision. With this plat it will be much easier to see just what you can and cannot do in regard to a new home addition.

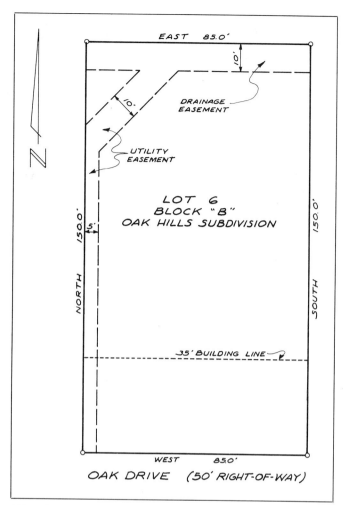

Although requirements vary from area to area, most plats will show lot line dimensions and bearings, the street setback or building line, and any easements which might be on the lot.

Find the side yard and rear yard requirements, if any, from the zoning ordinance and scale them on the plat. Although you may build a drive or walk across an easement or any of the yard requirement areas, you cannot build any type of permanent structure or pour any footings, such as for patios. (These requirements may vary slightly from area to area, so be sure to check for any differences in your locale.)

Next you need to locate the existing house on the plat. Measure the distance from your house to the side lot lines and the front and back lot lines. Then scale these dimensions on the plat, forming a box which should contain the outline of your house. Using the sketch of your existing house with the exterior dimensions that you made previously, carefully draw the house onto the lot. It it does not fit into the box there could be a mistake in your scaling (many plats are drawn with an engineer's scale, which is different from an architects' scale) in measuring from your house to the lot lines, or you may be unsure as to exactly where a lot line is. In the latter case you may need to seek the advice of a surveyor.

Once the house is drawn on the plat it will be easy to see where you can add on and where you cannot without a variance. You may be tempted to add-on in a particular direction if you have only a few feet clearance. But unless it is crucial to what you are doing inside the house, this may be unwise; long, narrow additions are more expensive to build and could be more expensive to heat and cool. Because determining just where you can and cannot add on is a very important step, it is advisable to have the building department or other qualified expert check your work on the plat.

DEED RESTRICTIONS

In some communities there are deed restrictions that usually go beyond the zoning ordinances which further limit the freedom you have in planning. Most often this is the case when a particular architectural style has been followed throughout the community. The restrictions may include not only where and what you build on your lot, but also what style the work will take. Before your plans begin to take concrete form, read your deed carefully to assure that your efforts will not be wasted.

BUILDING PERMITS

Before construction begins you may need to purchase one or more building permits from the building department. In some areas one permit will cover the entire job, while in others separate permits may be required for things such as electrical and plumbing work. The cost of the permit is usually based on the value of the work to be done. Since the purchase of the permit means that the job will be inspected for proper and safe construction, this money is well spent.

Copies of your plans, obtainable from a printing company, must be submitted to the building department for approval prior to issuance of the building permit. Since there may be a time lapse involved, be sure to submit the plans early enough to avoid holding up the start of construction.

10 Subcontracting and Starting Construction

With careful groundwork at the beginning of your remodeling, you can avoid problems that can increase your cost and delay completion of the job.

BEGINNINGS AND OPTIONS

Once plans and specifications are complete, you will have to deal with permits and inspectors. Although most contractors will handle the purchasing of building permits, it is advisable for the self-planner to purchase the permits himself in order to observe first-hand the review of his plans by the building department. Any changes necessary to comply with local regulations will thus not have to be passed on through a middle man. But after the permit is purchased, what comes next?

There are several ways your construction can be handled. You may:

(1) hire a general contractor to carry out the entire job;

(2) act as your own general contractor by hiring subcontractors for specific aspects of the job;

(3) perform all or part of the work yourself.

THE GENERAL CONTRACTOR

If you know little about construction or construction techniques, and do not have the time or inclination to supervise construction, then you should hire a reputable general contractor. He will oversee the job, hire and pay the subcontractors, work with building department inspectors, order and pay for supplies, and be solely responsible to you. Your payment(s) will be made to him and not to a series of subcontractors, for whose work he will be responsible. But it is very important that the contractor be an experienced, respected figure in his profession.

In most cases, the cost of the contractor's services will be about 10 percent of the total cost of the construction — this includes both his profit and his overhead. For smaller jobs, this percentage may be a little higher.

Selecting A General Contractor

There are several ways to check on the reliability of prospective contractors. Consider these factors when determining which contractors you wish to have bid on your job:

(1) Ask the contractor for several references from other homeowners for whom he has done work, and check the references.

(2) Check the contractor's financial references. This is done much less often than it should be, since a contractor's solvency is of utmost importance. This information can be gathered for a small fee from your proposed contractor's bank. If you are in a large city, run a credit check through a credit bureau.

(3) The contractor's place of business should be established and should be reasonably near your residence. (Not in another town, unless it is very close to your own community.)

(4) Check the contractor's professional affiliations and length of time in the business.

(5) If you have worked with an architect or other professional, solicit their suggestions as to a qualified contractor. Local builders' associations are another good source for recommendations.

(6) Be sure the contractor is insured for workmen's compensation, property damage, and personal liability. Don't hesitate to ask for proof.

(7) Talk with the prospective contractor to assure that your personalities will be compatible. Often, this factor can prove to be just as important as the contractor's ability or reputation.

(8) Make sure the contractor has time for your job when you want it done. Pay attention to local rumors regarding work completion time.

Soliciting Bids

Select three or four contractors who meet your criteria and ask them to bid on the job. Supply each with a set of plans and specifications and discuss them thoroughly with the bidders to assure there will be no misunderstanding. Ask them to break down the bids according to labor divisions. Have each bidder visit your home and look over the job site. This is the ideal time to go through a detailed discussion of the plans and specifications. Keep any material brochures for products you want to use close at hand.

Set a date, usually one to two weeks, for the contractor to call, mail, or bring by his bid. It is important that you do not automatically select the contractor with the lowest bid. There is an old saying in the construction business that goes: "Beware of the Low Bidder." This means that a bid that is far below the others could spell trouble. If a contractor has misunderstood the work to be done you could end up with less than you expect. And if a contractor takes a job at too low a price, it could mean a delayed finish, a poor job, or worse.

Look at the bids carefully, but weigh all the other factors such as the contractor's reputation, how well you get along with him, and so on. Then make your choice based on all these factors. (It should be noted here that a bid far higher than the others does not necessarily mean you will get a spectacular job. Again, it could be simply a misunderstanding or it could mean that the contractor is very busy and only wants your job if he stands to make a large profit. Either way, you are wasting money.)

The contract

No work should ever be done without a firm written agreement. Even the best of intentions cannot avoid a verbal misunderstanding. Most contractors will have a standard contract. This document need not be overly long, but should include:

(1) The total cost of the job and the schedule of payments. Don't pay the contractor in advance, and be sure to hold at least 10 percent of his money until all required final inspections are complete, including yours. This should be clearly stipulated in the contract.

(2) The contract must make reference to the plans and specifications. Include the original date of the plans and the latest revised date; in your files, retain a copy of the plans and specifications on which the contract was based.

(3) Insist that the contractor include a clause that all work will meet construction standards such as: "All work shall be carried out in an expedient and professional manner and shall conform to the standards as set forth by the Federal Housing Administration's *Minimum Property Standards,* and to all applicable building codes of the city of _____, county of _____, state of _____." As stated earlier you should include the reference to FHA's MPS whether or not your work is actually subject to federal inspection.

(4) A firm completion date should be included. Allow the contractor sufficient time to complete the job with a small cushion included for unforseeable problems.

Have your attorney study the contract before you sign. Once the contract has been signed any changes made should be written on the contract and then signed by both you and the contractor.

To protect yourself, require that the contractor furnish proof of construction insurance and a performance bond. Should the contractor default on the contract, the company furnishing the bond must either complete the job or pay the owner's loss.

Though you pay only the contractor, you should include in the contract that he must provide evidence that he is paying his subcontractor and has actually paid for the materials that are at the site. This will avoid liens against your property by material suppliers and subcontractors. You may wish to require proof of these payments before the final reimbursement to the contractor.

One good already-worked-up contract is the standard AIA contract. It can be obtained from the AIA for a few dollars or less. Even if you do not use it, you can compare it to any contract submitted by a prospective contractor.

SUBCONTRACTING THE JOB

You can save money by acting as your own general contractor; hiring, paying, and overseeing the subcontractors. But be realistic. You must have enough free time during normal working hours to deal with the subcontractors, oversee the work, order materials, and make sure everything needed is at the job site at the right time, so that workers are not held up. You should also be familiar with construction so that you can recognize whether something is being done correctly or incorrectly, as well as the labor sequence. This will avoid such disasters as pouring a concrete floor before putting in drains and plumbing lines — or applying wallboard before wiring.

Subcontracting the work may prove very difficult, if not impossible, on a large job. But it may be perfectly suited to a small remodeling. General contractors will often not handle small jobs, and if they do, the price is usually high. In this case you would be wise to act as your own general contractor.

The same selection techniques and contract items discussed under general contractor above will apply to the subcontractors, except that instead of going through the process once you would need to go through it separately for each subcontractor. Check labor organizations and trade associations for recommendations of subcontractors who can do your work.

DOING THE WORK YOURSELF

If you are handy with carpentry and construction, and can spare the time, you may consider doing all or part of the work yourself. This is a great way to save money. Again, however, it is very important that you be realistic about what you can and can't do.

On smaller jobs you might be able to handle it all yourself. But if not, consider working with the contractor to set aside certain items of work that you can do. This should be clearly understood before you take bids. The contractor can assist you in deciding which parts of the job you would be able to perform. But be careful not to interfere with the contractor's schedule. It is vitally important that you complete any work you are to handle as quickly as possible when the contractor is ready for that particular phase of construction. It is also important that your work is done properly and meets all code requirements. Plumbing and electrical are the most difficult to guarantee. Unless you have already had experience at this type of job, use a licensed professional rather than doing it yourself.

PREPARING FOR CONSTRUCTION

Areas of your home, which will be remodeled should be cleared of plants, furniture, drapes, and so on, prior to the start of construction. In other areas it would be wise to put protective coverings over furniture, carpet, and anything else you don't want harmed. Keep children and neighbors away from the job site. Not only will this interfere with the workers, but it is also unsafe and an invitation to a lawsuit.

LIVING WITH CONSTRUCTION

It doesn't take a very large remodeling job to disrupt your family life. Of course it is only a temporary inconvenience and will result in a more pleasant home, but you should be planning for it. Be prepared to live with the nuisance of construction, the noise of hammers pounding all day, the strong smell of fresh paint, workers constantly in your way, (or you in theirs).

If the job is so extensive that you will need to leave the house for a period of time, get an idea of when and how long you will need to be away and make prior arrangements for temporary living quarters. The workmen will occasionally need use of the telephone, electricity, water, and bath facilities, so furnish them with a key — whether you are moving temporarily or simply are going to be in and out.

FINANCING

Before getting bids, or working out detailed drawings, find out how much the bank will lend you. This prevents your designing in features you cannot afford. After you get your bids and have a firm price, make all financing arrangements. Do this before signing the contract. Be sure to build in a cushion in your financing for changes during construction, though these should be avoided as much as possible, and for furnishings once the job has been completed.

Check around for the best interest rate. The difference can be substantial over the term of the loan. You can obtain financing from commercial banks — both short-term commercial loans and long-term home improvement loans — from savings and loan associations, from credit unions, and from mortgage institutions which may offer Title I, HUD-insured home-improvement loans. Most general contractors can assist you in arranging financing, but shop on your own to get the best rate. Take the time to be positive of your decisions before you sign anything.

Do not allow an institution to get you to pay off a first mortgage and consolidate the loan. The first mortgage will almost always be at a lower interest rate and consolidation could cost you a great deal of money.

Glossary of Housing Terms

Attic ventilators.—In houses, screen openings provided to ventilate an attic space. They are located in the soffit area as inlet ventilators and in the gable end or along the ridge as outlet ventilators. They can also consist of power-driven fans used as an exhaust system. (See also *Louver.*)

Backfill.—The replacement of excavated earth into a trench around and against a basement foundation.

Base or baseboard.—A board placed against the wall around a room next to the floor to finish properly between floor and plaster.

Base molding.—Molding used to trim the upper edge of interior baseboard.

Base shoe.—Molding used next to the floor on interior baseboard. Sometimes called a carpet strip.

Batten.—Narrow strips of wood used to cover joints or as decorative vertical members over plywood or wide boards.

Beam.—A structural member transversely supporting a load.

Bearing partition.—A partition that supports any vertical load in addition to its own weight.

Bearing wall.—A wall that supports any vertical load in addition to its own weight.

Blind-nailing.—Nailing in such a way that the nailheads are not visible on the face of the work—usually at the tongue of matched boards.

Boston ridge.—A method of applying asphalt or wood shingles at the ridge or at the hips of a roof as a finish.

Brace.—An inclined piece of framing lumber applied to wall or floor to stiffen the structure. Often used on walls as temporary bracing until framing has been completed.

Brick veneer.—A facing of brick laid against and fastened to sheathing of a frame wall or tile wall construction.

Built-up roof.—A roofing composed of three to five layers of asphalt felt laminated with coal tar, pitch, or asphalt. The top is finished with crushed slag or gravel. Generally used on flat or low-pitched roofs.

Butt joint.—The junction where the ends of two timbers or other members meet in a square-cut joint.

Casement frames and sash.—Frames of wood or metal enclosing part or all of the sash, which may be opened by means of hinges affixed to the vertical edges.

Casing.—Molding of various widths and thicknesses used to trim door and window openings at the jambs.

Checking.—Fissures that appear with age in many exterior paint coatings, at first superficial, but which in time may penetrate entirely through the coating.

Collar beam.—Nominal 1– or 2–inch-thick members connecting opposite roof rafters. They serve to stiffen the roof structure.

Column.—In architecture: A perpendicular supporting member, circular or rectangular in section, usually consisting of a base, shaft, and capital. In engineering: A vertical structural compression member which supports loads acting in the direction of its longitudinal axis.

Combination doors or windows.—Combination doors or windows used over regular openings. They provide winter insulation and summer protection and often have self-storing or removable glass and screen inserts. This eliminates the need for handling a different unit each season.

Condensation.—In a building: Beads or drops of water (and frequently frost in extremely cold weather) that accumulate on the inside of the exterior covering of a building when warm, moisture-laden air from the interior reaches a point where the temperature no longer permits the air to sustain the moisture it holds. Use of louvers or attic ventilators will reduce moisture condensation in attics. A vapor barrier under the gypsum lath or dry wall on exposed walls will reduce condensation in them.

Construction dry-wall.—A type of construction in which the interior wall finish is applied in a dry condition, generally in the form of sheet materials or wood paneling, as contrasted to plaster.

Construction, frame.—A type of construction in which the structural parts are wood or depend upon a wood frame for support. In codes, if masonry veneer is applied to the exterior walls, the classification of this type of construction is usually unchanged.

Coped joint.—See *Scribing*.

Corner bead.—A strip of formed sheet metal, sometimes combined with a strip of metal lath, placed on corners before plastering to reinforce them. Also, a strip of wood finish three-quarters-round or angular placed over a plastered corner for protection.

Corner boards.—Used as trim for the external corners of a house or other frame structure against which the ends of the siding are finished.

Corner braces.—Diagonal braces at the corners of frame structure to stiffen and strengthen the wall.

Let-in brace.—Nominal 1–inch–thick boards applied into notched studs diagonally.

Cornice.—Overhang of a pitched roof at the eave line, usually consisting of a facia board, a soffit for a closed cornice, and appropriate moldings.

Cornice return.—That portion of the cornice that returns on the gable end of a house.

Counterflashing.—A flashing usually used on chimneys at the roof line to cover shingle flashing and to prevent moisture entry.

Cove molding.—A molding with a concave face used as trim or to finish interior corners.

Crawl space.—A shallow space below the living quarters of a basementless house, normally enclosed by the foundation wall.

Cripple stud.—A stud that does not extend full height.

d.—See *Penny*.

Dado.—A rectangular groove across the width of a board or plank. In interior decoration, a special type of wall treatment.

Decay.—Disintegration of wood or other substance through the action of fungi.

Deck paint.—An enamel with a high degree of resistance to mechanical wear, designed for use on such surfaces as porch floors.

Density.—The mass of substance in a unit volume. When expressed in the metric system, it is numerically equal to the specific gravity of the same substance.

Dewpoint.—Temperature at which a vapor begins to deposit as a liquid. Applies especially to water in the atmosphere.

Dimension.—See *Lumber dimension*.

Direct nailing.—To nail perpendicular to the initial surface or to the junction of the pieces joined. Also termed *face nailing*.

Door jamb, interior.—The surrounding case into which and out of which a door closes and opens. It consists of two upright pieces, called side jambs, and a horizontal head jamb.

Dormer.—An opening in a sloping roof, the framing of which projects out to form a vertical wall suitable for windows or other openings.

Downspout.—A pipe, usually of metal, for carrying rainwater from roof gutters.

Dressed and matched (tongued and grooved).—Boards or planks machined in such a manner that there is a groove on one edge and a corresponding tongue on the other.

Drip.—(a) A member of a cornice or other horizontal exterior-finish course that has a projection beyond the other parts for throwing off water. (b) A groove in the underside of a sill or drip cap to cause water to drop off on the outer edge instead of drawing back and running down the face of the building.

Drip cap.—A molding placed on the exterior top side of a door or window frame to cause water to drip beyond the outside of the frame.

Dry-wall.—Interior covering material, such as gypsum board or plywood, which is applied in large sheets or panels.

Ducts.—In a house, usually round or rectangular metal pipes for distributing warm air from the heating plant to rooms, or air from a conditioning device or as cold air returns. Ducts are also made of asbestos and composition materials.

Eaves.—The margin or lower part of a roof projecting over the wall.

Facia or fascia.—A flat board, band, or face, used sometimes by itself but usually in combination with moldings, often located at the outer face of the cornice.

Filler (wood).—A heavily pigmented preparation used for filling and leveling off the pores in open-pored woods.

Fire stop.—A solid, tight closure of a concealed space, placed to prevent the spread of fire and smoke through such a space. In a frame wall, this will usually consist of 2 by 4 cross blocking between studs.

Fishplate.—A wood or plywood piece used to fasten the ends of two members together at a butt joint with nails or bolts. Sometimes used at the junction of opposite rafters near the ridge line.

Flashing.—Sheet metal or other material used in roof and wall construction to protect a building from water seepage.

Flat paint.—An interior paint that contains a high proportion of pigment and dries to a flat or lusterless finish.

Flue.—The space or passage in a chimney through which smoke, gas, or fumes ascend. Each passage is called a flue, which together with any others and the surrounding masonry make up the chimney.

Flue lining.—Fire clay or terra-cotta pipe, round or square, usually made in all ordinary flue sizes and in 2-foot lengths, used for the inner lining of chimneys with the brick or masonry work around the outside. Flue lining in chimney runs from about a foot below the flue connection to the top of the chimney.

Fly rafters.—End rafters of the gable overhang supported by roof sheathing and lookouts.

Footing.—A masonry section, usually concrete, in a rectangular form wider than the bottom of the foundation wall or pier it supports.

Foundation.—The supporting portion of a structure below the first-floor construction, or below grade, including the footings.

Framing, balloon.—A system of framing a building in which all vertical structural elements of the bearing walls and partitions consist of single pieces extending from the top of the foundation sill plate to the roofplate and to which all floor joists are fastened.

Framing, platform.—A system of framing a building in which floor joists of each story rest on top plates of the story below or on the foundation sill for the first story, and the bearing walls and partitions rest on the subfloor of each story.

Frieze.—In house construction, a horizontal member connecting the top of the siding with the soffit of the cornice.

Frostline.—The depth of frost penetration in soil. This depth varies in different parts of the country. Footings should be placed below this depth to prevent movement.

Fungi, wood.—Microscopic plants that live in damp wood and cause mold, stain, and decay.

Fungicide.—A chemical that is poisonous to fungi.

Furring.—Strips of wood or metal applied to a wall or other surface to even it and normally to serve as a fastening base for finish material.

Gable.—In house construction, the portion of the roof above the eave line of a double-sloped roof.

Gable end.—An end wall having a gable.

Gloss enamel.—A finishing material made of varnish and sufficient pigments to provide opacity and color, but little or no pigment of low opacity. Such an enamel forms a hard coating with maximum smoothness of surface and a high degree of gloss.

Gloss (paint or enamel). A paint or enamel that contains a relatively low proportion of pigment and dries to a sheen or luster.

Girder.—A large or principal beam of wood or steel used to support concentrated loads at isolated points along its length.

Grain.—The direction, size arrangement, appearance, or quality of the fibers in wood.

Grain, edge (vertical).—Edge-grain lumber has been sawed parallel to the pith of the log and approximately at right angles to the growth rings; i.e., the rings form an angle of 45° or more with the surface of the piece.

Grain, flat.—Flat-grain lumber has been sawed parallel to the pitch of the log and approximately tangent to the growth rings, i.e., the rings form an angle of less than 45° with the surface of the piece.

Grain, quartersawn.—Another term for edge grain.

Grounds.—Guides used around openings and at the floorline to strike off plaster. They can consist of narrow strips of wood or of wide subjambs at interior doorways. They provide a level plaster line for installation of casing and other trim.

Grout.—Mortar made of such consistency (by adding water) that it will just flow into the joints and cavities of the masonry work and fill them solid.

Gusset.—A flatwood, plywood, or similar type member used to provide a connection at intersection of wood members. Most commonly used at joints of wood trusses. They are fastened by nails, screws, bolts, or adhesives.

Gutter or eave trough.—A shallow channel or conduit of metal or wood set below and along the eaves of a house to catch and carry off rainwater from the roof.

Gypsum plaster.—Gypsum formulated to be used with the addition of sand and water for base-coat plaster.

Header.—(a) A beam placed perpendicular to joists and to which joists are nailed in framing for chimney, stairway, or other opening. (b) A wood lintel.

Heartwood.—The wood extending from the pith to the sapwood, the cells of which no longer participate in the life processes of the tree.

Hip.—The external angle formed by the meeting of two sloping sides of a roof.

Hip roof.—A roof that rises by inclined planes from all four sides of a building.

Humidifier.—A device designed to increase the humidity within a room or a house by means of the discharge of water vapor. They may consist of individual room-size units or larger units attached to the heating plant to condition the entire house.

Insulation board, rigid.—A structural building board made of coarse wood or cane fiber in $1/2$- or $25/32$-inch thicknesses. It can be obtained in various size sheets, in various densities, and with several treatments.

Insulation, thermal.—Any material high in resistance to heat transmission that, when placed in the walls, ceiling, or floors of a structure, will reduce the rate of heat flow.

Interior finish.—Material used to cover the interior framed areas, or materials of walls and ceilings.

Jack post.—A hollow metal post with a jack screw in one end so it can be adjusted to the desired height.

Jack rafter.—A rafter that spans the distance from the wallplate to a hip, or from a valley to a ridge.

Jamb.—The side and head lining of a doorway, window, or other opening.

Joint.—The space between the adjacent surfaces of two members or components joined and held together by nails, glue, cement, mortar, or other means.

Joint cement.—A powder that is usually mixed with water and used for joint treatment in gypsum-wallboard finish. Often called "spackle."

Joist.—One of a series of parallel beams, usually 2 inches in thickness, used to support floor and ceiling loads, and supported in turn by larger beams, girders, or bearing walls.

Knot.—In lumber, the portion of a branch or limb of a tree that appears on the edge or face of the piece.

Landing.—A platform between flights of stairs or at the termination of a flight of stairs.

Lath.—A building material of wood, metal, gypsum, or insulating board that is fastened to the frame of a building to act as a plaster base.

Ledger strip.—A strip of lumber nailed along the bottom of the side of a girder on which joists rest.

Lintel.—A horizontal structural member that supports the load over an opening such as a door or window.

Lookout.—A short wood bracket or cantilever to support an overhang portion of a roof or the like, usually concealed from view.

Louver.—An opening with a series of horizontal slats so arranged as to permit ventilation but to exclude rain, sunlight, or vision. See also *Attic ventilators.*

Lumber.—Lumber is the product of the sawmill and planing mill not further manufactured other than by sawing, resawing, and passing lengthwise through a standard planing machine, crosscutting to length, and matching.

Lumber, boards.—Yard lumber less than 2 inches thick and 2 or more inches wide.

Lumber, dimension.—Yard lumber from 2 inches to, but not including, 5 inches thick and 2 or more inches wide. Includes joists, rafters, studs, plank, and small timbers.

Lumber, dressed size.—The dimension of lumber after shrinking from green dimension and after machining to size or pattern.

Lumber, matched.—Lumber that is dressed and shaped on one edge in a grooved pattern and on the other in a tongued pattern.

Lumber, shiplap.—Lumber that is edge-dressed to make a close rabbeted or lapped joint.

Lumber, timbers.—Yard lumber 5 or more inches in least dimension. Includes beams, stringers, posts, caps, sills, girders, and purlins.

Lumber, yard.—Lumber of those grades, sizes, and patterns which are generally intended for ordinary construction, such as framework and rough coverage of houses.

Mantel.—The shelf above a fireplace. Also used in referring to the decorative trim around a fireplace opening.

Masonry.—Stone, brick, concrete, hollow-tile, concrete-block, gypsum-block, or other similar building units or materials or a combination of the same, bonded together with mortar to form a wall, pier, buttress, or similar mass.

Mastic.—A pasty material used as a cement (as for setting tile) or a protective coating (as for thermal insulation or waterproofing).

Metal lath.—Sheets of metal that are slit and drawn out to form openings. Used as a plaster base for walls and ceilings and as reinforcing over other forms of plaster base.

Millwork.—Generally all building materials made of finished wood and manufactured in millwork plants and planing mills are included under the term "millwork." It includes such items as inside and outside doors, window and door frames, blinds, porchwork, mantels, panelwork, stairways, moldings, and interior trim. It normally does not include flooring, ceiling, or siding.

Miter joint.—The joint of two pieces at an angle that bisects the joining angle. For example, the miter joint at the side and head casing as a door opening is made at a 45° angle.

Moisture content of wood.—Weight of the water contained in the wood, usually expressed as a percentage of the weight of the ovendry wood.

Molding.—A wood strip having a curved or projecting surface used for decorative purposes.

Mullion.—A vertical bar or divider in the frame between windows, doors, or other openings.

Muntin.—A small member which divides the glass or openings of sash or doors.

Natural finish.—A transparent finish which does not seriously alter the original color or grain of the natural wood. Natural finishes are usually provided by sealers, oils, varnishes, water-repellent preservatives, and other similar materials.

Nonbearing wall.—A wall supporting no load other than its own weight.

Nosing.—The projecting edge of a molding or drip. Usually applied to the projecting molding on the edge of a stair tread.

O. C., on center.—The measurement of spacing for studs, rafters, joists, and the like in a building from the center of one member to the center of the next.

Outrigger.—An extension of a rafter beyond the wall line. Usually a smaller member nailed to a larger rafter to form a cornice or roof overhang.

Paint.—A combination of pigments with suitable thinners or oils to provide decorative and protective coatings.

Panel.—In house construction, a thin flat piece of wood, plywood, or similar material, framed by stiles and rails as in a door or fitted into grooves of thicker material with molded edges for decorative wall treatment.

Paper, building.—A general term for papers, felts, and similar sheet materials used in buildings without reference to their properties or uses.

Paper, sheathing.—A building material, generally paper or felt, used in wall and roof construction as a protection against the passage of air and sometimes moisture.

Parting stop or strip.—A small wood piece used in the side and head jambs of double-hung windows to separate upper and lower sash.

Partition.—A wall that subdivides spaces within any story of a building.

Penny.—As applied to nails, it originally indicated the price per hundred. The term now serves as a measure of nail length and is abbreviated by the letter *d*.

Perm.—A measure of water vapor movement through a material (grains per square foot per hour per inch of mercury difference in vapor pressure).

Pier.—A column of masonry, usually rectangular in horizontal cross section, used to support other structural members.

Pigment.—A powdered solid in suitable degree of subdivision for use in paint or enamel.

Pitch.—The incline slope of a roof or the ratio of the total rise to the total width of a house, i.e., an 8–foot rise and 24–foot width is a one-third pitch roof. Roof slope is expressed in the inches of rise per foot of run.

Pith.—The small, soft core at the original center of a tree around which wood formation takes place.

Plaster grounds.—Strips of wood used as guides or strike-off edges around window and door openings and at base of walls.

Plate.—Sill plate: A horizontal member anchored to a masonry wall. Sole plate: Bottom horizontal member of a frame wall. Top plate: Top horizontal member of a frame wall supporting ceiling joists; rafters, or other members.

Plough.—To cut a lengthwise groove in a board or plank.

Plumb.—Exactly perpendicular; vertical.

Ply.—A term to denote the number of thicknesses or layers of roofing felt, veneer in plywood, or layers in built-up materials, in any finished piece of such material.

Plywood.—A piece of wood made of three or more layers of veneer joined with glue, and usually laid with the grain of adjoining plies at right angles. Almost always an odd number of plies are used to provide balanced construction.

Preservative.—Any substance that, for a reasonable length of time, will prevent the action of wood-destroying fungi, borers of various kinds, and similar destructive agents when the wood has been properly coated or impregnated with it.

Primer.—The first coat of paint in a paint job that consists of two or more coats; also the paint used for such a first coat.

Putty.—A type of cement usually made of whiting and boiled linseed oil, beaten or kneaded to the consistency of dough, and used in sealing glass in sash, filling small holes and crevices in wood, and for similar purposes.

Quarter round.—A small molding that has the cross section of a quarter circle.

Rabbet.—A rectangular longitudinal groove cut in the corner edge of a board or plank.

Radiant heating.—A method of heating, usually consisting of a forced hot water system with pipes placed in the floor, wall, or ceiling; or with electrically heated panels.

Rafter.—One of a series of structural members of a roof designed to support roof loads. The rafters of a flat roof are sometimes called roof joists.

Rafter, hip.—A rafter that forms the intersection of an external roof angle.

Rafter, valley.—A rafter that forms the intersection of an internal roof angle. The valley rafter is normally made of double 2–inch–thick members.

Rail.—Cross members of panel doors or of a sash. Also the upper and lower members of a balustrade or staircase extending from one vertical support, such as a post, to another.

Rake.—Trim members that run parallel to the roof slope and form the finish between the wall and a gable roof extension.

Reflective insulation.—Sheet material with one or both surfaces of comparatively low heat emissivity, such as aluminium foil. When used in building construction the surfaces face air spaces, reducing the radiation across the air space.

Reinforcing.—Steel rods or metal fabric placed in concrete slabs, beams, or columns to increase their strength.

Relative humidity.—The amount of water vapor in the atmosphere, expressed as a percentage of the maximum quantity that could be present at a given temperature. (The actual amount of water vapor that can be held in space increases with the temperature.)

Ribbon (Girt).—Normally a 1– by 4–inch board let into the studs horizontally to support ceiling or second-floor joists.

Ridge.—The horizontal line at the junction of the top edges of two sloping roof surfaces.

Ridge board.—The board placed on edge at the ridge of the roof into which the upper ends of the rafters are fastened.

Rise.—In stairs, the vertical height of a step or flight of stairs.

Riser.—Each of the vertical boards closing the spaces between the treads of stairways.

Roll roofing.—Roofing material, composed of fiber and saturated with asphalt, that is supplied in 36–inch wide rolls with 108 square feet of material. Weights are generally 45 to 90 pounds per roll.

Roof sheathing.—The boards or sheet material fastened to the roof rafters on which the shingle or other roof covering is laid.

Rout.—The removal of material, by cutting, milling or gouging, to form a groove.

Run.—In stairs, the net width of a step or the horizontal distance covered by a flight of stairs.

Saddle.—Two sloping surfaces meeting in a horizontal ridge, used between the back side of a chimney, or other vertical surface, and a sloping roof.

Sapwood.—The outer zone of wood, next to the bark. In the living tree it contains some living cells (the heartwood contains none), as well as dead and dying cells. In most species, it is lighter colored than the heartwood. In all species, it is lacking in decay resistance.

Sash.—A single light frame containing one or more lights of glass.

Saturated felt.—A felt which is impregnated with tar or asphalt.

Scratch coat.—The first coat of plaster, which is scratched to form a bond for the second coat.

Screed.—A small strip of wood, usually the thickness of the plaster coat, used as a guide for plastering.

Scribing.—Fitting woodwork to an irregular surface. In moldings, cutting the end of one piece to fit the molded face of the other at an interior angle to replace a miter joint.

Sealer.—A finishing material, either clear or pigmented, that is usually applied directly over uncoated wood for the purpose of sealing the surface.

Semigloss paint or enamel.—A paint or enamel made with a slight insufficiency of nonvolatile vehicle so that its coating, when dry, has some luster but is not very glossy.

Shake.—A thick handsplit shingle, resawed to form two shakes, usually edge-grained.

Sheathing.—The structural covering, usually wood boards or plywood, used over studs or rafters of a structure. Structural building board is normally used only as wall sheathing.

Sheathing paper.—See *Paper, sheathing.*

Sheet metal work.—All components of a house employing sheet metal, such as flashing, gutters, and downspouts.

Shellac.—A transparent coating made by dissolving *lac,* a resinous secretion of the lac bug (a scale insect that thrives in tropical countries, especially India), in alcohol.

Shingles.—Roof covering of asphalt, asbestos, wood, tile, slate, or other material cut to stock lengths, width, and thicknesses.

Shingles, siding.—Various kinds of shingles, such as wood shingles or shakes and nonwood shingles, that are used over sheathing for exterior sidewall covering of a structure.

Shiplap.—See *Lumber, shiplap.*

Shutter.—Usually lightweight louvered or flush wood or nonwood frames in the form of doors located at each side of a window. Some are made to close over the window for protection; others are fastened to the wall as a decorative device.

Siding.—The finish covering of the outside wall of a frame building, whether made of horizontal weatherboards, vertical boards with battens, shingles, or other material.

Siding, bevel (lap siding).—Wedge-shaped boards used as horizontal siding in a lapped pattern. This siding varies in butt thickness from $^1/_2$ to $^3/_4$ inch and in widths up to 12 inches. Normally used over some type of sheathing.

Siding, Dolly Varden.—Beveled wood siding which is rabbeted on the bottom edge.

Siding, drop.—Usually $^3/_4$ inch thick and 6 and 8 inches wide with tongued-and-grooved or shiplap edges. Often used as siding without sheathing in secondary buildings.

Sill.—The lowest member of the frame of a structure, resting on the foundation and supporting the floor joists or the uprights of the wall. The member forming the lower side of an opening, as a door sill, window sill, etc.

Sleeper.—Usually, a wood member embedded in concrete, as in a floor, that serves to support and to fasten subfloor or flooring.

Soffit.—Usually the underside of an overhanging cornice.

Soil cover (ground cover).—A light covering of plastic film, roll roofing, or similar material used over the soil in crawl spaces of buildings to minimize moisture permeation of the area.

Soil stack.—A general term for the vertical main of a system of soil, waste, or vent piping.

Sole or sole plate.—See *Plate.*

Solid bridging.—A solid member placed between adjacent floor joists near the center of the span to prevent joists from twisting.

Span.—The distance between structural supports such as walls, columns, piers, beams, girders, and trusses.

Splash block.—A small masonry block laid with the top close to the ground surface to receive roof drainage from downspouts and to carry it away from the building.

Square.—A unit of measure—100 square feet—usually applied to roofing material. Sidewall coverings are sometimes packed to cover 100 square feet and are sold on that basis.

Stain, shingle.—A form of oil paint, very thin in consistency, intended for coloring wood with rough surfaces, such as shingles, without forming a coating of significant thickness or gloss.

Stair carriage.—Supporting member for stair treads. Usually a 2-inch plank notched to receive the treads; sometimes called a "rough horse."

Stair landing.—See *Landing.*

Stair rise.—See *Rise.*

Stile.—An upright framing member in a panel door.

Stool.—A flat molding fitted over the window sill between jambs and contacting the bottom rail of the lower sash.

Storm sash or storm window.—An extra window usually placed on the outside of an existing one as additional protection against cold weather.

Story.—That part of a building between any floor and the floor or roof next above.

Strike plate.—A metal plate mortised into or fastened to the face of a door-frame side jamb to receive the latch or bolt when the door is closed.

Strip flooring.—Wood flooring consisting of narrow, matched strips.

String, stringer.—A timber or other support for cross members in floors or ceilings. In stairs, the support on which the stair treads rest; also stringboard.

Stucco.—Most commonly refers to an outside plaster made with Portland cement as its base.

Stud.—One of a series of slender wood or metal vertical structural members placed as supporting elements in walls and partitions. (Plural: Studs or studding.)

Subfloor.—Boards or plywood laid on joists over which a finish floor is to be laid.

Suspended ceiling.—A ceiling system supported by hanging it from the overhead structural framing.

Termites.—Insects that superficially resemble ants in size, general appearance, and habit of living in colonies; hence, they are frequently called "white ants." Subterranean termites establish themselves in buildings not by being carried in with lumber, but by entering from ground nests after the building has been constructed. If unmolested, they eat out the woodwork, leaving a shell of sound wood to conceal their activities, and damage may proceed so far as to cause collapse of parts of a structure before discovery. There are about 56 species of termites known in the United States; but the two major ones, classified by the manner in which they attack wood, are ground-inhabiting or subterranean termites (the most common) and dry-wood termites, which are found almost exclusively along the extreme southern border and the Gulf of Mexico in the United States.

Threshold.—A strip of wood or metal with beveled edges used over the finish floor and the sill of exterior doors.

Toenailing.—To drive a nail at a slant with the initial surface in order to permit it to penetrate into a second member.

Tongued and grooved.—See *Dressed and matched.*

Tread.—The horizontal board in a stairway on which the foot is placed.

Trim.—The finish materials in a building, such as moldings, applied around openings (window trim, door trim) or at the floor and ceiling of rooms (baseboard, cornice, and other moldings).

Trimmer.—A beam or joist to which a header is nailed in framing for a chimney, stairway, or other opening.

Truss.—A frame or jointed structure designed to act as a beam of long span, while each member is usually subjected to longitudinal stress only, either tension or compression.

Turpentine.—A volatile oil used as a thinner in paints and as a solvent in varnishes. Chemically, it is a mixture of terpenes.

Undercoat.—A coating applied prior to the finishing or top coats of a paint job. It may be the first of two or the second of three coats. In some usage of the word it may become synonymous with priming coat.

Underlayment.—A material placed under finish coverings, such as flooring, or shingles, to provide a smooth, even surface for applying the finish.

Valley.—The internal angle formed by the junction of two sloping sides of a roof.

Vapor barrier.—Material used to retard the movement of water vapor into walls and prevent condensation in them. Usually considered as having a perm value of less than 1.0. Applied separately over the warm side of exposed walls or as a part of batt or blanket insulation.

Varnish.—A thickened preparation of drying oil or drying oil and resin suitable for spreading on surfaces to form continuous, transparent coatings, or for mixing with pigments to make enamels.

Vehicle.—The liquid portion of a finishing material; it consists of the binder (nonvolatile) and volatile thinners.

Veneer.—Thin sheets of wood made by rotary cutting or slicing of a log.

Vent.—A pipe or duct which allows flow of air as an inlet or outlet.

Water-repellent preservative.—A liquid designed to penetrate into wood and impart water repellency and a moderate preservative protection. It is used for millwork, such as sash and frames, and is usually applied by dipping.

Weatherstrip.—Narrow or jamb-width sections of thin metal or other material to prevent infiltration of air and moisture around windows and doors, Compression weather stripping prevent air infiltration, provides tension, and acts a counterbalance.

Appendices

Appendix A: Abbreviations

@	at
A/C	Air conditioner
Al.	Aluminum
B.R.	Bedroom
BD.	Board
CL.	Closet
COL.	Column
CONC.	Concrete
C.T.	Ceramic Tile
DBL.	Double
D.H.	Double Hung
D.O.	Ditto
D.R.	Dining Room
ENT.	Entrance
EXT.	Exterior
FHA	Federal Housing Administration (Also Farm Home Administration)
FL.	Fluorescent
F.R.	Family Room
FT.	Feet (')
FTG.	Footing
FUR.	Furnace
GYP.	Gypsum
H.C.	Hollow Core
IN.	Inches (")
INSUL.	Insulation
INT.	Interior
KIT.	Kitchen
LAV.	Lavatory
L.F.	Linear Feet
L.R.	Living Room
MAP	Manual of Acceptable Practices
MPS	Minimum Property Standards
O.C.	On Center
RM.	Room
R & S	Rod and Shelf
S.F.	Square Feet (⊓)
SHR.	Shower
S.H.	Single Hung
STL.	Steel
STO.	Storage
T & G	Tongue and Groove
VA	Veterans Administration
VAN.	Vanity
W/	With
W.C.	Water Closet
WD.	Wood
W.H.	Water Heater
W.W.M.	Welded Wire Mesh

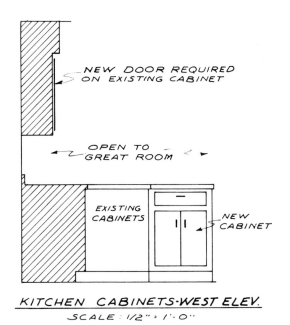

KITCHEN CABINETS·WEST ELEV.
SCALE : 1/2" = 1'-0"

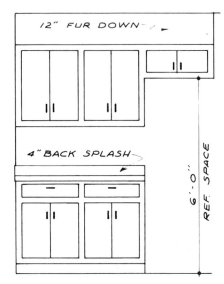

KITCHEN CABINETS - NORTH ELEV.
SCALE : 1/2" = 1'-0"

VANITY-BATH No. 2
SCALE : 1/2" = 1'-0"

LINEN CLOSET
SCALE : 1/2" = 1'-0"

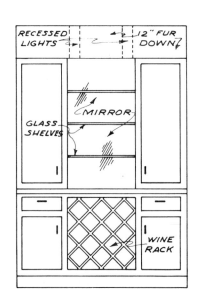

DINING ROOM CABINETS
SCALE : 1/2" = 1'-0"

NOTE : CONSTRUCTION DETAILS ARE ATTACHED TO THE SPECS.

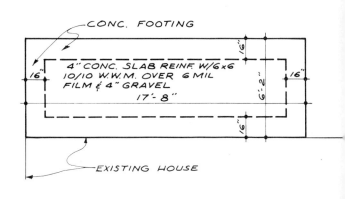

This reduced plan shows the layout on the sheet for the cabinet elevation and foundation plan components discussed in Chapter 7. This is the most common overall arrangement, and should be followed if possible.

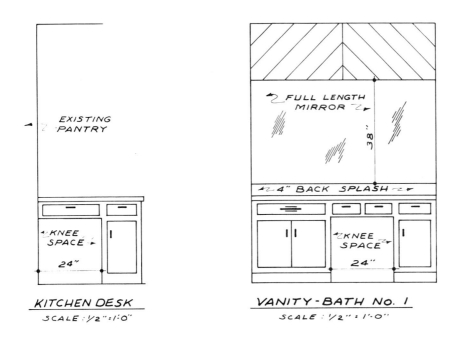

KITCHEN DESK
SCALE: 1/2" = 1'·0"

VANITY - BATH No. 1
SCALE: 1/2" = 1'·0"

NOTE: CABINET DOOR STYLES
SHALL BE SELECTED BY
OWNER. SEE SPECS FOR
ALLOWANCE.

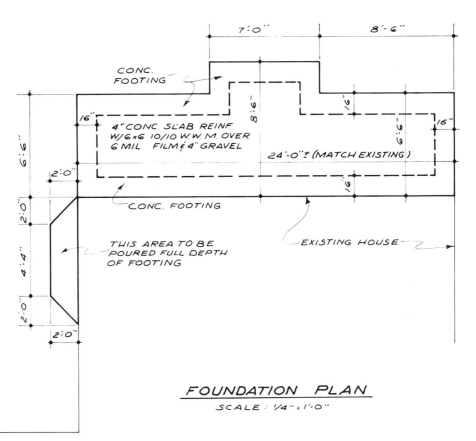

FOUNDATION PLAN
SCALE: 1/4" = 1'·0"

7 of 7

Appendix C: The Effects of Regional Weather on Building Time and Costs

**Average Percent Increase in Time by Type of Building Activity
for Worst Three Weather Months vs. Best Three Weather Months**

TYPE OF BUILDING ACTIVITY	NORTH	MID SOUTH	DEEP SOUTH	WEST			
				Mountain	Desert	North Coast	South Coast
Survey	4	4	3	4	5	8	3
Lot Layout	5	4	3	10	2	7	3
Clearing Lot	10	7	8	7		15	6
Stake Basement	9	5	5	7		5	3
Dig Basement	14	10	10	15		16	1
Insulate Basement	2	2	3	5		2	1
Form Ftgs.	8	8	8	9		15	8
Cast Ftgs.	8	7	7	10		12	8
Insulate Ftgs.	4	1	1	15		3	
Form Found. Walls	9	9	8	15	3	15	9
Cast Found. Walls	7	10	7	10		17	8
Strip Found. Walls	4	3	2	12	3	6	4
Lay Block Found. Wall	15	9	15	16	2	15	2
Drain Tile and Sump	10	8	10	12		15	3
Waterprfg. Found. Wall	8	10	10	3		8	4
Backfill	11	10	6	7		16	6
Gas Service	15	4	5	12	2	4	1
Electric Service	8	6	4	8	2	4	3
Water Service	12	5	4	7	2	12	3
Cast Basement Floor Slab	10	10	10	12		12	3
Decking	6	8	12	5	2	6	4
Rough Framing	8	8	10	9	3	5	9

Average Percent Increase in Time by Type of Building Activity (Continued)

TYPE OF BUILDING ACTIVITY	NORTH	MID SOUTH	DEEP SOUTH	WEST			
				Mountain	Desert	North Coast	South Coast
Chimney & Fireplace	10	8	12	12	2	12	4
Rough Plumbing (DWV)	3	4	5	8	2	7	4
Rough Plumbing (Water Piping)	3	3	5	4	2	6	4
Rough Heating	2	2	4	6	3	4	4
Rough Electric	1	2	4	1	3	1	4
Roofing	8	10	10	10	2	16	6
Install Windows and Doors	4	2	4	6	2	5	5
Furnace Hook-Up Gas or Oil	3		2	3	2	1	
Brick Veneer	15	16	12	15		12	3
Exterior Siding	10	8	6	10	2	10	8
Hang Drywall	3	3	4	6	2	5	6
Finish Drywall	5	8	12	12		9	10
Exterior Prime	11	8	11	10	2	10	10
Exterior Finish	14	10	12	8	2	14	10
Interior Paint	2	4	5	5			8
Electric Finish					2		1
Plumbing Finish					2		1
Heating Finish		1			2		1
Cast Garage Floor Slab	11	7	10	10	2	12	4
Cast Sidewalks and Porches	18	10	13	16	2	16	6
Cast Apron and Driveway	19	9	13	16	2	16	6
Finish Grade and Clean-Up	22	12	14	15	2	25	9
Landscape and Sodding	20	16	16	22	2	20	10

**Average Percent Increase in Cost by Building Elements
for Worst Three Weather Months vs. Best Three Months**

TYPE OF BUILDING ELEMENT	NORTH	MID SOUTH	DEEP SOUTH	WEST			
				Mountain	Desert	North Coast	South Coast
Excavation	16	15	10	15	3	18	16
Foundation	7	7	10	18	ND	15	15
Floors	7	8	5	20	ND	5	11
Rough Fram.	6	6	5	13	2	8	10
Electrical	0.5		1	7	ND		2
Plumbing	1	1	2	2	ND	2	3
Int. Finish	4	8	1	10	ND	4	8
Fin. Carp.	1	7		5	ND	3	6
Roof	7	5	3	7	ND	8	4
Siding	6	7	1	8	ND	8	8
Ex. Paint.	5	8	2	5	ND	8	6

(Source: HUD's 1975 Survey of Home Builders' All-Weather Building Practices by NAHB Research Foundation)

FHA Form 2005
VA Form 26-1852
Rev. 2 /74

U. S. DEPARTMENT OF HOUSING AND URBAN DEVELOPMENT
FEDERAL HOUSING ADMINISTRATION

For accurate register of carbon copies, form
may be separated along above fold.   Staple
completed sheets together in original order.

Form Approved
OMB No. 63—RO055

☐ Proposed Construction
☐ Under Construction

DESCRIPTION OF MATERIALS   No. _____

(To be inserted by FHA or VA)

Property address _____   City _____   State _____

Mortgagor or Sponsor _____   _____
                                    (Name)   (Address)

Contractor or Builder _____   _____
                                    (Name)   (Address)

INSTRUCTIONS

1.   For additional information on how this form is to be submitted, number of copies, etc., see the instructions applicable to the FHA Application for Mortgage Insurance or VA Request for Determination of Reasonable Value, as the case may be.

2.   Describe all materials and equipment to be used, whether or not shown on the drawings, by marking an X in each appropriate check-box and entering the information called for in each space.   If space is inadequate, enter "See misc." and describe under item 27 or on an attached sheet.   THE USE OF PAINT CONTAINING MORE THAN FIVE-TENTHS OF ONE PERCENT LEAD BY WEIGHT IS PROHIBITED.

3.   Work not specifically described or shown will not be considered unless required, then the minimum acceptable will be assumed.   Work exceeding minimum requirements cannot be considered unless specifically described.

4.   Include no alternates, "or equal" phrases, or contradictory items. (Consideration of a request for acceptance of substitute materials or equipment is not thereby precluded.)

5.   Include signatures required at the end of this form.

6.   The construction shall be completed in compliance with the related drawings and specifications, as amended during processing.   The specifications include this Description of Materials and applicable Minimum Property Standards.

1. EXCAVATION:

Bearing soil, type _____

2. FOUNDATIONS:

Footings: concrete mix _____ ; strength psi _____   Reinforcing _____

Foundation wall: material _____   Reinforcing _____

Interior foundation wall: material _____   Party foundation wall _____

Columns: material and sizes _____   Piers: material and reinforcing _____

Girders: material and sizes _____   Sills: material _____

Basement entrance areaway _____   Window areaways _____

Waterproofing _____   Footing drains _____

Termite protection _____

Basementless space: ground cover _____ ; insulation _____ ; foundation vents _____

Special foundations _____

Additional information: _____

3. CHIMNEYS:

Material _____   Prefabricated (make and size) _____

Flue lining: material _____   Heater flue size _____   Fireplace flue size _____

Vents (material and size): gas or oil heater _____ ; water heater _____

Additional information: _____

4. FIREPLACES:

Type: ☐ solid fuel; ☐ gas-burning; ☐ circulator (make and size) _____   Ash dump and clean-out _____

Fireplace: facing _____ ; lining _____ ; hearth _____ ; mantel _____

Additional information: _____

5. EXTERIOR WALLS:

Wood frame: wood grade, and species _____   ☐ Corner bracing.   Building paper or felt _____

　　Sheathing _____ ; thickness _____ ; width _____ ; ☐ solid; ☐ spaced _____ " o. c.; ☐ diagonal; _____

　　Siding _____ ; grade _____ ; type _____ ; size _____ ; exposure _____ "; fastening _____

　　Shingles _____ ; grade _____ ; type _____ ; size _____ ; exposure _____ "; fastening _____

　　Stucco _____ ; thickness _____ "; Lath _____ ; weight _____ lb.

　　Masonry veneer _____   Sills _____   Lintels _____   Base flashing _____

Masonry: ☐ solid ☐ faced ☐ stuccoed; total wall thickness _____ "; facing thickness _____ "; facing material _____

　　　　　　Backup material _____ ; thickness _____ "; bonding _____

　　Door sills _____   Window sills _____   Lintels _____   Base flashing _____

　　Interior surfaces: dampproofing, _____ coats of _____ ; furring _____

Additional information: _____

Exterior painting: material _____ ; number of coats _____

Gable wall construction: ☐ same as main walls; ☐ other construction _____

6. FLOOR FRAMING:

Joists: wood, grade, and species _____ ; other _____ ; bridging _____ ; anchors _____

Concrete slab: ☐ basement floor; ☐ first floor; ☐ ground supported; ☐ self-supporting; mix _____ ; thickness _____ ";

  reinforcing _____ ; insulation _____ ; membrane _____

Fill under slab: material _____ ; thickness _____ ". Additional information: _____

_____

7. SUBFLOORING: *(Describe underflooring for special floors under item 21.)*

Material: grade and species _____ ; size _____ ; type _____

Laid: ☐ first floor; ☐ second floor; ☐ attic _____ sq. ft.; ☐ diagonal; ☐ right angles. Additional information: _____

_____

8. FINISH FLOORING: *(Wood only.   Describe other finish flooring under item 21.)*

LOCATION	ROOMS	GRADE	SPECIES	THICKNESS	WIDTH	BLDG. PAPER	FINISH
First floor ____							
Second floor ____							
Attic floor ____ ____ sq. ft.							

Additional information: _____

9. PARTITION FRAMING:

Studs: wood, grade, and species _____ size and spacing _____ Other _____

Additional information: _____

10. CEILING FRAMING:

Joists: wood, grade, and species _____ Other _____ Bridging _____

Additional information: _____

11. ROOF FRAMING:

Rafters: wood, grade, and species _____ Roof trusses (see detail): grade and species _____

Additional information: _____

12. ROOFING:

Sheathing: wood, grade, and species _____ ; ☐ solid; ☐ spaced _____ " o.c.

Roofing _____ ; grade _____ ; size _____ ; type _____

Underlay _____ ; weight or thickness _____ ; size _____ ; fastening _____

Built-up roofing _____ ; number of plies _____ ; surfacing material _____

Flashing: material _____ ; gage or weight _____ ; ☐ gravel stops; ☐ snow guards

Additional information: _____

13. GUTTERS AND DOWNSPOUTS:

Gutters: material _____ ; gage or weight _____ ; size _____ ; shape _____

Downspouts: material _____ ; gage or weight _____ ; size _____ ; shape _____ ; number _____

Downspouts connected to: ☐ Storm sewer; ☐ sanitary sewer; ☐ dry-well. ☐ Splash blocks: material and size _____

Additional information: _____

14. LATH AND PLASTER

Lath ☐ walls, ☐ ceilings: material _____ ; weight or thickness _____ Plaster: coats _____ ; finish _____

Dry-wall ☐ walls, ☐ ceilings: material _____ ; thickness _____ ; finish _____

Joint treatment _____

15. DECORATING: *(Paint, wallpaper, etc.)*

ROOMS	WALL FINISH MATERIAL AND APPLICATION	CEILING FINISH MATERIAL AND APPLICATION
Kitchen ____		
Bath ____		
Other ____		

Additional information: _____

16. INTERIOR DOORS AND TRIM:

Doors: type _____ ; material _____ ; thickness _____

Door trim: type _____ ; material _____ Base: type _____ ; material _____ ; size _____

Finish: doors _____ ; trim _____

Other trim *(item, type and location)* _____

Additional information: _____

7. WINDOWS:

Windows: type _____ ; make _____ ; material _____ ; sash thickness _____

Glass: grade _____ ; ☐ sash weights; ☐ balances, type _____ ; head flashing _____

Trim: type _____ ; material _____ Paint _____ ; number coats _____

Weatherstripping: type _____ ; material _____ Storm sash, number _____

Screens: ☐ full; ☐ half; type _____ ; number _____ ; screen cloth material _____

Basement windows: type _____ ; material _____ ; screens, number _____ ; Storm sash, number _____

Special windows _____

Additional information: _____

8. ENTRANCES AND EXTERIOR DETAIL:

Main entrance door: material _____ ; width _____ ; thickness ____ ". Frame: material _____ ; thickness ____ "

Other entrance doors: material _____ ; width _____ ; thickness ____ ". Frame: material _____ ; thickness ____ "

Head flashing _____ Weatherstripping: type _____ ; saddles _____

Screen doors: thickness ____ "; number _____ ; screen cloth material _____ Storm doors: thickness ____ "; number _____

Combination storm and screen doors: thickness ____ "; number ____ ; screen cloth material _____

Shutters: ☐ hinged; ☐ fixed. Railings _____ , Attic louvers _____

Exterior millwork: grade and species _____ Paint _____ ; number coats _____

Additional information: _____

9. CABINETS AND INTERIOR DETAIL:

Kitchen cabinets, wall units: material _____ ; lineal feet of shelves _____ ; shelf width _____

Base units: material _____ ; counter top _____ ; edging _____

Back and end splash _____ Finish of cabinets _____ ; number coats _____

Medicine cabinets: make _____ ; model _____

Other cabinets and built-in furniture _____

Additional information: _____

10. STAIRS:

STAIR	TREADS		RISERS		STRINGS		HANDRAIL		BALUSTERS	
	Material	Thickness	Material	Thickness	Material	Size	Material	Size	Material	Size
Basement										
Main										
Attic										

Disappearing: make and model number _____

Additional information: _____

11. SPECIAL FLOORS AND WAINSCOT:

	LOCATION	MATERIAL, COLOR, BORDER, SIZES, GAGE, ETC.	THRESHOLD MATERIAL	WALL BASE MATERIAL	UNDERFLOOR MATERIAL
FLOORS	Kitchen				
	Bath				

	LOCATION	MATERIAL, COLOR, BORDER, CAP. SIZES, GAGE, ETC.	HEIGHT	HEIGHT OVER TUB	HEIGHT IN SHOWERS (FROM FLOOR)
WAINSCOT	Bath				

Bathroom accessories: ☐ Recessed; material _____ ; number _____ ; ☐ Attached; material _____ ; number _____

Additional information: _____

22. PLUMBING:

FIXTURE	NUMBER	LOCATION	MAKE	MFR'S FIXTURE IDENTIFICATION NO.	SIZE	COLOR
Sink						
Lavatory						
Water closet						
Bathtub						
Shower over tub △						
Stall shower △						
Laundry trays						

△☐ Curtain rod   △☐ Door   ☐ Shower pan: material _____

Water supply: ☐ public; ☐ community system; ☐ individual (private) system. ★

Sewage disposal: ☐ public; ☐ community system; ☐ individual (private) system. ★

★ *Show and describe individual system in complete detail in separate drawings and specifications according to requirements.*

House drain (inside): ☐ cast iron; ☐ tile; ☐ other _____   House sewer (outside): ☐ cast iron; ☐ tile; ☐ other _____

Water piping: ☐ galvanized steel; ☐ copper tubing; ☐ other _____   Sill cocks, number _____

Domestic water heater: type _____; make and model _____; heating capacity _____

_____ gph. 100° rise. Storage tank: material _____; capacity _____ gallons.

Gas service: ☐ utility company; ☐ liq. pet. gas; ☐ other _____   Gas piping: ☐ cooking; ☐ house heating.

Footing drains connected to: ☐ storm sewer; ☐ sanitary sewer; ☐ dry well. Sump pump; make and model _____

_____; capacity _____; discharges into _____

23. HEATING:

☐ Hot water. ☐ Steam. ☐ Vapor. ☐ One-pipe system. ☐ Two-pipe system.

☐ Radiators. ☐ Convectors. ☐ Baseboard radiation. Make and model _____

Radiant panel: ☐ floor; ☐ wall; ☐ ceiling. Panel coil: material _____

☐ Circulator. ☐ Return pump. Make and model _____; capacity _____ gpm.

Boiler: make and model _____   Output _____ Btuh.; net rating _____ Btuh.

Additional information: _____

Warm air: ☐ Gravity. ☐ Forced. Type of system _____

Duct material: supply _____; return _____   Insulation _____, thickness _____   ☐ Outside air intake.

Furnace: make and model _____   Input _____ Btuh.; output _____ Btuh.

Additional information: _____

☐ Space heater; ☐ floor furnace; ☐ wall heater. Input _____ Btuh.; output _____ Btuh.; number units _____

Make, model _____   Additional information: _____

Controls: make and types _____

Additional information: _____

Fuel: ☐ Coal; ☐ oil; ☐ gas; ☐ liq. pet. gas; ☐ electric; ☐ other _____; storage capacity _____

Additional information: _____

Firing equipment furnished separately: ☐ Gas burner, conversion type. ☐ Stoker: hopper feed ☐; bin feed ☐

Oil burner: ☐ pressure atomizing; ☐ vaporizing _____

Make and model _____   Control _____

Additional information: _____

Electric heating system: type _____   Input _____ watts; @ _____ volts; output _____ Btuh

Additional information: _____

Ventilating equipment: attic fan, make and model _____; capacity _____ cfm

kitchen exhaust fan, make and model _____

Other heating, ventilating. or cooling equipment _____

24. ELECTRIC WIRING:

Service: ☐ overhead; ☐ underground. Panel: ☐ fuse box; ☐ circuit-breaker; make _____ AMP's _____ No. circuits _____

Wiring: ☐ conduit: ☐ armored cable; ☐ nonmetallic cable; ☐ knob and tube; ☐ other _____

Special outlets: ☐ range; ☐ water heater; ☐ other _____

☐ Doorbell. ☐ Chimes. Push-button locations _____   Additional information: _____

25. LIGHTING FIXTURES:

Total number of fixtures _____   Total allowance for fixtures, typical installation, $ _____

Nontypical installation _____

Additional information: _____

26. INSULATION:

Location	Thickness	Material, Type, and Method of Installation	Vapor Barrier
Roof			
Ceiling			
Wall			
Floor			

HARDWARE: (*make, material, and finish.*) _____

_____

SPECIAL EQUIPMENT: *(State material or make, model and quantity.   Include only equipment and appliances which are accept-able by local law, custom and applicable FHA standards.   Do not include items which, by established custom, are supplied by occupant and removed when he vacates premises or chattles prohibited by law from becoming realty.)*_____

_____

_____

_____

_____

_____

_____

_____

27. **MISCELLANEOUS:** *(Describe any main dwelling materials, equipment, or construction items not shown elsewhere; or use to provide additional information where the space provided was inadequate.   Always reference by item number to correspond to numbering used on this form.)* _____

_____

_____

_____

_____

_____

_____

_____

PORCHES:

_____

_____

TERRACES:

_____

_____

GARAGES:

_____

_____

_____

WALKS AND DRIVEWAYS:

Driveway: width _____ ; base material _____ ; thickness _____ "; surfacing material _____ ; thickness _____ "

Front walk: width _____ ; material _____ ; thickness _____ ". Service walk: width _____ ; material _____ ; thickness _____ "

Steps: material _____ ; treads _____ "; risers _____ ". Cheek walls _____

OTHER ONSITE IMPROVEMENTS:

(Specify all exterior onsite improvements not described elsewhere, including items such as unusual grading, drainage structures, retaining walls, fence, railings, and accessory structures.)

_____

_____

_____

LANDSCAPING, PLANTING, AND FINISH GRADING:

Topsoil _____ " thick: ☐ front yard; ☐ side yards; ☐ rear yard to _____ feet behind main building.

Lawns *(seeded, sodded, or sprigged)*: ☐ front yard _____ ; ☐ side yards _____ ; ☐ rear yard _____

Planting: ☐ as specified and shown on drawings; ☐ as follows:

_____ Shade trees, deciduous, _____ " caliper.　　　　　_____ Evergreen trees. _____ ' to _____ ', B & B.

_____ Low flowering trees, deciduous, _____ ' to _____ '　　_____ Evergreen shrubs. _____ ' to _____ ', B & B.

_____ High-growing shrubs, deciduous, _____ ' to _____ '　　_____ Vines, 2-year _____

_____ Medium-growing shrubs, deciduous, _____ ' to _____ '　　_____

_____ Low-growing shrubs, deciduous, _____ ' to _____ '　　_____

IDENTIFICATION.—This exhibit shall be identified by the signature of the builder, or sponsor, and/or the proposed mortgagor if the latter is known at the time of application.

Date _____　　Signature _____

FHA Form 2005
VA Form 26–1852　　　　　　　　　　　　　　Signature _____

Appendix E: Bibliography

Callender, John Hancock, Editor-in-Chief. *Time Saver Standards for Architectural Design Data,* Fifth Edition, New York, 1974.

Harrison, Henry S. *Houses,* National Institute of Real Estate Brokers of the National Association of Realtors, Chicago, 1973.

Manual of Acceptable Practices (MAP). Department of Housing and Urban Development, Washington D.C., 1973.

Minimum Property Standards (MPS). Department of Housing and Urban Development, Washington D.C., 1973.

Ramsey and Sleeper. *Architectural Graphic Standards,* Sixth Edition, John Wiley and Sons, Inc., New York, 1970.

Roberts, Rex. *Your Engineered House,* M. Evans and Company, Inc., New York, 1964.

Seelye, Elwyn E. *Design: Data Book For Civil Engineers,* Third Edition, John Wiley and Sons, Inc., New York, 1967.

Ulrey, Harry F. *Building: Construction and Design,* Theodore Audel and Co., Indianapolis, 1970.

Walker, Les, and Milstein, Jeff. *Designing Houses,* The Overlook Press, Woodstock, New York, 1976.

Appendix F: Helpful Government Publications

INVESTMENT & CONSTRUCTION

Buying Lots from Developers
043G. $1.00. 28 pp. 1976.
What to ask about a property and contract before you sign; information the developer must give you under law.

Can I Really Get Free or Cheap Public Land?
632 G. Free. 12 pp. 1978.
What public lands are still available for purchase or homesteading; how to go about it.

Designs for Low-Cost Wood Homes
044G. $1.30. 30 pp. 1978.
Sketches and model floor plans; how to select economical, durable materials; order forms for working plans.

Drainage Around the Home.
045G. $.60. 6 pp. 1977.
How to identify drainage problems caused by flooding, seasonal high water tables, or density of the soil.

Finding and Keeping a Healthy House
091G. $1.25. 20 pp. 1978.
How to identify and protect your home from water damage, wood decay, and destructive insects such as termites, beetles, and carpenter ants.

Having Problems Paying Your Mortgage?
683G. Free. 5 pp. 1979.
Steps to take if you are having trouble making your mortgage payments on time; where to go for help.

Home Buyer's Vocabulary.
655G. Free. 14 pp. 1978.
Defines terms you need to understand when buying.

Home Buying Veteran
600G. Free. 36 pp. 1977.
Useful for non-veterans as well; choosing a neighborhood, a lot, a house; checklist for inspecting a house; financing.

House Construction; How To Reduce Costs
049G. $.80. 16 pp. 1977.
How to save in location, style, interior arrangements, and selection of materials and utilities.

Move in . . . with a Graduated Payment Mortgage
656G. Free. 2 pp. 1978.
How this new program enables you to buy a home and make lower monthly payments during the first few years of your mortgage.

Questions and Answers on Condominiums
602G. Free. 48 pp. 1979
What to ask before buying.

Remodeling a House — Will It Be Worthwhile?
670G. Free. 9 pp. 1978.
What to consider when deciding whether a wood-frame house is worth restoring.

Rent or Buy?
051G. $.80. 32 pp. 1979.
How to compare costs and returns of renting with owning a home; includes charts for estimating the monthly costs of each.

Selecting and Financing a Home
052G. $1.10. 23 pp. 1977.
Brief comparison of renting with buying; how to figure what you can afford; how to apply for a loan; what to look for in homeowners insurance.

Selling Property: Brokers, Title, Closing, and Taxes
671G. Free. 7 pp. 1978.
Advantages and disadvantages of using a real estate broker; some costs of selling; tax implications.

Settlement Costs
053G. $1.00. 40 pp. 1978.
What they are; documents to expect; sample forms and worksheets to compare costs; how to avoid unfair practices when purchasing a home.

When You Move — Do's and Don'ts
603G. Free. 6 pp. 1974.
Planning, what to expect during the move, and how to handle a loss or damage claim; tips for the do-it-yourselfer.

Wise Home Buying
657G. Free. 28 pp. 1978.
Discusses choosing a real estate broker, locating a house, inspecting an old house, and financing the purchase of a home.

Wood-Frame House Construction
054G. $4.25. 223 pp. 1975.
Comprehensive, illustrated handbook of detailed instructions and basic principles for building and insulating.

ENERGY CONSIDERATIONS

Buying Solar
055G. $1.85. 80 pp. 1976.
How solar energy can be used to heat and cool your house and heat your water; advantages of the different types of equipment and systems; designing a system; how to estimate costs and savings.

The Energy-Wise Home Buyer.
109G. $2.00. 59 pp. 1979.
Twelve energy features to look for in a home; detailed energy checklists; comprehensive charts and maps for figuring your energy needs and costs.

Firewood for Your Fireplace
047G. $.60. 7 pp. 1978.
Burning characteristics of various woods, where and how to buy firewood, and tips on safe fireplace use.

How To Improve the Efficiency of Your Oil-Fired Furnace
605G. Free. 12 pp. 1978.
What you and the service technician should check; adjustments that will cut costs.

Tips for Energy Savers
610G. Free. 46 pp. 1978.
How to save energy and money on home heating, cooling, lighting, appliances, etc.; how much insulation you need; lists annual electricity use for appliances.

MAINTENANCE

Controlling Household Pests
064G. $.50. 30 pp. 1977.
Procedures and proper pesticides for controlling rats, cockroaches, termites, clothes moths, carpet beetles, etc.

Corrosion
057G. $.80. 8 pp. 1978.
Causes of common corrosion problems; how to prevent and remove rust, tarnish, and other corrosion from silver and other metals.

Family Work and Storage Areas Outside the Home
672G. Free. 11 pp. 1978.
How to use the space you have more efficiently; build different types of storage sheds; and get financing.

How To Prevent and Remove Mildew
077G. $.90. 12 pp. 1978.
What it is; how to prevent and remove it from different surfaces; and how to get rid of dampness and musty odors.

Painting—Inside and Out
092G. $1.30. 32 pp. 1978.
Directions for doing a top-quality paint job, including surface preparation, paint selection, application, use of natural finishes; also lists references.

People and Fire
093G. $1.40. 27 pp. 1977.
Latest ideas on fire safety for homes, apartments, and mobile homes; includes household fire safety checklist and electrical troubleshooting guide.

Protecting Your Housing Investment
616G. Free. 32 pp. 1979.
Maintenance of heating systems, plumbing, and building structure; treatment of special problems such as pest control and moisture.

Appendix G: Metric Conversions

NAILS

NUMBER PER POUND OR KILO

LENGTH AND DIAMETER IN INCHES AND CENTIMETERS

Size	Weight Unit	Common	Casing	Box	Finishing	Size	Inches	Length Centimeters	Inches	Diameter Centimeters*
2d	Pound	876	1010	1010	1351	2d	1	2.5	.068	.17
	Kilo	1927	2222	2222	2972					
3d	Pound	586	635	635	807	3d	1/2	3.2	.102	.26
	Kilo	1289	1397	1397	1775					
4d	Pound	316	473	473	548	4d	1/4	3.8	.102	.26
	Kilo	695	1041	1041	1206					
5d	Pound	271	406	406	500	5d	1/6	4.4	.102	.26
	Kilo	596	893	893	1100					
6d	Pound	181	236	236	309	6d	2	5.1	.115	.29
	Kilo	398	591	519	680					
7d	Pound	161	210	210	238	7d	2/2	5.7	.115	.29
	Kilo	354	462	462	524					
8d	Pound	106	145	145	189	8d	2/4	6.4	.131	.33
	Kilo	233	319	319	416					
9d	Pound	96	132	132	172	9d	2/6	7.0	.131	.33
	Kilo	211	290	290	398					
10d	Pound	69	94	94	121	10d	3	7.6	.148	.38
	Kilo	152	207	207	266					
12d	Pound	64	88	88	113	12d	3/2	8.3	.148	.38
	Kilo	141	194	194	249					
16d	Pound	49	71	71	90	16d	3/4	8.9	.148	.38
	Kilo	108	156	156	198					
20d	Pound	31	52	52	62	20d	4	10.2	.203	.51
	Kilo	68	114	114	136					
30d	Pound	24	46	46		30d	4/4	11.4	.220	.58
	Kilo	53	101	101						
40d	Pound	18	35	35		40d	5	12.7	.238	.60
	Kilo	37	77	77						
50d	Pound	14				50d	5/4	14.0	.257	.66
	Kilo	31								
60d	Pound	11				60d	6	15.2	.277	.70
	Kilo	24								

*Exact conversion

LUMBER

NOMINAL SIZE (This is what you order.)	ACTUAL SIZE (This is what you get.)	METRIC CONVERSION OF NOMINAL SIZE	METRIC CONVERSION OF ACTUAL SIZE	AUSTRALIAN METRIC STOCK LUMBER SIZES
Inches	Inches	Millimetres*	Millimetres*	
1 x 1	¾ x ¾	25 x 25 mm	19 x 19 mm	19 x 19 mm
1 x 2	¾ x 1½	25 x 51	19 x 38	19 x 41
1 x 3	¾ x 2½	25 x 76	19 x 64	19 x 66
1 x 4	¾ x 3½	25 x 102	19 x 89	
1 x 6	¾ x 5½	25 x 153	19 x 140	
1 x 8	¾ x 7¼	25 x 203	19 x 184	
1 x 10	¾ x 9¼	25 x 254	19 x 235	
1 x 12	¾ x 11¼	25 x 305	19 x 286	
2 x 2	1¾ x 1¾	51 x 51	38 x 38	
2 x 3	1½ x 2½	51 x 76	38 x 64	41 x 66
2 x 4	1½ x 3½	51 x 76	38 x 89	
2 x 6	1½ x 5½	51 x 153	38 x 140	
2 x 8	1½ x 7¼	51 x 203	38 x 184	
2 x 10	1½ x 9¼	51 x 254	38 x 235	
2 x 12	1½ x 11¼	51 x 305	38 x 286	

*Some of these sizes have been adjusted from American stock lumber dimensions by up to 0.2 mm.; always measure before cutting or drilling in order to ensure exact fit.

Index

MORE BOOKS FOR THE CREATIVE HOMEOWNER

MODERN PLUMBING FOR OLD AND NEW HOUSES

Complete emergency plumbing repairs, plus improvements to update your plumbing system and make it more efficient, convenient and dependable. From the basics of working with all types of pipe and installing shutoff valves, to details of installing outdoor plumbing systems and solar collectors, author Jay Hedden converts professional techniques into layman's language. Step-by-step instructions are supplemented with over 200 photos and drawings. Author Hedden (editor of *Workbench* magazine) also offers a glossary and "Where to Write for Replacement Appliance Parts."
144 pp.; 8½" x 11", Creative Homeowner Press; paperback, $4.95; hardcover, $12.95.

175 HOME PLANS

Selected best-selling multi-level and two-story home plans, including dome styles and other specialties. Designs are by well-known architect William G. Chirgotis, with over 500 drawings — artist's renderings, floor plans, and supplemental sketches. Additional features: *House-Planning Guide, House Style Characteristics, How to Read a Floor Plan,* and *How to Arrange a Loan.* 192 pp.; 8½" x 11"; Index; Creative Homeowner Press; paperback, $4.95; hardcover, $12.95.

250 HOME PLANS

A diversified assortment of outstanding home plans, combined with much-needed guidelines for decisions related to planning financing, and building your home. Square footage ranges from 750 to 5,000 square feet in this collection designed by William G. Chirgotis. Contains over 700 illustrations, and discussions of the characteristics of each type of home. 240 pp.; 8½" x 11"; Creative Homeowner Press; $6.95.

HOME IMPROVEMENT/HOME REPAIR

A manual written in layman's language for over 300 interior and exterior repairs and improvements. Basics of tool selection and techniques, outdoor lot and garden repair projects, and extensive interior improvements are detailed with over 650 illustrations. Author Richard Nunn gives tools- and- materials lists and step-by-step instructions for each project. 288 pp.; 8½" x 11"; Creative Homeowner Press; paperback, $7.95; hardcover, $14.95.

DECKS AND PATIOS

Design aid and complete basic construction techniques for decks and patios, using all kinds of materials. Other features include roofings and coverings, planning and landscaping details, and materials recommendations. Additional projects to round off your recreative area include: screens, fences, outdoor furniture benches and built-ins, BBQ and firepit, lighting. Over 200 illustrations, many in color; 144 pp.; 8½" x 11"; Creative Homeowner Press; paperback, $4.95; hardcover, $12.95.